Myths & Realities of American Slavery

The True History of Slavery in America

By
John C. Perry

To Harvey Skinner !
Always seek the truth !
John C. Perry
3/15/03

BURD STREET PRESS
SHIPPENSBURG, PENNSYLVANIA

This Burd Street Press publication
was printed by
Beidel Printing House, Inc.
63 West Burd Street
Shippensburg, PA 17257-0708 USA

The acid-free paper used in this book meets the guidelines for permanence and durability of the Committee on Production Guidelines for Book Longevity of the Council on Library Resources.

For a complete list of available publications
please write
Burd Street Press
Division of White Mane Publishing Company, Inc.
P.O. Box 708
Shippensburg, PA 17257-0708 USA

Library of Congress Cataloging-in-Publication Data

Perry, John C., 1948-
    Myths & realities of American slavery : the true history of slavery in America / by John C. Perry.
        p. cm.
    Includes bibliographical references and index.
    ISBN 1-57249-335-6 (acid-free paper)
    1. Slavery--United States--History. I. Title: Myths and realities of American slavery. II. Title.

E441 .P46 2002
306.3'62'0973--dc21

2002032990

PRINTED IN THE UNITED STATES OF AMERICA

To My Precious Grandchildren:

Jacob Aaron Thompson
Adam Burke Agee
Landry Malynn Agee
Grace Ann Thompson
Joseph Perry Agee

May each of you always seek the truth
May each of you be blessed with wisdom
May each of you love life and God

Contents

Prologue

As I embarked on the writing of this book I knew going in that I was entering a very controversial topic, a topic that generates a lot of emotions. In fact that is one of the reasons that the topic appeals to me, as in this book I have endeavored to replace emotion with logic and an honest pursuit of the truth.

Some may attack this book as being biased and its author perhaps even labeled a racist. That is one of the major disadvantages of writing a book that deals with such an emotional topic as American slavery. Let me be perfectly clear on my personal views. I abhor slavery. It was wrong and is wrong; simply stated, slavery is an abomination. No person should ever, under any circumstances, be owned by another person. My position on the races is equally clear and simple, as stated in the Declaration of Independence, "all men are created equal." I believe that with all my heart and I firmly believe that God views us all as his children, equal in every respect.

Before we begin let me first set the stage. I am endowed, in the twenty-first century, with just about everything politically incorrect, for I am a white male Southerner. Growing up in the South in the 1950s and 1960s I lived through a most turbulent period, a period that saw the start of equality and justice for African Americans. As a small child in Atlanta, Georgia, I vividly remember being told to move out of the backseat of a city bus to allow the "colored people" to sit there. As children, when we boarded the bus, guess where we wanted to sit? We were told that we could not sit in the back of the bus, because that is where the "colored people" sat; so as children that is exactly where we wanted to sit. Most bus drivers would let us sit in the back of the bus until the first African American passengers boarded, and then the driver would tell us to move to the front.

As a child, I was never quite sure of my Southern past. My mother had told me about members of her family that had served in the Confederate army and the tremendous hardships the family suffered when General William T. Sherman's Union army came through Georgia in 1864. It was probably those stories and as a child being able to find Union and Confederate artifacts in our yard, relics from the Battle of Atlanta, which stirred a lifelong interest in the American Civil War, or as we called it when I was growing up, The War Between the States. I will use the term "War Between the States" throughout this book as it is a much more accurate description and title for the conflict.

Back in the 1950–60s, Southern history in the public schools was still taught, for the most part, in a pro-Southern perspective. In spite of that, I was taught that basically the main cause of the War Between the States was slavery. Even at a young age, it seemed an odd reason to fight a war. Why you would fight a war to keep a people enslaved, particularly if you personally owned no slaves? That always perplexed me. I had learned from my mother that no one in our family lines had ever owned slaves, yet all the military-aged males voluntarily served in the Confederate army.

By the time I graduated from college, in the 1970s, the interpretation of Southern history was rapidly changing. I received a degree in history and did a brief stint as a history teacher. While teaching, I began an initial effort to find out the true facts about slavery and what caused the War Between the States. After I left teaching and entered the business world, I got too busy earning a living and raising children to finish my research. In spite of a life in the corporate world, far away from academia, I have been a constant reader of books on the War Between the States and early Southern history.

Wow, have things really changed! Now, it seems to me that under the guise of political correctness, formerly revered Confederate symbols in the South are being attacked with a force and vigor I could have never imagined. Some even equate Confederate symbols with Nazi symbols. I have been appalled by the perception of Southern history, by not only people from outside the South, but by "folks" born and raised in the South.

Are common perceptions about the South and the Confederacy right? Should Southerners actually be ashamed of their Southern history? What was the world of the slave like? How harsh of a condition did the American slaves have to endure? As I now approach retirement and my children are educated and on their own, I have a bit more time on my hands. So, bottom line, the purpose of this book is to go back and find the facts. What is true about American slavery and what is pure myth?

Am I the right person to undertake this effort? That certainly can be argued either way. First I am not a professional historian. I have not spent a lifetime in academia. That perhaps is not all bad; it affords me absolute independence in my observations and conclusions. I have spent a lifetime studying Southern history, in particular, the time leading up to and including the War Between the States.

One friend of mine, from above the Mason-Dixon line, asked me the question, "How can a white Southerner write a book about slavery?" The obvious implication is, can you be unbiased? The answer is yes, to the degree humanly possible, otherwise this book would not have been written. I like the quote from Frank L. Owsley, when apparently he was challenged with a similar type question, "A Southern historian is, I suppose, as objective and impartial as a Northern historian,"[1] Owsley said. He added, "Every good historian tries to tell the truth. But historians are human, and, Northern or Southern, they are bound to have emotional reactions to every human situation, no matter how much they try to exercise self-restraint. When emotion is too much in the ascendancy, the historian may be accused of bias, sometimes more elegantly spoken of as 'point of view.'"[2] Following Dr. Owsley's caution, I have endeavored to be as impartial and unbiased as a human being can be.

Who is this book for? This book is not designed for the professional historian, although they are welcomed to read it, and I certainly would enjoy their professional opinion and constructive criticisms. There is no new research, other than some personal analysis and interpretations of the 1860 United States Census data as well as other studies, accounts, and research. This book is simply a summary, compiling the best thoughts, studies, and interpretations of

American slavery into a single, and hopefully easy to read source. Not being a professional historian, I do not have at my beck and call an army of graduate students to do research at my direction. Rather, I have attempted to sort through the reams of existing materials, hundreds and hundreds of books, various interpretations, studies, data, et cetera, to seek logic and the truth.

This book was designed for the average everyday reader. It is a book that I hope will enlighten the average reader on the truth of American slavery. One note here is that this book is a study of the entire institution of slavery in America, not just a study of the life of slaves. So in addition to information about the lives of slaves I have also included information from the perspective of the slave owner, the national political implications of slavery, as well as related topics.

One might ask, how can a book on American slavery be relevant in the twenty-first century? If for no other reason, this book perhaps will help as discussions take place regarding "Slave Reparations" to African Americans. Should such reparation payments be made? This book will certainly not answer that controversial question, but what this book can do is to arm all Americans with the facts so this issue can be discussed with, hopefully, a better understanding of the American institution of slavery.

Greater than that, this book hopefully will help remove historical inaccuracies heavily influenced by popular culture, political correctness, and those with specific social agendas.

One approach I have used is to introduce thirty-one "Slavery Facts." These are summary statements regarding some aspect of slavery. To many they may be very surprising, but they are true. For the most part, each "Slavery Fact" is an undisputedly true "nugget" of information about American slavery.

This is a journey to seek the truth. Let us take a look at the myths and realities of American slavery.

Acknowledgments

This book was a labor of love, and lots of people were part of the effort. I must first and foremost thank my wife, Sandra, for all the help and more importantly for all the support she has given me in this endeavor. She is clearly the most wonderful wife in the world.

I would also like to thank all those that helped me in the researching of this book. I received so much support and assistance from the Harold B. Simpson History Complex at Hill College in Hillsboro, Texas. To the dean, Dr. Buddy Patterson, thank you so much for your support and the opening of the doors to the research center to me. I couldn't have done it without your help. I also need to specifically thank Peggy Fox, at the History Complex, who went out of her way in helping me and also a special thanks to Dr. T. Lindsey Baker, for his assistance, as well as the other staff at the college.

Thanks should also go out to the library staffs at the University of Mary Hardin Baylor in Belton, Texas; Baylor University in Waco, Texas; and the University of Texas in Austin. Thankfully, all of these facilities were kind enough to allow a nonstudent use of their extensive resources.

Special thanks to Dr. Odie Faulk, from Waco, Texas, professor emeritus of history from Northeastern State University of Oklahoma. Dr. Faulk, author of fifty books including three Pulitzer Prize nominations, was kind enough to educate me in the goal of having a historically oriented book published. Also thanks to Scott Bowden of Arlington, Texas, coauthor of the excellent book on the Battle of Gettysburg *Last Chance for Victory*. Scott also was very helpful for his insight into historical book publishing.

I want to also thank all those that took the time to read and comment on the draft manuscript: Dr. Buddy Patterson of Hillsboro, Texas; Pete Orlebeke of Dallas, Texas; and Greg Manning of Salado, Texas. Thanks to each of you for your input and constructive comments.

I would also like to express my appreciation to the fine people at White Mane Publishing, especially my editor, Harold Collier, as well as Marianne Zinn in the Editorial Department, whose suggestions made this book much better. Also thanks to Nicole Riley for her help in keeping me on schedule.

Finally thanks to all my family members and friends who were always encouraging me and very positive when it came to the project. I appreciate the confidence and your support.

Chapter One
Which Version of History?

Scenario 1

The large white two-story mansion, with the huge white pillars on the front porch, glistened in the light of the full moon. The wind gently rustled through the large oak trees that graced the entranceway to the plantation with Spanish moss dangling from each. The wind brought forth the sweet smell of the magnolia blossoms over the well-manicured plantation grounds. Inside the plantation home was the very embodiment of high culture, a library filled with all the classical books, a music room with a fine grand piano, a grand staircase illuminated by a beautiful crystal chandelier, leading to the lavish bedrooms of the plantation master and his family.

To the back of the plantation home were the slave quarters, neatly constructed in a row, each containing an individual slave family. Their homes were made of stone and had plank floors and each had its own fireplace. They were modestly furnished with beds, tables, and chairs. The children had their own room, a small loft.

Surrounding the plantation home and slave quarters were other outbuildings, the central kitchen, barns, workshops, and even a small clinic-infirmary. There were also the homes of the white plantation employees and their families, the overseer, the tutor, and perhaps some artisans. The remainder of the land was made up of the massive cotton fields, thousands of acres bristling, at harvest time, with lily-white cotton balls.

At daybreak everyone stirred from the plantation home, the master arose, a kindly, but somewhat forgetful gentleman, known by the honorary title of "Colonel." His refined wife, the mistress of the plantation, and their well-educated children would arise as the sun rose over the stately live oak trees. The Colonel's wife was master of the plantation home and saw to it that everything was always in place. She also was in command of the many and varied social events, from parties to visits to town. The teenage son, who would someday inherit his father's plantation, was a perfect young gentleman, educated by the very best tutors, an excellent horseman, and well skilled in the art of firearms. The young daughter, also in her teenage years, was her father's pride and joy. She was the belle of the ball no matter where she went. She was beautiful, graceful, and aware of every social detail—she was indeed the plantation's princess.

The house servants also arose early from their quarters, in the back of the plantation home, to begin to prepare breakfast and lay out the wardrobes for the master and his family. The other slaves arose as well, prior to dawn, for a hearty breakfast and to prepare for the workday. The field hands, mostly the younger males, would soon head to the fields to tend to the crops, their duties varying depending on the time of the year. Other male slaves were assigned specific duties, like blacksmithing, carpentering, gardening, and tending to the livestock. The female slaves never worked in the fields, but would spend the day cooking, working as seamstresses, serving as nurses or tending to the children, both white and black. Still others were rewarded with duty as house servants. The children of the slaves were happy, spending their day playing, not only with each other, but with any small white children that lived on the plantation. In spite of the state laws to the contrary the kindly Colonel held school for the slave children, as well as providing them with religious instruction.

The overseers were hired to attend to the slaves, assigned duties, and enforced plantation regulations. Many times these were men imported from the North. The Colonel had strict rules for each overseer relating to the proper and kind treatment of his slaves. The tutors, also typically imported from the North, were responsible for teaching all the plantation children, regardless of race.

The workday would end around 5:00 P.M. during the weekdays. On weekends everyone was expected to put in a half day of work on Saturday but have a full day off on Sunday. On Saturday night, there was nearly always some event, both for the whites and the slaves. Whether it be a big dance, featuring various waltzes or the Virginia Reel, or a big cookout, some event would be held, typically the highlight event of the week on the plantation. Sunday was always a day of rest for all. Everyone on the plantation, slaves and whites, were expected to attend worship service on Sunday morning.

Life was good for all. The plantation would produce a bounty of cotton, and everyone, white or black, would receive a cash bonus when the crops were harvested. Everything was taken care of for everyone, and all, slaves and free, were happy, but then came the War Between the States and life would never be the same.

Scenario 2

The big plantation home was set on the edge of the cotton fields, a sea of misery for the oppressed slaves that were forced to work the fields from dawn to dusk six and a half days a week. The large extravagant plantation home sat in marked contrast to the miserable slave quarters that housed those in bondage.

Although well furnished, the plantation home was constantly being patched up due to the angry outbursts of both the master of the plantation and his spoiled and loathsome son. House servants were forced to deal with drunken stupors and irresponsible behavior of both the plantation's master and son. The mistress of the plantation was a pathetic woman who never crossed her husband or her children and pretended to ignore most of what went on around her. The master's teenage daughter was a spoiled brat that frequently abused the house servants assigned to meet her every whim.

The master was motivated only by greed. Slave families were broken up as he sold slaves, with no consideration for families, as someone would sell cattle. Mothers were separated from their children and husbands from their wives. Being "sold down the river" was a common occurrence. Some mothers never saw their children or husbands again.

The slave quarters were atrocious. Small cabins with dirt floors were crammed with the equivalent of two and three families.

Frequently, the cabins leaked when it rained, and the slaves were left to their own devices to make any needed repairs to the quarters.

The master ruled the plantation by absolute brute force. He imported Northern overseers who maintained tight control over the slaves. The overseers were typically very cruel and had the authority to use the whip as the primary form of discipline. Lashes were administered daily to those slaves whom the overseer perceived had broken the plantation's rules. At times the ultimate punishment, the sentence of death, could be carried out, with the master's approval.

Both the master and his son were morally corrupt. They had their way with the slave women, some as young as twelve or thirteen years old. They would brag to the other slaves of their sexual conquests, and numerous "mulatto" children were born, sired by either the master or his son.

All adult slaves, men, women and even children over the age of ten, except a select few household servants and coachmen, were required to work in the fields. Quotas were assigned to each slave and those that did not meet their quota were subject to a whipping. Life was hard and unrelenting; fieldwork lasted from sunrise to sunset. Upon return from the fields the slaves would have to prepare the food and do other tasks such as gardening and seamstress work.

Slaves would often try to escape, but the plantation owners had a network of men poised to chase down a slave as soon as he or she was reported missing. Yet the lure of freedom was strong. Many slaves tried to escape their chains of bondage, and some did make it north, to the land of the free. The slaves would often feign overseer and plantation compliance, while more often they would work to sabotage the plantation operations whenever they thought they could get away with it.

Life was almost unbearable, but most slaves kept their pride in spite of the frequent beatings. It was a living hell, and then came the Civil War and life would never be the same.

The Challenge

Which was it? Which scenario most closely resembled the actual way slaves in the South were treated? What was life truly like on the Southern plantation? Did the enslaved African Americans live a life that was brutal, a true "Hell on Earth," or was life better than the way one might expect a slave to live, "a kinder and gentler" form of slavery?

The purpose of this book is to answer those questions. Our goal is to seek out the truth. We will delve into the myths of American slavery and attempt to root out the realities of it. Myths are defined as untrue stories, legends, or even imaginary events. One historian's definition of a myth perhaps put it best. Thomas Bailey defined a historical myth as "an account or belief that is demonstrably untrue, in whole or substantial part."[1] We will find those historical myths, explain what parts are either partially true or totally false and then explain what really happened, as best we can determine.

The myths we will seek to debunk are with us for a number of reasons. We will see how popular culture's interpretation of history has created some myths—evidence the impact of two fictional works, the movie *Gone with the Wind* (1939) and the television mini-series *Roots* (1976) have had on our view of American slavery. Others are created by biased interpretations of history, for instance, the pro-slavery Southern accounts of slavery versus the Northern abolitionist accounts of slavery.

We are also looking for realities. If something is a myth, then alternatively what actually happened? What is the reality of the situation? That pursuit of truth is much easier said than done. We cannot simply go back in time and observe. We will have to rely on the writings of those from that period and we will have to sift through the biases of the writer, if any. We will have to examine the facts, records that have survived, United States census data, and more modern studies of various forms of economic data. We will also rely on past historical research and interpretations to give us a better understanding of the institution of slavery.

In no sense of the word is this book a defense of American slavery. It was evil and is an absolute blot on American history. One person "owning" another person is morally reprehensible and without defense. A modern-thinking person abhors slavery. With that said, we will however need to do a thought shift as we approach the issue of American slavery. We must try to put ourselves in the minds of white Americans, the "typical" slave owner, beginning in the seventeenth century when African slaves were first brought to the "New World" of North America. Slavery, up until about the 1830s was a universally accepted institution. As sure as people accepted the institution of marriage, citizens of the world accepted, almost without question, the institution of slavery. Although today we know they were wrong, slavery was accepted as being part of the natural scheme of things by virtually everyone in the world until the first half of the nineteenth century.

The other thought shift is much more difficult, that of trying to understand what being an American slave was like. We simply cannot be all together successful in that regard. No one truly knows what slavery was like except those that experienced the bonds of slavery. Fortunately, some narratives of slaves have survived, so we can get at least a brief glimpse of what their world must have been like.

With all that said let's embark on our journey and discover the myths and the realities of American slavery.

Chapter Two
How American Slavery Began (Ancient Times to 1773)

Early History of Slavery

First, let us define exactly what slavery is. Simply put, slavery is the practice where one individual owns another person or persons. The slave is the property of the slave owner, usually called the master, and is bound to the master. The slave is typically not paid for his labors, but is provided food, clothing, and shelter by the master. The slave has no promise of freedom unless the master grants the slave his or her freedom or allows the slave to purchase their freedom. Throughout most of history the institution of slavery has been officially sanctioned and protected by governments, religions, and virtually all cultures, and traditions.

To better understand American slavery let us briefly review the overall history of slavery to better put the American version of this ancient institution into a historical context. Slavery began, more than likely, before man began to record written history. One family, one tribe, would exert physical force on another group, and the conquerors would force the vanquished into servitude. It has been with us since the "dawn of civilization." It seems odd to us today to even associate the word slavery with a "civilized society." We must remember, however, what we said in the previous chapter, that virtually all peoples accepted slavery without question, until the nineteenth century. Even Aristotle said, "From the hour of their birth, some are marked out for subjection, others for rule." Some historians even claim that slavery is an example of the

growth of civilization, in that
prior to the advent of slavery
captured prisoners were killed
rather than enslaved.

> *Slavery Fact #1*
> *Until the nineteenth century, the inhabitants of the world practiced and accepted the institution of slavery as a normal part of life.*

Incidents of slavery were
recorded in some of the earliest historical recordings. The
Bible, in both the Old Testament and the New Testament, contains
numerous instances of slavery, from the story of Joseph, who was
sold into slavery by his brothers, to the entire Hebrew race, who
were enslaved by the ancient Egyptians. The Bible actually does not
prohibit slavery, in fact prior to the onset of the War Between the
States, some Southern theologians made attempts to justify slavery
by using the Bible as their source.

The Bible, in the Old Testament, actually does list the laws to
follow for appropriate enslavement. For example, kidnapping is
forbidden as a means of obtaining slaves. There are four "acceptable" ways of obtaining slaves, (1) purchased (Leviticus 25:44–46),
(2) captured in war (Numbers 31:32–35), (3) as punishment for theft
(Exodus 22:1–3), and (4) as payment of debt (Leviticus 25:39 and
Exodus 21:7).[1]

In the Old Testament there are also laws relating to the treatment of slaves. In Exodus, chapter 21, a number of different rules
relating to slavery are listed, including specifics on slave punishment. According to the Bible, it is allowable to beat a slave, as a
method to produce the desired level of slave labor (Exodus 21:20–
27). However, if a master murdered his slave, then the master could
be executed (Exodus 21:20). A slave could gain his freedom if he or
she was seriously injured by the master (Exodus 21:26–27). Other
biblical laws provided that a slave of the same race as the master
should be set free after six years and any foreign slaves liberated
twice every one hundred years.

In the New Testament of the Bible, the Apostle Paul discusses
the duties of both the slave and the slave owner. In the book of
Ephesians, verses 6:5–8, Paul instructs all slaves to serve their masters, "Slaves obey your earthly masters with respect and fear, and
sincerity of heart, just as you would obey Christ." He goes on to say,

"Serve wholeheartedly, as if you were serving the Lord, not men." Paul also instructs the slave owners, admonishing them to treat their slaves well (Ephesians 6:9).

Islam, which was established in the seventh century, also recognized the institution of slavery. Moslems were encouraged by the Prophet Mohammed to treat slaves kindly. Most slaves, held by followers of Mohammed, were used as domestic servants. Moslem law decreed that slave children were not to be separated from their mothers until they had reached the age of seven, that slaves were not to be treated as if they were animals, and that slaves and freemen were equal in the eyes of Allah.[2]

The ancient Egyptians built much of their great culture on the backs of slaves. Some of the Hebrew tribes made their way into Egypt in the 1600s B.C. and became slaves. Their exodus from Egypt and their gaining their freedom are important parts of Hebrew history. The Babylonian Code of Hammurabi, from the 1700s B.C., made provisions for slavery, including a sentencing of death to anyone who helped a slave escape.

Across the Mediterranean Sea from Egypt, the ancient Greeks reached intellectual greatness with a society built on slavery. In Homer's works one finds that a natural byproduct of being captured in warfare is to become a slave. Aristotle said, "Humanity is divided into two: the masters and the slaves," and called slaves "living tools." By 600 B.C., slavery was widespread among the Greeks, with the slave population approaching one-third of the population in some city-states. Greek slaves were slaves for life, and children born into slavery would remain slaves for life. Both the Greek city-states and the religious temples owned their own slaves. Athens had 60,000 slaves at one time, including the Athens police force with three hundred slave archers. One quarter of the workers who built the Parthenon were slaves.[3]

The city-state of Sparta had a special category of slaves, known as "helots." These were typically prisoners captured during warfare. They were assigned to individual homes in Sparta where they would do the menial tasks and chores. The use of slaves would free Sparta parents to raise strong children and allow the fathers to train their male offspring as warriors.

Slavery perhaps reached its peak in the very early stages of the Roman Empire. By the fifth century B.C. slavery was already part of Roman law. The Twelve Tables, Rome's first codified body of law, recognizes the presence of slaves. There are provisions in the Twelve Tables, for instance, that if an ex-slave died without a will and had no heirs, his estate would go to his former owner, and a provision that allowed for a slave to be set free in a will on payment of a cash sum to an heir.[4]

Rome took its slaves from a number of sources. Slaves were procured from the ranks of those people Rome had conquered. Those who became slaves as a result of warfare could experience rather brutal treatment from the "enlightened" Romans. One account describes what became of slaves taken as prisoners in 359 A.D. A number of the slaves were older men and women. When they could no longer produce work or keep up, their calves would be severed and they were left behind to die or fend for themselves.[5]

Roman slaves also came from the ranks of debtors, who sold themselves or members of their families into slavery, or from criminals. Slavery was far more important to the Romans than to the Greeks. To the Romans slavery was an important part of their economic system. As the Roman Empire began to expand they needed laborers, mainly to help Rome meet its immense agricultural needs.

Roman slaves were owned by wealthy landholders. They worked in the fields, the mines, on merchant ships, and as gladiators to amuse the Roman populace. It has been estimated that at one time three out of four residents on the Italian peninsula were enslaved, approximately twenty-one million people.[6]

Roman slave status was quite severe. Under Roman rule, a child would follow the status of his or her mother. Even if the father was free, if a child was born to a slave mother then the child would be a slave and the property of the owner of the mother. Consequently, if the child's father was a slave, but the mother was free, then the child would be free. All children of slaves were the property of the owner of the mother. The splitting up of families would occur, and many Roman slave owners would buy and sell slaves without regard for the slave's family members.

In spite of the harshness of the Roman system, unlike the Greeks, the Roman slaves could potentially become citizens of Rome. Even though they were considered to be the property of the slave owner, the slaves had certain rights in the Roman judicial system; however, the right to marry was not one of them. A marriage would be immediately terminated if either party to the marriage became a slave. If there was infidelity between slaves, under Roman law it would not be considered adultery.[7]

The freeing of slaves by the slave owner was allowed. Some Rome slave owners would free their slaves in return for their faithful service. In fact, with time, Roman slavery would evolve into more of a form of servitude, thus ending at least some of the harsher elements of traditional slavery.[8]

In Europe, a limited form of slavery, serfdom, arose. The word "serf" comes from the Latin word *servus*, which means slave. Serfdom differed from slavery. To be a serf was to be bound to a master to provide services and payments. Typically in the Middle Ages, the serf would work land owned by the master and they would provide payments to the owner of the estate. They were not bound to the master but rather bound to the land which they worked. In time, most European law recognized the serf as a free person and England ended serfdom in the seventeenth century.

Although serfdom dominated, slavery still did occur in Europe. During the Crusades, the religious wars between Christians and Moslems, both sides made slaves of captured soldiers. Moors, captured in northern Africa, were held in slavery in Italy, Spain, Portugal, and France.[9]

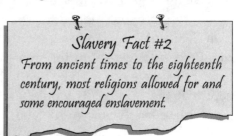

Slavery Fact #2

From ancient times to the eighteenth century, most religions allowed for and some encouraged enslavement.

African Slaves

The export of slaves from Africa began long before the slave trade to either Europe or the Western Hemisphere. People in western Africa had been selling slaves across the Sahara and south of Egypt as far back as several millennia. Slaves would be transported to northeastern Africa and moved east from there. The ancient Egyptians, the Turks, and others also captured slaves from the Nile Valley area, particularly from Nubia. Nubia was located in northeastern Africa, roughly between what is now Egypt and Sudan. A treaty in 651 A.D. required the Nubians to deliver three hundred and sixty slaves a year to Egypt.[10] Most of the slaves would be transported to the Red Sea and to distant locations in ancient Arabia and even into southern Asia.

Because of the lack of written records and due to a massive time span, the historical estimates of the number of slaves taken and transported through the trans-Saharan and Red Sea routes vary greatly. Some historians estimate that as many as eight to ten million Africans were sold into slavery, many by the time the slave trade to the Western Hemisphere began. Others put the number at half that amount. The trans-Saharan and Red Sea slave trade predated the rise of Islam, although some historians incorrectly refer to the North African slave trade as the "Islamic Slave Trade."

The trans-Saharan and Red Sea slave trade varied greatly from European slave trade to the Western Hemisphere. It was not nearly as formal or institutionalized, being operated mainly by small-scale slave traders. Unlike the western slave trade, the slaves being taken were thought to be predominately female, perhaps as high as two-thirds. The females would be used as domestics or concubines.

The trans-Saharan and Red Sea slaves journeyed mainly by foot to slave markets in Mediterranean port cities. After being sold, they would typically be shipped to the eastern Mediterranean, the Arabian Peninsula, the Persian Gulf area, and even as far away as India. Perhaps it was with the trans-Saharan slave trading that the concept of slave began to be tied to black-skinned Africans, a concept that the Europeans would soon pick up on and much later Americans. The Arabic word "abd," which originally meant slave, evolved to have the single meaning of a black-skinned person.[11] The exact origin of racism against black-skinned peoples can be debated, but early on we see hints of it.

Some slaves from Africa were also found in the Greek and Roman periods. Artistic representations of Africans are found on Greek vases, on Alexandrian terracottas, and on a Pompeii mosaic, a black slave serving at a banquet.[12] The Romans seemed to prize slaves from Africa, paying higher prices for them. Apparently the Romans felt more comfortable with them in positions of trust due to their being so far from home.[13]

It was the Portuguese that made the first major effort in enslaving Africans to the rest of the world. African slaves had been in Portugal for many years; as early as the mid-1200s Moorish traders were selling slaves from Africa.[14] By the fifteenth century the Portuguese had made great maritime strides. They had developed the caravel, a sleek and fast-sailing vessel, and one that could utilize the power of the wind, regardless of the direction the wind was blowing.[15] By 1415, the Portuguese had captured the key Mediterranean port of Ceuta, just across the Straight of Gibraltar, on the northern tip of northwest Africa.

The Portuguese king, John I, appointed one of his son's, Henry, later to be known as "Prince Henry the Navigator," in control of the North African region. Henry won his title not by his own exploration or voyages, but rather by encouraging the exploration of the west coast of Africa, which would eventually become the gateway for African slave traders. Henry's motivation to explore down the African western coast was to search for the source of gold that had been coming out of the African interior, the opportunity to find peppers, and perhaps to search for sources of African slaves.[16]

The Portuguese, in the fifteenth century, captured several Moors, from the Sahara Desert, as prisoners. The Moors bartered with the Portuguese and offered to provide them with some black Africans, who were non-Moslems, in exchange for their freedom. The deal was made and ten Africans were sent to Portugal.[17] African slave trade was now "officially" under way. As they worked their way down the African west coast, the Portuguese would capture slaves. A Venetian traveler on one of the Portuguese vessels described their slave-catching routine, "The Portuguese caravels, sometimes four, sometimes more, used to come to the Gulf of Arguin, well armed and landing by night, surprised some fishermen's villages. . . ."[18] The Africans would resist the Portuguese efforts to capture them. One African's gallant attempt to escape slavery was described, "For he was so valiant that two men, strong as they were, could not drag him into the boat until they took a boathook and caught him above one eye, and the pain of this made him abate his courage, and allow himself to be put inside the boat. . . ."[19]

During the first fifty years of the European slave trade, up until about 1500, most of the African slaves went to the European continent.[20] Slaves were brought to Portugal and Spain, where there was a labor shortage due to a rapid economic expansion. The slaves were employed in both rural and urban areas. By the middle part of the sixteenth century, ten thousand Africans or people of African descent lived in Lisbon, making up 10 percent of the total city's population. Likewise, in Seville the slave population had already reached about six thousand.[21] But the number of slaves coming to Europe would begin to slow. The labor shortage on the European continent began to decline in part due to its increased populations, beginning as early as in the late 1400s.

The focus of slave exportation switched and most of the slaves that were captured were sent not to Europe but rather to islands like Madeira, the Canaries, off the northwest coast of Africa.[22] Just before 1500, the Portuguese captured the island of São Thomé, in the Gulf of Guinea. On São Thomé the Portuguese developed large sugar cane plantations which were manned by African slaves. These plantations would become the prototype of future sugar plantations in the Western Hemisphere using the African slaves as the preferred method of labor. It has been estimated that perhaps as many as 125,000 slaves were exported to islands like São Thomé, Madeira, and the Canaries.[23] Between 1451 and 1559, the vast majority of the slaves went to the islands with the remainder going into Europe.[24]

As early as 1435, the Portuguese had established trading posts in Senegal, on the west coast of Africa.[25] Their purpose was to either capture or barter for Africans to be sent back to Europe as slaves. Their effort was made all the easier due to the fact that slavery already existed in the African tribes and certain tribal chiefs were eager to trade with the Portuguese.[26]

U. B. Phillips's book *American Negro Slavery* is an account of an official member of the Portuguese court, Azurara, who went on one of Prince Henry's slave-catching expeditions in 1452. Azurara thought that the effort to catch slaves was noble and just, using the rationalization that they were winning "savages" over to Christianity. Azurara did express regret over the Africans that were killed or suffered in the slave-capturing process, but thought that overall the Christian redemption that the slaves would receive made it all worthwhile.[27]

Once in Portugal, Azurara described the African slaves, "they never more tried to fly, but rather in time forgot all about their own country," and that "they were very loyal and obedient servants, without malice."[28] Azurara described that some of the Africans were unable to adjust to their new land, but that at least they died "happily" as Christians. He mentions how others flourished, eventually integrating into the Portuguese society. Some of the slaves were married to men and women that owned land, thus acquiring "comfortable estates."[29]

The Portuguese effort of enslaving Africans was sanctioned by the Catholic Church. In 1455, the Pope "blessed" Portugal's efforts to garner African slaves, when it authorized Portugal to reduce to servitude all "infidel" people.[30] In fact, not only was the Catholic Church not opposed to the institution of slavery, the Church owned large numbers of slaves.[31] As late as the 1750s, no church had discouraged its members from owning and participating in slave trade. The Portuguese were only more than willing to answer the call of the Church, as the enslavement of Africans enhanced their pocketbooks and met the desire of the Church to spread the word of Christianity. By Christopher Columbus' 1492 "discovery" of the "New World," a little more than twenty-five thousand Africans had been enslaved and transported to Europe.[32] Most of the Portuguese African slaves worked either as domestic servants in Lisbon or other Portuguese towns. Other slaves worked on the large estates in the countryside. Some were sold and taken to Spain.

Spain, like Portugal, was long active in slave trade. For many years, the Spanish had used Moslems captured in Crusades warfare as slaves. Málaga, in southern Spain, had been one of the last Moslem strongholds on the Iberian Peninsula. In 1487, the Spanish captured Málaga, taking prisoner about four thousand Moslems in the process. About one-third of the prisoners were exchanged for Christian slaves in Africa, but the remainder became slaves. Spain sold about one-third as slaves and the remaining third were sent as slaves across Europe. About one hundred were sent to Pope Innocent VIII in Rome in 1488. The Pope dispersed his share of the slaves as presents to various Roman clergy.[33]

Columbus, two years before his historic voyage across the Atlantic, was aware of the African slave trade, writing about the cost of slaves in the Cape Verde Island, a small island chain off the coast of West Africa.[34] Some historians have even speculated that Columbus may have had some African slaves on board one of his famous voyages to the "New World," but there is certainly no proof of such. On Columbus's second voyage, which began in 1493, he used the indigenous people, the Native Indian population, to help build the settlement of Isabela on the island of Hispaniola, the present-day countries of the Dominican Republic and Haiti. The indigenous people were also enslaved to help Columbus and his men search for gold on the island.

It was during Columbus's second voyage that the very first cargo of slaves was sent across the Atlantic Ocean. Instead of coming from Africa, these slaves were the indigenous people of the "New World," sent by Columbus from the Western Hemisphere to Europe. The slaves were under the command of Antonio de Torres. History does not tell us what became of these slaves, both males and females, from the "New World." Antonio de Torres brought a second group of four hundred slaves shortly after the first group. About half of the slaves died on the trans-Atlantic voyage, and the remainder of the slaves were received in Spain by Amerigo Vespucci, the Italian navigator for whom the continents of North and South America were named.[35] It is interesting to note that America was named for at least a part-time slave trader. The slaves were ordered to be put on sale in Seville, Spain, in April of 1495, but the sale was annulled, due to its possible illegality.

Columbus returned to Spain, ending his second voyage in 1496, with thirty Native Indians. Columbus called the indigenous people the Taínos. They were actually the Arawak Indians, who were inhabiting an area that stretched from present-day Florida down through the islands of the West Indies and even down into the coastal areas of South America. The Arawaks were sold at 1,500 maravedís each, but again the legal issues of "New World" slaves caused the Spanish royal government to delay the sale until the legal issues could be resolved. As late as the 1490s, Columbus was developing a business plan to send to Spain four thousand "New World" slaves a year. He calculated that would bring him twenty million maravedís at a cost of only three million maravedís. Some additional slaves were transported back, but the riches Columbus expected never came to fruition.[36]

The native Western Hemisphere's indigenous peoples were proving not to be very good slaves, from the Europeans' perspective. Diseases, like smallpox, were taking a heavy toll on the Native Indians as well as harsh labor conditions imposed by the Spanish. By 1510 there were only twenty-five thousand people able to work on the island of Hispaniola. A 1511 report to the Spanish royal government noted that the work of one black slave was equal to that of four Native Indians.[37] The Arawak Indian population, in the West Indies, fell from an estimated two to three million to no more than a few thousand by the early sixteenth century. By the end of the sixteenth century, the island-dwelling Arawaks were virtually extinct.

Now, with the advent of new lands, no longer were slave traders limited to importing African slaves just to Europe. The Western Hemisphere offered a huge new African slave trade market. With a virgin land needing to be conquered, cleared, settled, and cultivated, most of the slaves would soon be headed westward to the labor-intensive Western Hemisphere. In January of 1510 Spanish King Ferdinand granted authority for fifty slaves to go to Hispaniola, and although the decree does not specify that the slaves be African, clearly it was intended that they were to be African. The Spanish crown would also share in any slave trade, as the sale of any slave would require a tax per slave to be paid to the Spanish royalty.[38]

Over the next several years African slaves were imported each year into the Western Hemisphere, but in relatively small numbers. The demand was certainly there and it was building. The Spanish crown was consistently being petitioned by "New World" colonists for the authority to import more and more Africans to replace the dwindling Native Indians. On Vasco Núñez de Balboa's expedition that "discovered" the Pacific Ocean, he had with him an African slave, Nuflo de Olano, in 1513.

Some African slaves entered the Western Hemisphere probably as early as 1501. That year the Spanish government allowed "Christian" slaves in her American colonies. Initially, the Spanish government prohibited the direct importation of slaves from Africa to the Americas. The idea of the Spanish government was to prevent non-Christian slaves from uniting with the native population and thus threaten the Catholic Church in the Western Hemisphere.

By 1518 the new Spanish king, Charles I, had authorized four thousand African slaves to be brought into Spain's Western Hemisphere territories.[39] Slaves, indigenous or African, were initially being used in building infrastructure and mines, but with the advent of the planting of the sugar cane in the Spanish territories the need for labor began to grow dramatically. In the 1520s sugar became a major "New World" crop. In Puerto Rico, the first mill was built and by 1530, there were already nearly three thousand slaves and only three hundred twenty-seven whites. The first sugar mill in Mexico was built in 1524 and in Jamaica by 1527.[40]

Just who were these Africans that the Spanish and Portuguese sought? They had a variety of indigenous names, the Bambara, the Mende, the Ewe, the Akan, the Kimbundi, the Zulu, the Hausa, and the Teso, as well as others.[41] They came from many diverse tribes with different cultures and languages.

An estimated fifty million people were in Africa at the time of Columbus's "discovery" of America. The Africans were as diverse culturally as was the geography of the continent. Africa is the second largest continent and has a land area of over 11.7 million square miles. With a diverse geography, varying climatic conditions, and nearly completely surrounded by oceans and seas it produced a variety of unique civilizations.

A great kingdom, Ghana, had developed in West Africa until it was overrun by the Moslems in the eleventh century. Ghana was located in Western Africa between the Sahara Desert in the north and the tropical rain forest in the south. It should be noted that the current nation of Ghana is not the location of ancient Ghana, rather it was located in the present-day countries of Mauritania and Mali. The civilization that was Ghana developed as early as 300 B.C. Ghana controlled much of the trans-Sahara trade routes with East Africa and the Mediterranean and on to Europe and imposed a tariff on goods being traded, becoming quite wealthy in the process.[42] Key products traded were gold and salt. An Arab writer in 1067 described a prosperous civilization, with the ruler, Tenkamenin, having a castle with painted windows and adorned with sculptures. Tenkamenin enforced his rule with an imperial army of two hundred thousand men.[43] Ghana flourished for nearly three hundred years, reaching its zenith in power in the eleventh century.[44] Ghana was eventually overrun by Moslem invaders in the twelfth century.

Succeeding Ghana in power and influence was the Kingdom of Mali, which reached its height of power by the thirteenth century.[45] It was located in West Africa, in what today is modern Senegal, Mauritania, Guinea, and Mali. Mali's glory days lasted for a much shorter time period than Ghana's, about two hundred years. It is perhaps best known for the key commercial city of Timbuktu, now known as Tombouctou, Mali. Timbuktu, on the southern edge of the Sahara Desert, was the end city in West Africa for the trans-Sahara trade routes. At Timbuktu was the noted Moslem school of Sankoré. Islamic scholars from across North Africa and the Middle East came to Sankoré to study.

Mali was primarily Moslem and history records the journey of the Mali ruler, Mansa Kango Musa, to Mecca in 1324. He was accompanied on his journey by sixty thousand others, including twelve thousand servants. He took with him and left along the way, from Mali to Mecca, twenty-four thousand pounds of gold as homage.[46] Musa ruled over a nation that some historians say rivaled any nation then in existence in Europe.[47]

When Mali's power reign ended in the fifteenth century, West Africa saw the rise of yet another kingdom dominated by the Moslem faith, that of Songhai or Songhay. The Songhai developed a kingdom along the Niger River in present-day Mali and northwestern Niger. Originally it was part of the empire of Mali, but in 1335

Songhai broke away from Mali, doing so with a strong military. Like Ghana and Mali, the success of the Songhai stemmed mainly from the Saharan trade in salt and gold. One key Songhai city was Gao, on the Niger River. The old Mali city of Timbuktu flourished under Songhai rule. There were one hundred and eighty schools in Timbuktu under the Songhai and the population grew to around one hundred thousand people.[48] The university at Timbuktu, Sankoré, had grown to be recognized internationally, with European scholars journeying to study there.

Songhai fell when attacked by Moroccans in the late 1500s. With the Moroccans were Spanish mercenaries, and the Moroccans had one definite advantage in the war: firearms. The Songhai fought valiantly but were never able to recover from the damage inflicted upon them.

In the Kingdom of Benin further to the south, agriculture had been developed to a high level, and the natives were well known for their pottery and metal work. These politically well-organized kingdoms had their own legal codes. The land between the rivers Senegal and Zambia had iron and copper industries with the quality of African metal work approaching that found in Europe. Because of this technology, most of the African households had knives, spears, axes, and hoes.[49]

Trading centers had developed in Africa and the Portuguese were the first to tap into the African trade potential. From Africa, Europeans would import gold, spices, rice, grain, ivory, and eventually slaves.

The Europeans labeled the west coast of Africa as Guinea. Most of the slaves that would eventually end up in the Western Hemisphere were from three distinct geographical areas of Africa: upper Guinea, lower Guinea, and further south, the area of the Congo (Angola).[50] Except for the extremely old and those ill or with debilitating problems, no one was spared from being a slave. Men, women, and children were all open to the snare of the slave trader.

Initially, the Portuguese attempted to capture the Africans themselves. This was a very dangerous endeavor for them; one of Prince Henry's protégés was killed in a slave-catching raid. The crew of a

Spanish vessel, in search of Africans to capture, was captured them-selves in 1475 in Guinea, and apparently later eaten by the Afri-cans.[51] Not only was it a very dangerous business endeavor, it was also very labor intensive. The Africans had practiced slavery for generations, mainly as the result of military conquest. So the Portu-guese, and later the Spanish and English, Dutch, French, and New Englanders, acquired slaves by either trading with African chiefs for their existing slaves or by hiring African "middle men" to raid interior villages for slave prospects. Men, women, and children were sold into bondage for cloth, beads, firearms, and alcohol, predomi-nately rum.[52] Even horses were traded for slaves. At one time, the Portuguese could trade with African tribal leaders—one horse for ten to fifteen slaves.[53]

Hugh Thomas, in his book *The Slave Trade*, cites a survey of slaves taken by Sigismund Koelle in the Sierra Leone area. Accord-ing to Koelle, for the Sierra Leone region in the 1850s, which may or may not be typical for other regions or for other times, 34 percent of the slaves had been taken as prisoner of war by other Africans, 30 percent had been kidnapped by other Africans, 11 percent became slaves as the result of committing a crime, 7 percent had been sold to pay debts, and another 7 percent had been sold into slavery by relatives or friends. The remaining 11 percent fell into a variety of other categories.[54]

In the early stages of slave trading, many of the slaves that the Europeans would trade for would be those captured in the various tribal wars. As the demand for slaves increased, the tribes began to launch slave-raiding parties. When fewer slave prospects were found along the coastal regions they began to move to the West African interior. In the region of Dahomey, today the West African nations of Benin and Togo, the tribes reorganized their army around the slave-capturing business. By the late eighteenth century, Dahomey had refashioned its economy into one centered on slaves as a commodity. One observer wrote in 1804 that the Dahomean slave

> *Slavery Fact #3*
> The majority of the original African slaves were captured by and sold into slavery by other Africans.

trade was "carried on by a chain of merchants as it were, from the Coast indefinitely in many directions towards the interior."[55]

Newly captured Africans would then begin a journey toward the African west coast, a forced march to the seaports. Many would not survive the perilous trip. One can imagine the fear, panic, and horror that these African men, women, and children faced. They were forcefully removed from their homes and perhaps their families. On the journey from their homes to the coast, it was not unusual for a new slave to be sold from one slave trader to another, or to one of the African tribes in need of a slave or two.

When they arrived at a West African seaport, many had never seen a town, or even the ocean for that matter. They may have been branded and chained and were being sold to strange-looking white men, the likes of which they had never set eyes on. These white men spoke a different language, totally incomprehensible to them. The slaves would be penned up until enough of them had been accumulated to fill an incoming slave cargo ship. When the time came, they would be forced into large canoes to make their way to the tall ships in the bay.

To The "New World"—The Middle Passage

By the close of the 1500s, the Portuguese and Spanish dominated the African slave trade. The Portuguese transported their slaves mainly to Brazil, and the Spanish shipped slaves to their far-flung Western Hemisphere colonies. The African slave trade business was highly profitable. In the 1500s, a Spanish slave trader could buy slaves in Europe or Africa for about forty-five or fifty pesos each and then sell them in the Western Hemisphere for, at a minimum, double that amount.[56] The lure of high profits soon attracted others into the slave trade business. By the 1600s, the British, Dutch, and French had gotten involved in the lucrative slave trade business. The British transported their slaves to their colonies in Jamaica and Barbados, and the Dutch and French moved slaves to their Caribbean colonies.[57] In 1672, with its dominant naval force, Britain formed the Royal African Company for the purpose of slave trading. The Royal African Company had a monopoly on British slave trade until 1749, after which slave trading was opened to all British citizens. The British, in 1713, had signed an *asiento* treaty with Spain, securing them the right to supply the Spanish colonies with slaves,[58] and enabling Britain to become the dominant world slave trader.

Historical records show that the first African slaves were brought into the Western Hemisphere in 1502.[59] For the next three hundred years or so, before slave trade formally ended, a minimum ten million Africans were enslaved and forcibly transported to the Western Hemisphere. Some historians' research has upped the estimate to somewhere between thirteen and fourteen million; in fact some estimate the number as high as twenty-five million,[60] but that number seems highly inflated. The editors of the new Trans-Atlantic Slave Trade Database (see appendix A for additional information) estimates the number to be 11.8 million slaves taken from Africa. It is noteworthy that they also estimate that of the 11.8 million taken only 10.3 million arrived in the Western Hemisphere.[61] That departure number would seem to be a more realistic number. Historical consensus is that somewhere around ten million to twelve million Africans were removed from Africa.[62]

The single largest recipient of the slaves might surprise the casual reader, it was Brazil. Thirty-eight percent of the African slaves were transported to that South American territory. Collectively, the many and far-flung Spanish colonies received about half of the total import of slaves. The remaining balance of 12 percent was split between the Dutch, Danish, and Swedish colonies and with what would eventually become the United States.[63] The exact number of slaves that entered what is now the United States will never be known for sure. Historians have estimated anywhere between 550,000 and 650,000 Africans were transported to what would become the United States.[64]

What was called the "Middle Passage" was the transportation of the new African slaves to the Western Hemisphere. The journey would typically last at least fifty days or perhaps

Slavery Fact #4

The majority of African slaves were sent to Western Hemisphere locations outside of what would become the United States. Only six percent were sent to the U.S.

much longer, depending on the weather and the final destination point. It was a horrific experience for the Africans. The Africans were crammed together in very unsanitary conditions and sometimes given only subsistence food and water rations.

Men were typically held in chains and were placed "'tween decks." Most ships of the day had two decks; the space between the first deck and the lower deck was called the upper hold or more commonly "between decks." It was in this area that the slaves were held. The between deck area would range from two and one-half feet high to five feet high, depending on the individual ship. A slave ship built in Rhode Island was to be "ten feet in the hold, with three feet ten inches betwixt decks."[65] On the Rhode Island slave ship, which was typical of the slave ships of the era, the slaves would be confined to the deck that was as long as the boat, but less than four feet high.

On the between deck the slaves would typically be chained together two by two at the ankles. All the male slaves were required to lie down with their backs on the deck floor. Their feet would usually be secured to chains or iron rods that were roved through staples in the deck. On some ships they were forced to lie on their sides, in a spoonlike position, so more slaves could be crammed on board. The slaves were squeezed so tightly together that the average space per man was only sixteen inches wide by five and a half feet long.[66]

Slave women and children, considered a lesser threat to the ship's crew, were usually allotted more freedom. Weather permitting, the male slaves were allowed on deck once a day and required to "dance," a painful experience for those in chains. The slaves that did not survive typically died from sickness. One can imagine the horrific conditions of being held in the hull of a slave ship. With extremely foul air and with the potential of extreme heat the conditions made survival a challenge. Sanitation was a major problem for the slaves. Men, in the hulls, would be forced to lie in their own defecation; obviously disease would occur. Vinegar would often be used in the hulls to combat the stench.

Death rates, for both slave and crew, on the "Middle Passage" voyages would range from 5 percent to 20 percent.[67] As time progressed,

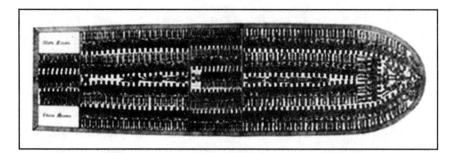

Cut-away depiction of the slave ship Brooke

National Archives

mortality rates dropped. By the early 1800s, the mortality rate on British slave ships was down to about 4 percent per voyage.[68] It is both interesting and praiseworthy of the hardiness of these Africans that the death rate for them during the Middle Passage was not much different than for white immigrants making the same voyage, but under far better circumstances than the slaves.[69] Often the death rate among crew members of slave ships was higher than that of the death rate of the slaves,[70] perhaps as high as 30 percent, likely due to crew members contracting diseases from their captives.[71]

In reviewing the slave trade in the eighteenth century from Africa to Brazil, Herbert S. Klein in his book, *The Middle Passage, Comparative Studies in the Atlantic Slave Trade*, found a direct correlation between death rates and the length of the voyage from Africa to the Western Hemisphere.[72] One slave boat captain, who lost nearly 84 percent of his nearly six hundred slaves in 1717, blamed the loss on the "length of the voyage" and "the badness of the weather."[73] Surprisingly, the number of slaves on board seemed to have no effect on the mortality rates, but there was a slight seasonal effect. Ships arriving in the summer months seemed to have slightly improved death rates than those ships that reached Brazil in the winter months.[74] One of the major causes of death during the Middle Passage was dysentery. A less common but more devastating event on a slave ship was an outbreak of highly communicable diseases, such as measles or smallpox. Nearly an entire "cargo" of slaves could potentially be lost.

Slave revolts on board the slave ships would sometimes occur. According to the Trans-Atlantic Slave Trade Database, between 1750 to 1794 54 percent of all recorded slave-ship revolts occurred, including 75 percent of all successful uprisings. Prior to the 1800s more young males, ideal candidates for slave rebellion, were being carried to the Americas, but by the 1800s nearly half of the slave "cargo" were children, making slave revolts less likely. All slave-trading nations experienced on board slave revolts, but France seemed to have the fewest per capita.[75]

A slave revolt occurred on board the British ship *Marlborough* in 1752. The ship carried about four hundred slaves, and as the crew was washing down the slave deck, a group of the slaves on main deck captured some of the arms on board and took over the ship. All but eight of the thirty-five-man crew were shot by the rebellious slaves. The surviving crew were ordered to turn the ship around and head back to Africa. A dispute broke out on board between slaves from different regions of Africa, and nearly one hundred were killed in warfare between the slave factions. The winning faction made it home.[76] Most slave revolts were not so successful and often typically ended in a very brutal fashion.

One effort to help prevent slave ship revolts was through the use of guardians. Guardians were slaves taken on board slave ships for the clear purpose of controlling the other slaves. The use of guardians was a standard operating procedure from the late seventeenth and early eighteenth centuries. Typically they were not armed, but would take leadership and supervisory roles over the other slaves. They were very successful in accomplishing their tasks; according to the Trans-Atlantic Slave Trade Database, no slave ship revolt data appears to have originated among the guardians. What was the guardians' reward? Although they received better treatment on board the slave ship, that was about the extent of their reward. Almost without exception, the guardians would be sold into the same slavery, just as the other slaves on board would be.[77]

The first African American slaves were brought into what is now Virginia in August of 1619. A ship approached the colony of Jamestown with its historic cargo. John Rolfe, the man that married Pocahontas, briefly described the first slave ship in America. Rolfe wrote, "a dutch man of warre that sold us twenty Negars."[78] The twenty African slaves were all sold in Jamestown. This would be the first of many visits up and down the American eastern seaboard. The slave ships would be ships of call originating from the British ports of London, Liverpool, and Bristol, and later from New England, most notably from Newport and Providence, Rhode Island, and Salem and Boston, Massachusetts. The African slave trade reached its peak in 1734 when approximately 70,000 slaves were imported into North America.[79]

The first slave ship, from what would become the United States, was called *The Desire*. The one hundred twenty-ton vessel was built at Marblehead, Massachusetts in 1636, and would soon embark on the profitable slave-trading business, sailing out of Salem, Massachusetts. One account of one of her voyages, in 1638, is recorded in a maritime journal, "Mr. Pierce in the Salem ship, the *Desire*, returned from the West Indies after seven months. He had been at Providence, and brought some cotton and tobacco and negroes, etc., from thence, and salt from Tortugas."[80]

The New England slave-trading industry grew quite rapidly, as large financial rewards awaited a successful "slave run." A "rum run" would have a slave ship leave New England bound for Africa with a cargo of rum. The rum would be used in trade for the slaves in Africa. The ships would be loaded with slaves and would then set sail for the Caribbean where the slaves would be sold, molasses would be loaded on board and taken to New England, where it would be turned into rum and the cycle began anew.

The importation of African slaves grew very slowly at first. From the twenty African slaves that came in 1619, the number of slaves in Virginia had grown to only three hundred, thirty-one years later, out of a white population of approximately fifteen thousand. In 1671, Virginia's Governor William Berkeley reported some two thousand slaves, six thousand white servants (indentured servants) out of

> *Slavery Fact #5*
>
> *Virtually all slave trade was done initially by the Portuguese and Spanish and later by the British, French, Dutch, and those from the New England colonies.*

a total population of forty thousand. Governor Berkeley wrote, "yearly, we suppose, there comes in of servants about fifteen hundred, of which most are English, few Scotch and fewer Irish; and not above two or three ships of negroes in seven years."[81]

Slave trading had a devastating effect on Africa. In 1850, it has been estimated that West Africa had a total population of about twenty-five million people. Had there been no slave-trading, historians have estimated that the West African population would have been around fifty million. Other historians point out the lost opportunities for African economic, social, and cultural growth with the loss of such massive numbers of peoples. What civilizations might have developed had not commerce with the Europeans been based on normal trade commodities rather than on a cargo of human lives?

There is also an emotional wound that the native Africans suffered with the loss of family members, friends, and other loved ones. A Yoruba saying bemoans the fact, "my child is dead is better than my child is missing." The loss of a loved one, never to know their fate, is painful indeed. Literally hundreds of thousands, if not millions, of Africans from young children to adults were snatched away from their homes and families never to be heard from again by those left behind. A true assessment of Africa's loss, as a result of the Atlantic slave trade, perhaps will never able to be determined, but if it could be measured would be absolutely staggering.

The Story of Gustavus Vassa

Unfortunately, few firsthand accounts of those slaves captured in Africa and brought to the American colonies survive. One account that did was written by Gustavus Vassa. His story was first published in London and eventually included in thirty-six editions published between 1789 and 1857.

Vassa was born about 1745 in the Benin Kingdom, located in what is now Nigeria on the Gulf of Guinea. The Benin Kingdom was well established in western Africa and established trade with Portugal during the reign of King Ozolua, who reigned from about 1480 to 1504. Vassa was part of the Ibo tribe within the Benin Kingdom. The Ibo tribe lived along the Niger River, further into the African interior. A number of the Ibo tribe who lived along the Niger

River became slave traders. Vassa's own father owned many slaves and had sold some of them to the slave traders.

Although his father was one of the Ibo tribal leaders, Vassa and his sister were kidnapped and sold to slave traders. Vassa described the capture: "One day, when all our people were gone out to their works as usual, and only me and my dear sister were left to mind the house, two men and a woman got over our walls, and in a moment seized us both; and, without giving us time to cry out, or make resistance, they stopped our mouths, tied our hands, and ran off with us into the nearest wood: and continued to carry us as far as they could, till night came on. . . ."[82]

Vassa's life as a slave had begun at age eleven. After about seven months, Vassa was sold several times and separated from his sister. He eventually ended up on the coast and recalled seeing for the first time the strange-looking white men. He was frightened by the tall ships that he saw in the harbor. Vassa described these strange sights, "The first object which saluted my eyes when I arrived on the coast was the sea, and a slave ship, which was then riding at anchor, and waiting for its cargo. These filled me with astonishment, which was soon converted into terror, which I am yet at a loss to describe, nor the then feelings of my mind. When I was carried on board I was immediately handled, and tossed up, to see if I were sound, by some of the crew; and I was now persuaded that I had got into a world of bad spirits, and that they were going to kill me. Their complexions too differing so much from ours, their long hair, and the language they spoke, which was very different from any I had ever heard, united to confirm me in this belief."[83]

The "Middle Passage" for Vassa was difficult, to say the least. Having enough food was a constant problem. Vassa described some of the meanness of the sailors: "One day they had taken a number of fishes; and when they had killed and satisfied themselves with as many as they thought fit, to our astonishment who were on the deck, rather than give any of them to us to eat, as we expected, they tossed the remaining fish into the sea again, although we begged and prayed for some as well as we could, but in vain; and some of my countrymen, being pressed by hunger, took an opportunity, when they thought no one saw them, of trying to get a little privately; but they were discovered, and the attempt procured them some very severe floggings."[84]

Vassa greatly feared that he would be eaten by the white sailors on board the slave ship. When he saw a pot of boiling water on the deck of the ship he fainted in fear, because he thought the pot was for him to be cooked. He saw one set of slaves, who were chained together, jump overboard in either a desperate escape attempt or perhaps to commit suicide.

He arrived in the Western Hemisphere in Barbados. Again Vassa, and apparently others, felt that they were going to be eaten by the whites. "There was much dread and trembling among us," Vassa said. The fear remained until some slaves, who spoke their language, came on board and explained that they were there to go to work for the white men, would not be eaten, and would join others that spoke their language.

Seeing horses and men riding them was the most amazing thing Vassa saw in this New World. He had never seen a horse, much less a man riding one, and considered it "magical arts." He was also amazed by the brick homes and the multiple stories of some of the buildings.

He was held in a stockade initially until the public slave sale. In a few days, Vassa was sold by way of a "shout" method. At the sound of a drum the slave buyers would rush in and select the slave that they want to purchase. As Vassa described it, "In this manner, without scruple, are relations and friends' separated, most of them never to see each other again."[85]

Vassa's journeys were not yet done. Several days later he and a few other slaves, "that were not saleable," were bound for Virginia on another ship. Vassa described this journey as much easier, both in terms of treatment and they had plenty of food to eat. He ended up on a Virginia plantation, but he was unable to converse with anyone, as no one spoke his language. "I was now exceedingly miserable, and thought myself worse off than any of the rest of my companions; for they could talk to each other, but I had no person to speak to that I could understand. In this state I was constantly grieving and pining, and wishing for death, rather than anything else," Vassa wrote.[86]

He spent the first few days weeding grass and gathering stones. He then was called into the slave owner's home where one of his duties was to fan the slave owner. He was amazed at the furnishings in the house. He had little or no understanding of the functions of the items in the house. The clicking clock scared him, and he feared a portrait hanging on the wall was watching his every move and would report his actions to the slave owner.

Vassa was called various names, depending on who owned him, including Jacob and Michael. He eventually was bought by an Englishman, Michael Pascal, and Vassa was renamed for the final time, Gustavus Vassa. He initially disliked the name, but later in life he used it exclusively. He served as a seaman with Pascal and eventually made it to England where he was converted to Christianity and received a formal education.

In 1763, Vassa was sold by Pascal to an American and continued to labor as a seaman for his new owner. He was able to purchase his own freedom in 1766 and he continued to work as a seaman. Vassa returned to England in 1777 where he married an English woman and lobbied for anti-slavery efforts. He died in 1797.

The Slave Traders

As we have seen, the West African slave trader originated from the Iberian Peninsula, with traders first coming from Portugal, followed by those from Spain. These two nations dominated the slave trade business in the fifteenth and sixteenth centuries. Both nations lost the slave trade crown in the seventeenth and eighteenth centuries, but the two nations that initiated African slave trading to the Western Hemisphere would be the last to end the trading in the 1800s.

The Portuguese initially began bringing African slaves into Europe. They were joined in the slave importing business by Spain, Sicily, and Italy. As many as fifty thousand Africans may have been brought into Europe as slaves.[87] Most of Portugal's imports went to the Western Hemisphere, mainly to Brazil. Almost two million African slaves had been exported to Brazil by 1810.[88] Slightly more than a million more African slaves would go to Brazil from 1811 to 1870, although not exclusively by way of the Portuguese.[89]

The Spanish enslaved about fifty-one thousand Africans from 1521 to 1595.[90] The numbers dramatically increased over the next two hundred years. By 1773, the Spanish had imported about another six hundred and fifty thousand African slaves to their far-flung Western Hemisphere colonies.[91] Mexico received about 50,000 African slaves and Peru around 100,000.[92]

Taking over the slave trade leadership from Portugal and Spain were England, France, and the Netherlands, beginning in the seventeenth century. The British had begun dabbling in African slave trade as early as 1562 when Sir John Hawkins, backed by British financiers, set sail for Africa with three ships and one hundred men. He and his crew were able to capture three hundred African slaves, "partly by the sword and partly by other means." He sailed to Hispaniola where, without any official hindrance from the authorities, he traded them for goods, and a year later sailed back to England proclaiming his slave voyage a financial success with much "gain to himself."[93]

With the British having naval superiority over the rest of the world, it was only natural that they enter the lucrative African slave business. A slave-trading company, the Royal African Company, was chartered in 1672, with the Duke of York at its head. Like the East India Company, the Royal African Company was a "royal monopoly," a private company given exclusive rights to trade by the monarchy in a particular region or field of commerce. The British now officially viewed slaves as a commodity, mere chattel property, on par with other goods eligible for international trade.

The Royal African Company had exclusive rights to trade for slaves from the Moroccan coast to the Cape of Good Hope.[94] Most of the slaves were sent to British colonies in the Caribbean to work on the labor intensive sugar plantations. The Royal African Company had exclusive rights to slave trading until 1698, when slave-trading rights were granted to all Englishmen. Beginning in 1698, for only a payment of ten pounds to the British crown, to help support British forts and garrisons on the African west coast, any British citizen could become a slave trader.[95]

The British, beginning in 1761, began a major effort in slave trading. Within only nine years they had taken over three hundred thousand Africans and transported the survivors of the Middle Passage to their colonial holdings in the Western Hemisphere. Before they ceased the slave-trading business in 1807, they took an additional one million two hundred thousand Africans to the "New World."[96] Nearly three quarters of the Africans that the British took came from three African regions, Bight of Biafra, the Congo (Angola), and the Windward Coast.[97]

The British wanted the slaves for their sugar plantations in the British West Indies. They had taken control of the island of Barbados by 1650 and began exporting sugar and tobacco. Jamaica came under British control in 1655 and would soon become the leading sugar producer in the world by 1700.[98] The sugar plantations needed labor and the African slave was the least expensive source to use.

The British made an excellent return on their slave trade investment. Roger Anstey, in one of the chapters in the book *Race and Slavery in the Western Hemisphere: Quantitative Studies*, did an analysis of the British slave trade. He found that during the forty-six years of British slave trade they averaged a 9.5 percent return per year.[99] Returns reached their peaks in the nineteen years between 1781 and 1800, averaging about 13 percent per year. The returns reached their lowest levels in the last six years of British slave trade, averaging only a bit more then 3 percent per year.[100]

The two banner years for the British were in 1792 when they captured over fifty-three thousand Africans, utilizing 186 ships, and in 1798 when they captured over fifty-six thousand Africans, utilizing 163 ships for transportation.[101] The British averaged 120 ships per year, from 1781 to 1807, for slave transportation.

The British greatly improved on the death rate of the "Middle Passage" sea journey form Africa to the Western Hemisphere. Anstey estimates a mortality rate of between 8 and 9 percent up to about 1792. The rate then improved to between about 3 percent to 4 percent, averaging about 4 percent the last ten years of British slave trade.[102] The improved rates were likely the result of improvements in hygiene and sanitation.

The French also imported slaves to their Western Hemisphere colonies. Following the British example they developed the island of Saint Domingue, the present-day Haiti. In just fifty years the slave population in Saint Domingue increased from only 20,000 to 230,000 by 1750.[103] Saint Domingue became the world's largest producer of lost cost sugar until 1790. Beginning in the 1790s, a slave revolt occurred in Saint Domingue, eventually led by Toussaint L'Ouverture. The result was the independent nation of Haiti in 1804, the fall of Haiti as a leading world producer of sugar, and the end of France as a major slave trader. Brazil and Cuba would eventually replace Haiti as leading sugar producers. Over one million three hundred thousand African slaves were brought to the French Caribbean colonies between 1701 and 1810,[104] although these were not exclusively French traders bringing in the slaves.

The Dutch began slave trading as early as 1629 and continued until 1795. They established a number of slave-trading posts in a large geographical area on the African west coast, stretching in the north from modern-day Senegal to modern-day Gabon, further south. At the onset the Dutch slave-trading was done exclusively through the Dutch West India Company. In return for subsidies to the Dutch government the company was given exclusive trading rights for Africa and America.

This is the company that helped to form and administer the colony of New Amsterdam, later to be known as New York City. Slaves were most likely introduced into what would become New York City by the Dutch shortly after the first slaves were brought into Jamestown. In a document dated 1629, the Dutch seemed very interested in African slaves, "The company will use their endeavors to supply the colonists with as many blacks as they conveniently can."[105] In 1991, the remains of over four hundred slaves were found in lower Manhattan. The slaves' well preserved remains were examined by anthropologists. According to Howard University anthropologists, the remains indicated that half of the populations died before they became teenagers, with others dying within the first two years of their arrival in New York.[106]

The Dutch captured and exported to the Western Hemisphere nearly a half million slaves in the nearly 165 years they were involved in slave trading. The peak years for the Dutch were in the

1760s when they captured and exported nearly sixty-three thousand Africans.[107]

Other European nations dabbled in the slave trade business. The Germans, the Danish, and others were minor players in the slave trade business. Slave trading was not an exclusive European enterprise. In the United States, slave traders could be found from what would become the New England states, particularly from Rhode Island and Massachusetts. New England's maritime industry could not avoid the potential profits that could be made from the slave trade business. It has been estimated that the New England slave traders brought in over 200,000 slaves to the United States.[108] Initially, the New England slave trade business was dominated by traders from Massachusetts. Traders from Rhode Island would soon challenge those in Massachusetts and would, by about 1770, dominate the New England slave trade business. As one historian noted, "American Slave Trade" perhaps should be re-titled "Rhode Island Slave Trade," as the Rhode Islanders dominated the American slave trade throughout the eighteenth century and into the nineteenth century. From about the early 1700s to 1807 there were nearly a thousand slave trade voyages out of just Rhode Island. Those voyages carried over 106,000 Africans to the Western Hemisphere, many dropped off in the Caribbean.[109]

The British ended slave trade in 1807 and strongly encouraged other nations to do likewise. Within the next ten years or so, most other nations followed the British example, also banning slave trade. Initially, the British ban on slave trade was somewhat ignored. The British navy, however, put the teeth into the ban. The Royal Navy began to patrol the western coast of Africa to stop slave traders, and they continued those patrols for forty-five years.

By 1865, the British navy had captured fifteen hundred ships and "rescued" approximately 160,000 slaves.[110] It has been estimated that the British naval patrols, as well as the international political influence it exerted on various nations, perhaps prevented as many as 820,000 Africans from being enslaved and sent to the Western Hemisphere.[111] It should be pointed out that of the Africans "rescued" many were not returned home, but ended up in the Western Hemisphere in places like Cuba as slaves.

The suppression of slave trade by the British had a curious negative side effect. Because slave traders had to evade the British naval patrols, it typically meant longer voyages so as to avoid detection. The longer voyages caused slave mortality rates to increase. No longer was it a straight trip from Africa to the Western Hemisphere, but a zigzag nondetection course would be required. The basic rule of thumb was, the longer the "Middle Passage" journey the fewer number of slaves survived.

It should be noted that for all the terrible suffering inflicted by the slave traders on the people of Africa, the slave traders also paid a high price for their efforts. Of the 598 slave trader voyages between 1748 and 1792, by the French, one crew member in six died. This was a higher death rate than that of the slaves.[112] It only got worse for the Europeans that manned the various slave outposts on the West African coast. In his book, *Atlantic Slave Trade*, Phillip Curtin estimated that half of all the European merchants, officials, and soldiers sent to man these posts died while in Africa.[113] It seems that the hostile African environment and diseases had a deadly effect on the Europeans. Another study of Europeans involved in slave trade on the African continent, indicated that half the men died within a year and scarcely one-tenth ever returned home.[114]

The Slave Coast

The Africans that were taken as slaves came from or near the western coast of Africa. Beginning as far north as the modern-day country of Senegal and then down the coast as far south as Gabon and the Congo this was African slave territory.

The majority of slaves came from an area known as the Bight of Benin, sometimes referred to as the "Slave Coast." This region is named for a large bay that is a portion of the western part of the Gulf of Guinea. The Bight of Benin extends from the mouth of the Volta River to the mouth of the Niger River. The slaves came from what are today the countries of Togo, Benin, and part of Nigeria. From the 1700s on this was the primary source of slaves for the Portuguese. From 1711 to 1810 nearly half of all the slaves taken were from this region.[115] This area was also the largest source of slaves for

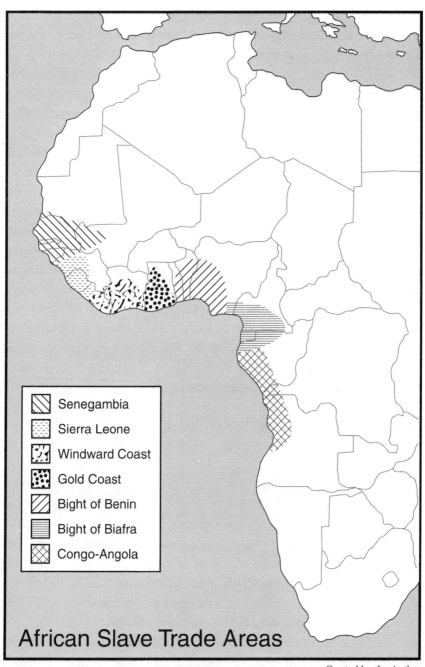

	Senegambia
	Sierra Leone
	Windward Coast
	Gold Coast
	Bight of Benin
	Bight of Biafra
	Congo-Angola

African Slave Trade Areas

French slave traders.[116] Some estimate that nearly one-third of all Africans taken came from the Bight of Benin area.[117] Many of these captured were from the Yoruba ethnic group in southwest Nigeria and some from the Hausa and Nupe.

The area that furnished the second largest number of slaves was the area known as the Bight of Biafra. This area is named for the bay that is a portion of the eastern part of the Gulf of Guinea. It would include the present-day nation of Nigeria, the southern half south of the Niger River, as well as the countries of Equatorial Guinea, Cameroon, Gabon, and parts of the Congo, and Angola. The British dominated this region drawing most of their slaves from this area. The Dutch seemed to avoid this area, finding the slaves from this region undesirable because of their "malicious" and "stubborn" nature.[118] The Trans-Atlantic Slave Trade Database statistics indicate that slaves taken from this region, had the highest death rates on the passages to the Western Hemisphere. Between 1663 and 1713 about a third of all the slaves taken from this region never made it to the Western Hemisphere, by far the highest mortality rate of any region. Apparently most of the slaves died from dehydration, resulting from gastrointestinal disease, and those that did survive the voyage would typically arrive very emaciated.[119] Many slave buyers viewed slaves from this region as the least desirable slaves. In spite of that, still an estimated 25 percent of all the slaves taken from West Africa were from this region.[120]

The Gold Coast, labeled by the Portuguese in 1471 when they were the first Europeans to arrive, was the third highest region for slaves. This West African coastal region was named not for the value of the slaves exported from it, but rather for the nearby trans-Saharan trade in the precious metal of gold. This area hit its peak for slave exports in the 1730s. This area includes the land around the modern-day country of Ghana. The principal cultural group in this area was the Ashanti, who had dominance in the region. The area was in dispute between the Portuguese, Dutch, and British, until the British gained superiority over the other European nations by the early 1800s. The British drew the majority of slaves from this area, followed by the Dutch and the French.[121] The British and the

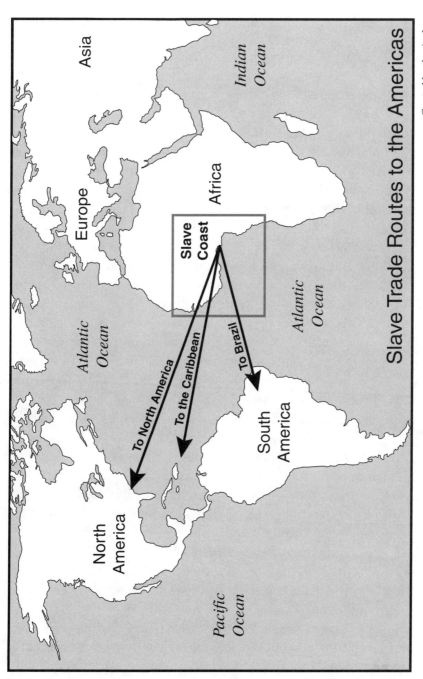

Slave Trade Routes to the Americas

Created by the Author
Drawn by Jim Robinson

Ashanti fought from the 1820s until a peace treaty was signed in 1831.

Three other West African coast areas were the source of slaves: the Windward Coast, Sierra Leone, and Senegambia. Collectively about a quarter of all slaves came from these areas. The Windward Coast is the area around the present-day coastal nations of Senegal and Côte d'Ivoire. Initially, this area was the major source of slaves for the French slave traders, who dominated until the 1740s. This area peaked in slave exports in the 1760s, after the British and the Dutch began to purchase or capture slaves from this region. Collectively, most of the slaves on the Windward Coast were taken by the British, followed by the French and the Dutch.

The Sierra Leone region includes what is now the country of Sierra Leone plus parts of Guinea and Liberia. In reviewing slave data this was the smallest of the areas in producing slaves. Again this was an area that was dominated by the British, reaching its peak in slave exports between 1761 and 1780. The French and the Dutch also drew slaves from this area, but in relatively small numbers.[122]

One of the first sources of slaves was the area of Senegambia, which is the area now occupied by Senegal and the Gambia plus a portion of western part of Mali. New England slave traders concentrated in Senegambia and Sierra Leone for slaves, as well as along the Gold Coast.[123] The British again dominated this region, but the French also used Senegambia as a source for slaves.

Another major source for slaves was the area of Congo-Angola. This is an area made up of the current nations of parts of Gabon, the Republic of the Congo, the Democratic Republic of the Congo, and northern Angola. Although the British were strong in this area, the Portuguese, who were the first to reach this region, dominated Angola slave trade, with most of the slaves going to Brazil.[124] Most historians include this region with the slave trade numbers from the Bight of Biafra.

Table 2.1 shows the African West Coast slave trade regions and the corresponding percentage of slaves taken by the four primary European nations that were involved in slave trade. As you will note, the British dominated all regions of slave trade with the exception of the Bight of Benin.

Table 2.1—Percentage of Slaves Taken by Region and
by European Nations from 1711 to 1810.

Region	British	French	Dutch	Portuguese
Senegambia	57.32%	42.68%	0	0
Sierra Leone	92.01%	4.97%	3.03%	0
Windward Coast	51.74%	26.87%	21.39%	0
Gold Coast	75.22%	9.87%	14.91%	0
Bight of Benin	25.93%	23.50%	4.94%	45.63%
Bight of Biafra	93.85%	6.15%	0	0

It should be mentioned that some African slaves came from the East Coast of Africa, although their numbers pale in comparison to the number originating from the West Coast of Africa. The Portuguese explorer Vasco da Gama rounded the Cape of Good Hope in 1498 and explored the East Coast of Africa on an expedition that eventually took him as far as India. As early as 1505 the Portuguese had established a trading post, at Sofala, in present-day Mozambique on the Indian Ocean. Later, further to the south, the Portuguese found an excellent deep water harbor, Delagoa Bay, and set up a post there, which they used for their slave trade efforts. Most of the slaves from this area were sent to Brazil.[125]

Non-African "Slaves"

As indicated by Virginia Governor William Berkeley in the 1600s, the largest segment of those with limited freedom in the colonies were not slaves, but rather indentured servants. Indentured servants were men and women who had signed an agreement to work without pay for a specific period of time in return for passage to America, typically from Europe. At the end of the specified time period the indentured servant was free to pursue whatever line of work they chose. In some cases, the departing indentured servant would be guaranteed land and tools.

The indentured servant approach was the manner in which many Europeans came to the English colonies. For the colonies it meant a cheap form of labor, and for many Europeans it meant an opportunity to come to the Western Hemisphere and begin a new life. Most came on a voluntary basis, although there were instances where individuals were kidnapped and forced into indentured servitude. Characteristically, an adult would serve a five-year indentured period and a child would serve for seven years. Terms of service could be extended for criminal behavior. The early tobacco-growing industry in Virginia and Maryland was initially built on a white indentured servitude labor force.[126]

What was the difference between being a slave and being an indentured servant in America? There were four major differences. First was the fact that an indentured servant was not property that could be sold. Indeed, the indentured servant's contract could be sold, but it was the time of service being sold, not the person. The second difference was the limited time period that the indentured servant would have to serve. The slave, of course, was a slave for life, unless freed by the master. The indentured servant was for all practical purposes a slave, answering in every way to his or her "employer," but only for the term of the indentured service. Like the master for the slave, the "employer" was required to furnish food, clothing, and shelter for the indentured servant. The third difference was that the children born to the indentured servant were not bound to the master, unlike those children born to slave women. Finally, the other difference was race, although this was not an absolute. The overwhelming majority of indentured servants were white and the vast majority of the slaves were of African descent.

Most of the early indentured servants were from England, but by the 1700s the indentured servant numbers swelled by new indentured servants from Ireland, Germany, Scotland, and Switzerland. A minority number of indentured servants were native born, choosing to serve out criminal punishment as an indentured servant. Most of the indentured servants were males; they outnumbered females three to one.[127] It has been estimated that perhaps as many as half of the white immigrants to the original thirteen colonies came as indentured servants.[128]

When the Europeans arrived in the Western Hemisphere, slavery was already in existence. Many Native American societies enslaved their enemies, although often the slaves would eventually be assimilated into the conquering tribes. This meant that not all of the slaves in the Western Hemisphere were of African origin. The Portuguese, Spanish, and English each enslaved native-born

American Indians. Many were originally captured as the result of military action. They were soon sold on the open market. The Native Americans did not adjust well to slavery; disease and hard work took a horrific toll. The other problem that slave owners had with Native American slaves was that they knew the lay of the land. Unlike the African slaves, who had been uprooted from their native lands, the Native Americans knew the territory and would frequently run away.

Native American slaves were found in each of the thirteen colonies, but the numbers were never very large. In 1708, the governor of South Carolina, which probably had the largest number of Native American slaves in the colonies, estimated that out of a population of 12,580 only fourteen hundred were Native American slaves.[129]

Sugar and Slaves

Most of the African slaves being imported into the Western Hemisphere were going to Brazil, Mexico, and the Caribbean colonies. What was the reason? It was the sweet tooth of Europeans. Europeans were first exposed to sugar when the Crusaders found it being grown in Palestine and Syria, in the late Middle Ages. The Europeans tried to cultivate the product, first on the islands in the eastern Mediterranean, Cyprus, then later on Crete and Sicily. It was on Cyprus that the forerunner to the plantation developed, where serfs worked land owned by someone else.[130] Some of those that worked the plantations were Eastern Europeans from the area of the Black Sea. The Slavs began to be identified with the bound labor and the word "slave" was born.[131]

Sugar grows best where it is warm year round. In their search for land best suited for sugar production, the Europeans moved westward out of the Mediterranean Sea to the northwest coast of Africa, in the Atlantic Ocean. The Portuguese introduced sugar growing on the island of Madeira by 1455, and for a time that island was the leading sugar producer for Europe. When the Spanish introduced sugar cultivation to the Canary Islands, the sugar production there soon rivaled Madeira's. Other warm weather locations were also found further south on islands off the west coast of Africa. There the Portuguese found one of the best locations for sugar cultivation on the uninhabited island of São Tomé off the coast of the present-day nation of Gabon in the Gulf of Guinea.

Slave labor was perfect for sugar cultivation. As early as 1100 A.D., Albert of Aachen described slave labor as the preferred method of labor for production that was hard and difficult, and high enough wages could not be paid to attract the workers. Albert of Aachen saw sugar cultivation as the perfect crop for slave labor because it was difficult to grow and the suspected demand it would one day have.[132]

Sugar production has intense and demanding labor requirements associated with it. First, the fields must be cleared and then planted by deeply burrowing under the old sugar cane. Once the plant begins to grow it must be constantly weeded and trimmed. Unwanted shoots must be cut back and the entire crop periodically fertilized. Perhaps the most difficult task is the harvest, where the cane must be cut. All of this is done in tropical or semi-tropical climates. Once cut, the cane must be quickly sent to the mill to be processed. From there the process starts anew.[133]

Slave labor was used in sugar production from the early days on Cyprus. Early on captured Moslems were used as slave labor in Cyprus. As the sugar production moved westward other slaves were used, including Africans, Berbers from northern Africa as well as others. The plantation system of labor also advanced as sugar production moved westward. By the time of the development of sugar cultivation in São Tomé the prototype plantation was in full operation. Slaves from the nearby west coast of Africa became the primary labor force. By the 1520s, São Tomé's sugar industry had begun to rapidly grow, and was importing about two thousand slaves a year.[134] São Tomé also served as an excellent slave trade port with its close proximity to the African West Coast and its navigable harbor.

Sugar plantations were the prime crop south of the thirteen original British colonies. It has been estimated that of the total number of African slaves who reached the Western Hemisphere between 60 percent and 70 percent ended up in one of the sugar colonies in the Caribbean, or in Central or South America.[135] By 1650, people of African descent made up 25 percent of the total population of the

British Caribbean, compared to only 4 percent of the total population in the British North American colonies.[136]

The Growth of African Slaves in the American Colonies

By 1624, according to the census of the Virginia colony, there were only twenty-two slaves, and the following year only one more. It is interesting to note that in the 1624 census the full names of white people are listed, but for the African Americans complete names are not listed at all, sometimes listing only a reference to "one Negor."[137] Is this a hint that a racist attitude was already in existence in the colonies?

As the original thirteen colonies began to grow, a critical need for labor developed. Settling new territories, clearing land, and farming took manpower. The indentured servant approach was not keeping pace with the overall need for additional labor. As Peter Kolchin points out in his book *American Slavery, 1619–1877*, the population of Virginia tripled from 1650 to 1700, and if indentured servants were to continue to provide the agricultural labor required their numbers would need to come close to tripling.[138] Fewer people, not more, were choosing the indentured servant method as their method of immigrating to the colonies. Since the Native Americans did not make good slaves the colonist began to look for another source of inexpensive labor. They had only to look towards Africa and the slave traders.

Starting in the 1670s a major labor force shift from indentured servants to African slaves had begun.[139] From 1700 to 1710 more than twice the number of African slaves were imported into Virginia and Maryland as in the entire previous century. Why weren't the indentured servants coming anymore? What forced the switch to slave labor? In his excellent book, *Black Southerners 1619–1869*, John Boles explains why. At least partly due to the English Civil War, the birthrate in England fell dramatically in the 1640s. By the 1660s the pay scales in England had improved and coupled with a shortage of workers, fewer people decided to journey to the colonies.[140] Planters began to complain about the American labor shortage, and even lowering of standards, using younger workers and less skilled indentured servants, was not enough to meet their labor needs. This created a ready-made opportunity for the slave traders to enter the picture with African slaves.

The majority of the African slaves found themselves on tobacco farms in Virginia and Maryland. In 1690 those two states had about two-thirds of the entire American slave population. Most of the slaves in the Chesapeake area were working on tobacco farms. The growth of the tobacco crop had been dramatic. In the mid-1630s Virginia produced a million pounds of tobacco per year; thirty years later the annual production had increased to fifteen million pounds.

Slavery was also beginning to take root in the Carolinas. Around 1670, British immigrants from Barbados arrived in what is now South Carolina. With them they brought their slaves. By 1690 rice production, which was very labor intensive, had begun to become a major crop in South Carolina.

Slavery was not limited to Virginia, Maryland, or the Carolinas. Slavery was sanctioned in all of the original thirteen colonies,[141] and slaves were found in each of the colonies.[142] In 1700, 42 percent of all the households in New York City possessed slaves, and even as late as 1770 twice as many slaves were in the colony of New York as in the colony of Georgia.[143] Also, by 1770, the percentage of slaves in the total population of the colonies had grown from 4 percent in 1650 to 22 percent. If you look only at the southern colonies the percentage was even more dramatic, from a level of 3 percent in 1650 to 50 percent, fifty years later.

It was in Virginia and Maryland that the first clear racial distinction between servants was made. In the 1660s laws went into effect that decreed that black slaves would be slaves for life and that any child would have the same status as his or her mother. Laws also went into effect stating that even a Christian baptism would not change the status of a slave.[144] These laws would make unborn children future slaves and upped the ante in slave investment. An investment in a slave was now ownership for life, including any and all of the slave offspring.

Slavery began to rapidly grow. In 1670, Virginia had an

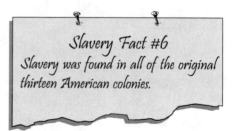

Slavery Fact #6

Slavery was found in all of the original thirteen American colonies.

estimated population of 40,000, which included six thousand white servants and two thousand African slaves. By 1700, the number of Virginia slaves had grown to 16,000 and by 1750 the number of African slaves in Virginia had reached 120,000.

African Adjustment

For the most part, the African slaves adapted to their new world setting. Family units typically remained together. Having a large family was a source of recognition both within the slave community and by the slave owners. For the most part they adopted the English language and soon embraced Christianity.

In a few instances, African slaves revolted. In 1739, twenty slaves near the Stono River in South Carolina rebelled. They were able to seize some weapons and killed several whites as they attempted to escape into Spanish-held Florida. Within a matter of days the "rebellion" was quashed, with the slaves either shot or hung.

The post-Revolutionary War period would see continued growth in the number of slaves and some dramatic changes in the way people viewed what some called "the peculiar institution" of slavery.

One major difference between slavery in what would become the United States, compared with the rest of the Western Hemisphere, was the relatively quick decline of slaves native to Africa. This caused a more rapid loss of the slaves' native roots and culture than elsewhere in the Western Hemisphere. Late into the nineteenth century, the majority of the slave populations in the British and French Caribbean islands and of Brazil were born in Africa. With a much higher death rate in these areas, compared to the United States, slave traders were constantly bringing in new African slaves to meet the labor demands.

In his book *Without Consent Or Contract: The Rise and Fall of American Slavery*, Robert Fogel points out that by the time George Washington had become president the native-to-Africa portion of the United States African American population had shrunk to slightly over 20 percent. It hovered near that range from 1780 to 1810 and then dramatically moved towards zero. By 1850, all but a minute fraction of slaves in the United States were native born.[145] By the outbreak of the War Between the States most slaves were third, fourth, or fifth generation Americans. Their native languages, religions, social mores, and much of their cultural heritage were gone, as they were assimilated into the European-based culture.

Chapter Three
The Growth Period (1774 to 1830)

Slavery and the Revolutionary War

The new nation proclaimed by the Declaration of Independence had a peculiar problem. The Declaration of Independence boldly proclaimed that "all men are created equal," yet within what would become the borders of the United States of America were many that were not treated as equals but rather as mere servants. Who to blame? Thomas Jefferson wanted a paragraph added to the Declaration of Independence that blamed the British. He wanted to point the finger of blame towards King George III, wanting to include, "He has waged a cruel war against human nature itself, violating its most sacred rights of life and liberty in the persons of a distant people who never offended him, captivating & carrying them into slavery in another hemisphere, or to incur miserable death in their transportation . . ."[1] The paragraph was never added, and the problem which was not resolved would become a thorn in the side of the new nation.

The greatest threat to the institution of slavery in North America, up to this point in time, was the American Revolutionary War. By the time of the war there were an estimated half million slaves in the colonies. The British immediately tried to disrupt the colonies' slave system. As they did with Native Americans, the British saw the slaves as a potential ally against the rebellious colonists. The British would promise freedom to the slaves in return for their support.

Some claim that the first person killed during the 1770 Boston Massacre was an African American, Crispus Attucks. Would this be a war that involved all Americans or would it exclude African Americans? The American colonies made counter offers to the British offer of freedom to the slaves, but did so in varying degrees, and it varied by colony. New York offered freedom for slaves in return for three years of military service. Maryland authorized slave recruitment into the military.

The Continental Army's official position on African American enlistments varied with time. The Continental Army seemed not to know what to do with African Americans willing to serve. There were sprinklings of African Americans with the Continental Army at the Battle of Bunker Hill in June of 1775. Following General George Washington's assumption of command, an order was issued, on July 10, 1775, forbidding the recruitment of African Americans, as well as British deserters and "vagabonds."[2]

In the Continental Congress an effort was made to discharge all African Americans serving in the army, but the motion was defeated. However, Congress did affirm the army's prohibition on any additional African American enlistments.[3] That was short-lived, as Washington reversed himself and allowed free African Americans, "who have served faithfully . . . may be re-enlisted therein, but no others." In spite of the limitations, which meant no slaves and no new free African Americans allowed, the need for troops overrode the prohibition. In various locations both slaves and free African Americans were allowed to enter the military. The exact number of slaves serving the colonial side is uncertain; some estimate as many as five thousand served.[4] Although some African Americans saw combat, most of them served in a support capacity. It is likely that some slaves from all states, except for South Carolina and Georgia, served on the American side.[5]

What is clear is that there was not a mass uprising of slaves against their owners, although tens of thousands of slaves did flee and follow the British army. Like their colonist counterparts, most of the African Americans serving with the British were used not in combat, but rather in an ancillary capacity. After the fighting had ended and the colonists had won, the British faced a dilemma. As they began to withdraw to return home to England, what would they do with the slaves that had followed and supported them? The Americans demanded that since the slaves were property they should be returned to their owners. The British, for the most part, would not agree and perhaps as many as 50,000 slaves were evacuated.[6] Some of the ex-slaves who followed the British in search of freedom ended up in Canada and England, but unfortunately, some of them ended up again as slaves in Britain's Caribbean colonies.

Perhaps the most profound effect of the Revolutionary War on slavery was the change of mindset that occurred with many after the war was over.

Beginnings of Opposition to Slavery

As we mentioned earlier, slavery was accepted by most people as a normal course of events in human life as long as history has been recorded. That would begin to change after the Revolutionary War, and would greatly accelerate in the nineteenth century.

Some of the earliest opponents of slavery were the Quakers. The Quakers first arose as a religious sect in the early 1600s in England, called the Society of Friends, founded by George Fox. They had no ministers and downplayed the importance of the Bible, rather relying on revelations received directly from God. In 1688, the Quakers made their first public statement against slavery. They held that God did not view people as inferior based on skin color. They would play an important role in the antislavery movement in the nineteenth century.

The American Revolutionary War brought new meaning to words such as freedom, liberty, and equality. Where did slavery fit in with the noble ideas of the Revolutionary War? Patrick Henry asked of slavery, is it not "repugnant to humanity . . . and destructive to liberty?" Some in the new American republic answered yes to Henry's question. Even George Washington, a slave owner himself, referred to slavery as a "misfortune." Washington's last will and testament would provide for the freeing of his slaves, after his death.

Slavery in the North, post-Revolutionary War, represented the easiest opportunity to end slavery. The smaller number of slaves and the small economic effect that they had on the Northern economy allowed the North to be the ideal location for an emancipation effort. Still, it took nearly thirty years for all the slaves to be freed in the North. In some states it happened rather quickly; Vermont prohibited slavery with its 1777 constitution.

The judicial system outlawed slavery in Massachusetts. In April of 1771, a slave in Massachusetts, Quok Walker, ran away from his owner. He took shelter at the home of a neighbor sympathetic to Walker's situation. Several days later the slave owner found Walker and subjected him to a beating. Walker, however, held his ground and sued his owner. Walker contended that the Massachusetts state constitution proclaimed all men are born free and equal. The Massachusetts State Superior Court in 1783 ruled in favor of Walker, which marked the beginning of the end for slavery in the state of Massachusetts.

In other Northern states, particularly where there were substantially more slaves, the process took much longer. Some of these states granted gradual emancipation. Typically these laws would allow slave children to become free after reaching a certain age: males usually at age twenty-eight and females at age twenty-one or twenty-five. New Jersey was the last of the Northern states to free its slaves with its gradual freedom act of 1804.[7]

One should not confuse the emancipation of slaves in the North with racial equality. A French writer commenting on 1830's America said, "race prejudice seems stronger in those states that have abolished slavery than where it still exists, and nowhere is it more intolerant than in those states where slavery was never known."[8] Prior to 1860, African Americans in the North were not always allowed to vote, they could not serve on a jury, children were usually educated in separate schools, and they worshipped in separate churches. Being a freed slave in the North meant spending your life in a world of racial discrimination.

A Quaker schoolteacher, Prudence Crandall, caused a national fury in 1832 when she admitted to her Connecticut school the daughter of a free African American farmer. After the white parents withdrew their students, she attempted to turn the school into a school for free African American children. The school's students were harassed, school windows were broken out and the school's well was contaminated. The next year the Connecticut legislature made it a crime to educate African American students who were not state residents. Ms. Crandall was arrested twice, convicted, and jailed. A mob eventually attacked the school, and even upon her release from jail the school was never reopened.

Compromise

In 1787, representatives from the various states met in Philadelphia originally to revise the young nation's Articles of Confederation. What came out of the nearly four-month meeting was the blueprint of a new national government. The delegates were a who's who of the day: George Washington, Alexander Hamilton, James Madison, and Benjamin Franklin, just to name a few. They, through compromise after compromise, were able to produce the Constitution of the United States. One of the issues that they had to wrestle with was the institution of slavery.

In spite of South Carolinian Pierce Butler's pronouncement that the North and the South were "as different as . . . Russia and Turkey," a compromise was made, as the young nation struggled to devise a government. The "slavery compromise," made at the Constitutional Convention, called for the United States Constitution to be purposely vague on the topic of slavery. The new Constitution neither specifically allowed for slavery nor denied its citizens the right to own slaves. The words "slave" or "slavery" were never used in the new Constitution, they chose the kindler and gentler terminology of "person held to service or labor."[9]

Slaves under the Constitution were to be counted as three-fifths of a person in population numbers used to determine the number of seats in the United States House of Representatives. This would allow the Southern states to have a higher representation versus the slaves not being counted, but it meant that the South would have to pay more in taxes.

Finally, there was the sticky issue of slave trade. The founding fathers agreed that there would be no national prohibition on the importation of African slaves until 1808. In other words, states, unless they chose individually to ban slave trading, could import as many slaves from Africa as they chose for the next twenty years. It was not only Southerners that supported the continuation of slave trade, Northern slave merchants also supported the continuation of American slave trading. In fact, many Southerners did not support the continuation of slave trade at all. In total opposition to the continuation of slave trade, the State of Virginia banned all slave imports in 1778. Other Southern states followed along: Maryland in 1783, South Carolina in 1787 (although South Carolina reopened slave trade between 1803 and 1808), North Carolina in 1794, and Georgia in 1798.[10] Certain New England commercial interest, however, wanted slave trading to continue, which would afford them to continue to see the excellent slave trade profits.

In spite of the Constitution not addressing the issue of slavery, the Continental Congress did, in the same year. The Continental Congress in the 1787 Land Ordinance Act forever barred slavery from the Northwest Territory. It would be the first of many future bills that would determine where slavery would be allowed and where it was prohibited.

The "Cotton Kingdom"

Prior to the 1800s, tobacco was the predominate crop in the upper states of the South, while rice and indigo were the major crops further south. A change was soon to come upon the Southern states that would dramatically affect slavery in the South. In 1793 a young Northerner had just graduated from Yale College. Upon graduating he had accepted a position as a tutor on a South Carolina plantation. On his passage southward he met the charming widow of Revolutionary War hero Nathanael Greene. Mrs. Green invited the young man to visit her plantation. There he heard planters complaining about the need to have a device that would separate the green seed from the white cotton fiber.

The young man decided it was a project worth tackling. Within ten days he had a design and a model of the machine that would solve the planters' dilemma. It was really rather simple—it was a roller with wire teeth attached that would separate the cotton fiber from the seeds. The young man was Eli Whitney, and the cotton gin, patented in 1794, was born. It was Whitney's "engine," where

Slave trader in Atlanta, Georgia

the word "gin" comes from, that would revolutionize the production of cotton. His original cotton gin, with a hand crank, could gin fifty pounds of cotton a day, compared to one pound a day, prior to his invention.[11]

Cotton, which was a minor crop in the South prior to the 1800s, would quickly grow to replace tobacco as the South's major crop. Whitney's invention alone is not totally responsible for the dramatic change. A number of other factors helped spur the production of Southern-grown cotton. A strong worldwide demand for cotton products developed, which had been aided by the development of steam-powered spinning and weaving machines, particularly in Britain and later in New England. Also the continued improvement in the South's transportation system—riverboats and railroads—which made the transportation costs much more reasonable, helped spur the cotton crop.[12] In addition, more land suitable for the growing of cotton was available as the South expanded westerly into states like Alabama (statehood in 1819), Mississippi (statehood in 1817), and Louisiana, (statehood in 1812). In fact by 1834 those three states grew more than half of all the United States cotton.[13]

United States cotton production went from about three thousand bales in 1790 to 178,000 bales twenty years later. By 1830 it had increased to 732,000 bales and by the eve of the War Between the States had grown to about 4,500,000 bales in 1860.[14] By 1860, cotton was the leading American product, accounting for half of all United States' exports.[15]

A world hungry for cotton products was waiting to receive the Southern-produced product. The raw cotton would be sent to be spinned and weaved, mainly in Britain and in the northeastern part of the United States. Some historians overlook the fact that some of the Southern cotton stayed in the South. In fact the South ranked sixth in the world as a manufacturer of cotton textiles, just ahead of Germany, Austria-Hungary, and Russia.[16]

The growth of cotton had a dramatic effect on American slavery. One effect was the change in the geographical location of slaves. Old tobacco states like Virginia and Maryland, which had two-thirds of the total African American population in 1690, saw that percentage begin to slip, as cotton became king and the South expanded westward. By 1820, Virginia and Maryland's share of African Americans had declined to only 35 percent and by the outbreak of the War Between the States it was down to only 15 percent.[17]

It is not known exactly how many slaves were uprooted from the upper South and moved to states like Alabama, Mississippi, or Louisiana, the lower South. Historians have estimated that from 800,000 to around one million slaves moved west and south between 1790 and 1860. One analysis, done in the 1970s, suggested that about 84 percent of the slaves that migrated moved with their slave owners,[18] as entire families, slaves and all, migrated west and south into cotton country.

During this time period not only was there a movement in slaves there was dramatic growth in the number of slaves in the United States. Slave trade in the United States officially ended in 1808. The first United States census, complete in 1790, counted a total of nearly 700,000 slaves in the nation, out of a total population of 3,929,214. But only twenty years later, the number of slaves had increased by more than 70 percent. This increase was due to slave trade still occurring until 1808, but a much greater cause was the large increase in the number of slave births.

The natural population growth of slaves, an excess of births over deaths, in the United States was most unique when compared to other slave societies. Elsewhere in the Western Hemisphere, when slave importations ended, slave

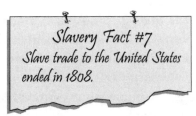

Slavery Fact #7
Slave trade to the United States ended in 1808.

populations decreased. But in the United States the exact opposite occurred. In Jamaica the slaves were freed in 1834. There were approximately 311,000 freed slaves, but over the slave-trading years nearly 750,000 had been brought into Jamaica. Numbers were similar in Brazil and other Caribbean colonies. The number of freed slaves in the United States in 1865 was six times the number of slaves that had been imported from Africa.[19] This obviously reflects a better quality of life for slaves in the United States versus other areas. This will be discussed in more detail in chapter six.

Although cotton farms were typically somewhat larger than tobacco farms, cotton could be grown on small farms with profitable results. As cotton production was beginning to rapidly grow in the South, most of the cotton farms were very small. For slaves this meant that they typically would be a part of a small farm, in very close contact with the slave owner and his family.

Slave Revolts

Unlike other parts of the Western Hemisphere, the United States did not experience slave revolts to any great degree. In 1791, the slaves in the French colony of Saint-Domingue, on the western side of the island of Hispaniola, began a revolt. The revolt lasted for thirteen years and culminated in 1804 with a slave victory over the French and the formation of a new independent nation: Haiti. Nothing like that happened in the United States, although it is only fair to point out that the slaves greatly outnumbered whites on Hispaniola.

In the United States, most of the slave revolts were insignificant in number of slaves involved. Many were foiled before they ever began, in New York in 1741 and in Virginia in 1800.

By far, one of the largest slave revolt attempts was organized by a free African American named Demark Vesey. Vesey was either born in Africa or in the then Danish, now U.S., Virgin Islands. He originally was a slave, serving a Bermuda slave trader, Joseph Vesey. He won, in 1800, enough money in a lottery to purchase his freedom. He opened a carpentry shop in the Virgin Islands and did rather well. Unfortunately for Vesey, his children, born of a slave mother, remained in slavery. He immigrated to the United States, settling in Charleston, South Carolina. In Charleston, he was a free man, but he was angered over the city's closing of his independent African American church. Vesey, inspired by the events in Haiti, realized that African Americans had a very large population in Charleston. He began to recruit other African Americans in a plot to take over the city. Most of the leaders of his band were, like Vesey, not native to the United States, but from either the Caribbean or directly from Africa.

Vesey recruited anywhere from several hundred to as many as a couple of thousand slaves and free African Americans—the exact number will never be known. It is likely that most of the members were free African Americans and not slaves. One problem that Vesey's band had was a lack of weapons. Homemade knives, spikes, and the like were fashioned. Their plan was to use the homemade weapons until they could seize an arsenal.

Their plan was violent. They intended to attack Charleston at seven different points, capture the arsenals in Charleston, kill all the white citizens, and then burn the city. Their target date was June 16, 1822. In the month before the planned date, a slave reported that the group had attempted to recruit him in the revolt effort. The

Charleston authorities recruited another slave to join the conspirators as a spy. With the help of the spy, Charleston authorities learned enough to crack the slave conspiracy.

Vesey initially evaded capture but eventually was caught at the home of his wife and was arrested by authorities. Vesey was hanged, as were thirty-four more of his band. The bodies of those executed were turned over to the Charleston city surgeons for dissection. A total of 131 were arrested with some of these being deported.

Better known than Vesey's attempt is the Nat Turner Slave Revolt, about nine years later. Turner, a slave in Southampton County, Virginia, felt led by God to lead a slave revolt. Turner, a Baptist minister, led five other slaves into the home of Turner's owner on August 22, 1831, and brutally killed his owner and the owner's family.

Turner was able to recruit other slaves from neighboring farms, but his force never exceeded more than about eight men. They attacked other whites in the area, and over several days killed nearly sixty white people. A local militia was able to stop the revolt and attacked Turner and his men. Although Turner escaped, the revolt was crushed. Turner remained on the loose for over two months before being captured. Turner went to trial in November and was convicted, in a one-day trial. He was hanged six days after the trial. About twenty other slaves were also executed.

There were other minor slave revolts, in 1848 in Kentucky and in 1860 in North Carolina, but in comparison to the rest of the Western Hemisphere, there were relatively few slave insurrections in the United States. Those that did take place involved very small numbers of men and in every case were quickly ended.

"Slave Codes"

As slavery came to an end in the Northern states, in the South the status of slaves began to be defined in a legal sense. As mentioned in the previous chapter, Virginia and Maryland led the way as early as the 1660s with laws that defined what a slave was and the rights of the slave's owner. These laws related to slave status, owner rights, etc. and were collectively referred to by most historians as "slave codes." They were enacted first by the individual colonies, and later as states.

It took many years for the "slave codes" to evolve and some of the codes were influenced by slave revolt attempts. From initially defining that African American slaves would be slaves for life to conferring disciplinary power to the slave owner, to even regulating the movement of slaves within the states, a varying mix of laws were passed by the slave states. In all of the slave states, except Louisiana, slaves were considered personal property. In Louisiana and in Kentucky, prior to 1852, they were considered property, in the same vain as real estate.[20]

State statutes would prohibit a slave from being taught to read, marry other slaves or marry a non-African American, freedom of travel prohibitions, and others. States could pass whatever laws they deemed necessary, but enforcement was a very different matter. Whether a slave was a single slave owned by a family or part of a large number of slaves on a plantation, enforcement of slave laws were usually administered by the slave owner. If the slave owner chose to teach his slave(s) to read and write then it would be done regardless of the state's statute prohibition. It was the law of the slave owner, not the law of the land that was typically adhered to. There was very little state enforcement of the "slave codes."

Not only were many of the laws not enforced, many were largely ignored, for instance the prohibition of slave marriages. Most slave owners encouraged slave marriages; a stable family relationship would benefit the slave owner. In fact on most plantations a slave couple's marriage, in spite of not having any legal precedent, was a widely celebrated event. Many were performed with the traditional marriage rituals and the ceremonies held in a church or in the plantation home.[21]

Chapter Four
Sectional Polarization

The Antislavery Movement Begins

Perhaps the seeds were planted with the Revolutionary War, but a major social and cultural shift began in the later half of the eighteenth century, blossomed at the turn of the century, and began to rapidly grow by the 1830s. The rise of the antislavery movement is made all that more amazing because it was a reversal of literally thousands of years of history. One man having the right to own another man, woman, or child was virtually accepted by all nations and all institutions within each nation, prior to this movement. Enlightened thought, wherever it had been hiding for all those years, was about to come into full bloom and raise havoc in the United States of America.

As mentioned in the previous chapter, the Quakers were early opponents of American slavery. Other denominations also came out against slavery. The Presbyterian Church, as early as 1787, had the first of several pronouncements against slavery. The slavery issue divided what is now the United Methodist Church in 1844. The church had gone on record against slavery, but when one of its bishops was suspended for refusing to free slaves his wife had inherited, the church split into two, a northern branch and a southern branch.

The enlightened view was not just an American invention. All across the world, slavery, as a culturally, socially, religiously, and governmentally approved institution, was coming to an abrupt end. Denmark ended slave trade as early as 1792. Britain ended slave trade in 1807 and the United States the next year. By 1833, Britain had freed its nearly 800,000 slaves in the British West Indies. Both France, in 1848, and Denmark, in 1863, followed suit. One of the holdouts was Brazil. Brazil's economy was so dependent on slavery that its slaves were not formally freed until 1888, twenty-three years after they were freed in the United States.

Those who opposed slavery in the North were certainly not in the majority. There was widespread concern throughout the United States about the ability of the black and white races to successfully live together. Virtually no one in the Anglo community was calling on the two races to integrate into one society, rather those that called for the freeing of the slaves wanted only for the slaves to be freed and live in a segregated world.

In fact, there were calls for the deportation of freed slaves back to Africa or to other locations. The American Colonization Society was formed in 1816, under the patronage of two wealthy New York merchants and philanthropists, Arthur and Lewis Tappan, to promote slave owners to free their slaves so that they could be relocated in western Africa. The society, which had prominent ministers as its organizers, had a parallel purpose. They saw the opportunity for slaves to be freed and then to go to Africa and spread their Christian beliefs across the African continent.

The African re-settlement approach had many prominent supporters, including Thomas Jefferson, James Monroe, John Marshall, James Madison, and Francis Scott Key. Thomas Jefferson said in 1781, "Among the Romans emancipation required but one effort . . . the slave, when made free, might mix with, without staining the blood of his master. But with us a second (step) is necessary, unknown to history. When freed, he is to be removed beyond the reach of mixture." He called the growing African American population, whether slave or free, a "blot in this country."[1]

Congress would eventually help fund some of the cost of transporting freed slaves to a new colony in western Africa, Liberia. The colony was established in 1820 and Liberia became an independent republic by 1847.

The idea that produced the nation of Liberia never produced either the freeing of the slaves nor the mass exodus of freed slaves back to Africa. In the slave states, slave owners were unwilling to free their slaves, where they had substantial investment, simply for ideological reasons or for religious reasons. Some free African Americans supported the concept and immigrated to Liberia, but the numbers were not very large. In 1830, the American Colonization Society helped 259 immigrate, bringing the total number of freed slaves in Liberia to only about fourteen hundred. One estimate is that only about twelve thousand African Americans went to Africa, even though the organization was in existence as late as 1912.[2]

> *Slavery Fact #8*
>
> A major effort was made by Northerners to relocate all freed slaves to Africa in the early 1800s.

As early as 1829, a free African American, David Walker in Boston, issued an appeal for armed insurrection against slave owners, but his call for the ending of slavery was not heeded. Beginning the next year, a series of annual conventions with free African American delegates from Northern states began. These meetings called for an end to racial discrimination in the North and denounced slavery in the South.

In contrast to the abolitionists' views in the North, there were defenders of slavery in the South that espoused the views of freedom and liberty, but with a twist. Southern intellectuals proclaimed freedom as their ultimate goal, but only when people were ready for it. In their view, freedom could not be granted to all, but it could be extended to an ever-increasing number. In spite of those not free, the process could be expected to result in a better life for those who remained enslaved. They viewed slavery actually as a positive force that produced an ideal social order for civilized progress.[3]

The Abolitionists

Some historians cite the birth of "abolitionism" from 1831 with the founding of the newspaper *The Liberator*, published by William Lloyd Garrison. The word "abolitionist" of course comes from the desire of the abolitionist to *abolish* slavery in the United States. A former indentured servant, Garrison was born in Massachusetts and, in his twenties, began to speak out against slavery. On January 31, 1831, he published the first edition of *The Liberator* which called for an immediate end to slavery. His publication was one of, if not the first, to formally call upon an end to slavery in the United States.

A coalition of three abolitionist groups formed the American Anti-Slavery Society at the end of 1833. The Tappan brothers, along with Theodore Weld, were instrumental in the formation of the group.[4] The American Anti-Slavery Society grew and by 1838 had nearly fourteen hundred chapters with about one

The abolitionist William Lloyd Garrison
National Archives

hundred thousand members.[5] Garrison joined with them and would serve as the president of the organization from 1843 to 1865. Although one of the most important groups, the American Anti-Slavery Society was not the sole voice of the antislavery movement. The American Anti-Slavery Society would be only one of around two hundred different antislavery groups that would form in the United States. In 1835, the American Anti-Slavery Society launched "the greatest pamphlet campaign in evangelical history." It has been estimated that collectively the various abolitionists groups produced over one million pieces of abolitionist literature, thousands of which were sent into the South.[6]

The initial efforts of the abolitionists produced a harsh response from the general public, in both the North and the South. In the 1830s, abolitionists would frequently receive the wrath of irate anti-abolitionist mobs. A riot occurred in Philadelphia in 1834 and forty-five homes of free African Americans were destroyed. The same year in New York City a mob gutted the home of Lewis Tappan. Even Garrison himself was dragged through the streets in Boston and nearly lynched until rescued by authorities. In Alton, Illinois, the editor of a more militant abolitionist newspaper was taken by a mob and shot and killed in 1837. His lifeless body was dragged through the streets as crowds cheered and his presses were destroyed.[7]

One of the splits in the abolitionist movement was just how to accomplish the goal of eliminating slavery. Some like Garrison, who was a pacifist, sought to use moral persuasion to end slavery. Others wanted more of a political approach, while still others took a more militant view. By 1840, the American Anti–Slavery Society had split over how the movement should continue and other social issues.

Frederick Douglass
Library of Congress

Frederick Douglass was another well-known abolitionist, who at first supported Garrison in the moral persuasion route of ending slavery. But by the 1840s, Douglass supported strong political action to end slavery. Douglass brought a new perspective in the predominately white abolitionist movement, as Douglass was a former slave.

Born a slave in Maryland, Douglass, who was half white, was able to learn to read and write. He also was a slave on a large plantation and claimed he had been subjected to many cruelties. In 1838, at the age of twenty, he escaped Maryland and slavery with the help of a free African American sailor. In 1841, Douglass attended the meeting of the Massachusetts Anti-Slavery Society and was asked to speak. The personal and moving story he told motivated the group to hire him as a spokesman for the group and later the larger American Anti–Slavery Society.

Douglass soon crisscrossed the North telling audiences about slavery and urging their support to end slavery in the United States. He was quite eloquent in the delivery of his talks and was able to emotionally move many of his listeners. By 1845, he had published a book, *Narratives of the Life of Frederick Douglass*, in which he recounted his life as a slave. Douglass's book had a strong impact on public thinking in the North, as he painted a very harsh picture of slavery in the South. The book became one of the primary sources about slaves.

Since Douglass was a runaway slave, he feared that he might be captured and returned to Maryland and back to slavery. In 1845, he fled the United States and went to Britain where he continued to lecture and speak out against slavery. He returned to the United States in 1847, after friends in Britain formally purchased his freedom. He formed his own abolitionist newspaper, which he continued until 1863. He was active in the political movement against slavery and also began to call for a more physical resistance to slavery. Douglass became acquainted with John Brown, who represents the extreme militant element in the abolitionist movement.

John Brown was born in Connecticut in 1800, but moved to Ohio at an early age. Brown became an abolitionist at a very young age, perhaps developing the sentiment from his father who was very antislavery. As a young man, Brown drifted aimlessly about the country, apparently unwilling to settle in any one place or with any one trade for very long. Brown had been a tanner, cattleman, wool merchant, shepherd, postmaster, horse breeder, and real estate speculator, failing at each. A Bible-quoting divinity school dropout, Brown soon felt that he was personally responsible for ending the institution of slavery. Brown had become a member of the militant wing of abolitionist thought.

In Kansas in 1856, his personal war was launched. Brown and six of his followers were able to drag five proslavery men and boys from their beds at Pottawatomie Creek on May 24, 1856. The attack was extraordinarily gruesome. Brown and his men split the heads of the men and boys with an axe, then cut off their hands, and finally cut open their stomachs and laid out their entrails.

Brown was not yet done, as he decided that he would help end slavery by an armed slave insurrection. He was well financed by six prominent abolitionists in the North: Dr. Samuel G. Howe, Thomas

W. Higginson, Theodore Parker, Franklin B. Sanborn, Gerrit Smith, and George L. Stearns.

Brown also sought the support of Frederick Douglass. They were friends, having first met in 1847. Brown and Douglass met at least at couple of times to discuss a slave revolution plot to be led by Brown. Brown outlined his plan of insurrection to Douglass and attempted to solicit Douglass's assistance. Brown hoped that he and his men would be able to seize a Federal arsenal, which would provide Brown with the weapons to arm the slaves and create a slave revolt. Douglass questioned Brown's plan, thinking that he was overestimating the inclination of slaves to revolt. Douglass told Brown that the slaves wanted freedom, but not suicide. Douglass thought Brown's plan represented suicide for all its participants.[8]

Finally at a secret three-day meeting in Pennsylvania in August of 1859, Brown told Douglass, "When I strike the bees will begin to swarm, and I will need you to help hive them." Douglass, perhaps seeing the futility of Brown's plan, declined. Douglass said that Brown "was going into a perfect steel trap, and that once he would get in he would never get out alive."[9]

Brown had hoped to capture the massive Federal Arsenal at Harpers Ferry, Virginia (now West Virginia). He and his men would then distribute the captured guns from the arsenal to slaves in the western Virginia area. There were approximately 18,000 slaves in the six-county area around Harpers Ferry, of which five thousand were men. Brown would then lead his slave "army" south, capturing other arsenals and arming new slave recruits as they went. Eventually, Brown thought he could free all the slaves in the South.

Brown and eighteen men, on the night of October 16, 1859, launched their attack at Harpers

John Brown, circa 1856

National Archives

Ferry. They were armed with approximately two hundred Sharps rifles and two hundred revolvers. They easily captured the unsuspecting town and the arsenal with little opposition. Ironically, the first person that Brown's group killed was an African American. Haywood Shepherd, a free African American, who was working at the railroad station, approached some of Brown's men. He was ordered to halt, but instead chose to return to the station. He was shot in the back and killed. The first casualty of John Brown's war to free the slaves was a free African American.

A memorial marker to honor the memory of Shepherd was placed in Harpers Ferry in 1931. In one of the extreme examples of political correctness, the marker which described the death of an African American at the hands of Brown and his men, the National Park Service, which controlled much of downtown Harpers Ferry, chose to build a wooden box around the marker to completely hide it from public view. It was so hidden from public view for a number of years. After numerous complaints, the box around the monument was removed in 1995, but only after an "interpretative" marker was placed by the Park Service. The "interpretative" marker attempts to explain that the Shepherd monument was originally erected by the United Daughters of the Confederacy and seems to attempt to justify the death of Shepherd, because it was at Harpers Ferry that "John Brown aimed a blow at human slavery that woke a guilty nation."

The residents of Harpers Ferry learned that the town and arsenal had been captured when they awoke on the morning of October 17. The townspeople quickly armed themselves with whatever

> *Slavery Fact #9*
> The first person killed in John Brown's Raid, by Brown's men at Harpers Ferry, was a free African American.

they could find and countered Brown and his men. Word was sent out on what had happened and within hours various local militia units surrounded Harpers Ferry, cutting off Brown's escape routes. Brown and his men hunkered down in the arsenal.

By October 18, Federal forces were sent in, a unit of marines that were under the command of Colonel Robert E. Lee and Lieutenant J.E.B. Stuart. Brown and his men had taken sanctuary in the arsenal's fire station. The marines stormed the building, and the slave war was quickly over. Brown was knocked unconscious in the fight and captured. He was put on trial in nearby Charles Town, where Brown refused to plead insanity. On November 2, 1859, he was found guilty of treason, conspiracy, and murder and was ordered to be executed.

December 2, 1859, the Northern abolitionists had a new martyr as John Brown was hung in a field near Charles Town. No civilians were allowed at the execution site; the field was surrounded by fifteen hundred cadets from the Virginia Military Institute under command of one of the VMI professors, Thomas J. Jackson, later to be known as "Stonewall." Also in one of the VMI companies was another person that would be later known to history, John Wilkes Booth.[10]

Many in the North as well as most in the South viewed Brown's execution as fitting for a traitor and murderer, in effect, the work of a madman. However, for many of the abolitionists he died a hero. Ralph Waldo Emerson compared Brown's death to that of Jesus Christ, and Henry Wadsworth called the date of his death the new great date in American history, "the date of a new Revolution." Even Garrison, who had preached a peaceful end to slavery, had succumbed to the radical antislavery views when he said that Brown's death had convinced him that that there was a need to use violence to end slavery. Abraham Lincoln, however, probably expressed the view of the majority in the North when he denounced Brown's actions as an act of "violence, bloodshed, and treason." According to Lincoln such acts deserved to be punished by death. Even Lincoln concluded that Brown was "insane."[11]

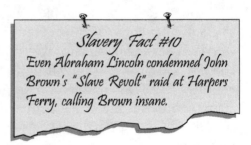

Slavery Fact #10
Even Abraham Lincoln condemned John Brown's "Slave Revolt" raid at Harpers Ferry, calling Brown insane.

The Little Lady That Started the War

In contrast to John Brown, there was one abolitionist who demonstrated that the pen indeed was mightier than the sword. Harriett

Beecher Stowe was born in 1811 and educated in Litchfield, Connecticut. She moved to Ohio when her father became president of the Lane Theological Seminary in Cincinnati. In Cincinnati, she had occasion to see slaves escaping from the South, across the Ohio River. She made at least a couple of trips into the slave-holding state of Kentucky.

Sometime around 1850, Stowe moved to Brunswick, Maine, where she became determined to write an antislavery book. She wrote *Uncle Tom's Cabin*, which was first published, in 1851–52, as a serial in the antislavery newspaper, *National Era*. The newspaper version had little impact, but when *Uncle Tom's Cabin* was published as a book it had a pronounced effect on the American people.

The book version of *Uncle Tom's Cabin* was published in 1852 and was an immediate success. It became what we would describe today as a runaway best seller. It sold 50,000 copies in eight weeks, an unprecedented number, and 300,000 copies in one year. Within sixteen months a million copies were printed and the book was translated into over twenty different languages. The book's characters have become legend in American literature, from Little Eva and Topsey to literature's ultimate villain, the infamous Simon Legree. In a twist of irony, the villainous character, Legree, was from the North. The term "Uncle Tom" became a part of our vernacular and has come to mean a form of subservient behavior of African Americans towards certain whites.

Although the book rambled and was rich in melodrama, it did catch the attention of the American people and helped to crystallize Northern sentiment against slavery. In response to Southern outcries that the book was pure fiction and grossly misrepresented slavery, Howe published in 1853, *A Key To Uncle Tom's Cabin*. This book attempted to document the fictional account of slavery described by Howe in the original book. When Abraham Lincoln met Howe for the first time he said, "So this is the little lady who made this big war?"[12]

As pointed out in volume two of *Myths of Southern History* by Patrick Gerster and Nicholas Cords, a number of stereotype views of the South can be traced back to the Stowe book. As pointed out, Stowe, who had limited firsthand experience with slavery, helped develop the "faithful darkey" image of some slaves, the virtuous southern belles, the cavalier men of the South, and the evil and sinister overseer.[13] Following Stowe's book at least six novels came out with a proslavery plot. These were direct responses to *Uncle Tom's Cabin*. None had anywhere near the effect on American public opinion as Stowe's book.[14]

Books by Ex-Slaves

There were other books about slavery that had an influence on the American public. Books written by former slaves, describing their "personal" recollections of the horrors of slavery, were very popular in the North prior to the War Between the States. Like *Uncle Tom's Cabin*, these books helped to stir up strong antislavery emotions.

Nearly one hundred of these former slave autobiographies were written prior to the beginning of the War Between the States. Is this what it seems, a treasure trove of firsthand information of which we can get a true and accurate glimpse of the life of a slave? Sadly, they probably are not. One of the first "scientific analysis" historians, U. B. Phillips, said, "ex-slave narratives in general . . . were issued with so much abolitionist editing that as a class their authenticity is doubtful."[15] There are a number of reasons why Phillips and other historians have taken this position.

The abolitionists saw the success of Frederick Douglass both as a lecturer and as a writer. The freed slave lecture and the freed slave writings became staples of the abolitionist propaganda. It would appear that many of the writings range from outright frauds, such as the account by James Williams and perhaps accounts by Charles Ball and Harriet Jacobs, to certainly highly embellished tales of the life of a slave.

First and foremost of the reasons why we cannot rely on the writings of these freed slaves prior to the War Between the States is that they were typically financed and strongly edited by the abolitionists. They were more a political document than they were a historical document. Most historians do not refute the fact that the ex-slave narratives were edited by the abolitionists.

A number of clues are evident when one reads the narratives. The reader quickly discovers an air of philosophy, religion, and moral persuasion that would appear to be well beyond the scope of the typical ex-slave. A reader will also see that many of the accounts are highly romantic, written in the same style as that of the popular novels of the day.

Another very important clue is that many of the ex-slave accounts are nearly identical. After reading several of these narratives, most readers will be amazed by the uniformity and the repetitive nature of each. The lack of uniqueness alone causes one to doubt the authenticity of the accounts. Some historians have suggested perhaps a master outline existed that all the ex-slave narratives followed. The basic outline apparently comes from the Douglass book, and organizationally most all of the ex-slave narratives follow the identical structure from the beginning of the first sentence to the end where the former slave takes a new name, from a white abolitionist.

The basic outline is listed in the book *The Slave's Narrative*. Each narrative starts off with a portrait of the ex-slave, followed by a title page that always includes the claim that it was written by the former slave. Each then has a testimonial or introduction, typically by a well-known abolitionist, followed by a poem. Next came the narrative that included the details of the slave's life in slavery, incredibly similar in each account. The ex-slave always began with "I was born . . . ," followed by the details of his or her family line, usually with a white father. Next, came the account of the cruel master, overseer, etc. with a description of the whippings that the ex-slave had to endure. Following the horrific accounts of beatings, always came the story of one slave, usually, "pure African," one who was extremely strong and who stood up and challenged any whippings.

After that came the details of how the ex-slave was not allowed to learn to read and write. Following that was usually some account of their former Christian master who labored over the fact that his or her ownership of slaves was at odds with his or her religion. A description of the food, clothing, and shelter was next. One of the abolitionist's strong propaganda tools was next in the narrative, the story of slave auctions and how families were broken up, children separated from parents, and husbands and wives permanently separated from each other.

Then came the escape, first a description of the slave owners' attempts to prevent slaves from running away, the use of patrols, dogs, etc. Next came the actual successful escape itself. Many of the narratives dwelled on the thrilling and successful escape. Using the North Star and being taken in, usually by a Quaker family, and fed a wonderful "freedom" breakfast were common themes in each account. The narrative ends with the ex-slave taking a new last name and finally some reflections on the institution of slavery.[16]

Seemingly a good source of slave detail, unfortunately they are not. As we look into the lives of the slaves beginning in chapter six we will have to find other ways of determining the truth. In spite of their not being a good source of accurate information, the ex-slave narratives were important. Along with the lecturers that usually preceded the book, the former slaves were able to help the abolitionists rally support for the antislavery movement. Like the novel *Uncle Tom's Cabin*, the ex-slave narrative would be one more polarizing factor between the North and the South.

The Underground Railroad

The Underground Railroad was a rather loose network of abolitionists who helped slaves escape from the slave states to either Northern states or to Canada. It may have originated with the Quakers, but by 1830 it had become a coalition of ex-slaves, free African Americans, and staunch abolitionists.

A slave would run away from his or her slave owner, headed in a northerly direction, and reach "safe houses," or "stations," along the way. At the "stations" the slaves would be given food, water, and rest by antislave sympathizers. Most of the slaves that fled were from the northern tier of slave-holding states, such as Maryland, Virginia, and Kentucky. Most of the Underground Railroad activity had northern entrance points in Ohio and Pennsylvania. It has been estimated that as many as 60,000 slaves were freed through the Underground Railroad, but that number is likely greatly exaggerated.

One of the best known "conductors" on the Underground Railroad was Harriet Tubman. Tubman was born a slave in Maryland. In her twenties, she received permission from her slave owner to marry a free African American. Legally she remained a slave, but was allowed to live with her husband. When her owner passed away in 1847, followed by the unexpected death of the owner's heir in 1849, Tubman became concerned over her status. She fled to the North, but her free husband chose to remain in Maryland. Tubman journeyed back to Maryland in 1851 to try to persuade her husband to join her in Pennsylvania, but found that he had no interest in leaving Maryland and had even remarried.

Beginning in 1850, Tubman made a decision to help other slaves escape. She journeyed south and first brought out her sister and her sister's children. Later she was able to lead out her brother and her parents. The Fugitive Slave Law of 1850 made it a crime, with severe penalties, to aid a slave in flight. Fearing that she might be arrested, Tubman fled to Canada. Her stay in Canada was short-lived, as many Northern states passed laws that circumvented the Federal Fugitive Slave Law. Tubman felt it was safe to return to the United States, settling in New York State.

Tubman became the "Moses" to slaves for leading them out of slavery, similar to the biblical Moses leading the Hebrews out of Egyptian slavery. She is credited, by some historians, as having led as many as three hundred slaves northward, in approximately nineteen trips. She was labeled as "General Tubman" by the fanatical John Brown, and even discussed with Brown his "slave revolution" ideas prior to Brown's attack on Harpers Ferry. Some historians speculate that Tubman may have joined with Brown, had not personal illness prevented her from doing so.

During the War Between the States, Tubman served as a cook and a nurse for the Union army. She was recognized for her efforts on behalf of the Northern army. Post War Between the States, she not only championed African American rights but she also was a strong advocate of women's rights. She died in 1913.

Although technically not part of the Underground Railroad, one of the most ingenious and interesting escapes from slavery was accomplished by Henry Brown. Brown was born a slave in Virginia and was working in a tobacco factory in Richmond. In 1848 he decided to escape slavery with a plan that he claimed was divinely inspired. With the help of a white antislavery friend, he had himself crated up in a large box. The box was two feet eight inches deep, two feet wide, and three feet long and was lined with a feltlike material. For air, the box had one large hole and for food Brown had a container of water and several biscuits.

The friend then took the box, with Brown inside it, to an overland express company for shipment to a Philadelphia, Pennsylvania, address. For the next twenty-seven hours, Brown remained in the box. The box made the journey to Philadelphia by way of a train, steamboat, and a wagon. He claimed to have spent much of the time upside down in the box. When he arrived, the handlers in Philadelphia rapped quietly on the lid of the box and asked if Brown was "All right!" From within the crate came the answer, "All right, sir!" When the box was uncrated, Brown, soaking wet, rose from the box. Brown reached out his hand to his amazed abolitionists handlers, asking, "How do you do, gentlemen?"[17]

He promptly earned the nickname of "Box" Brown. He relocated, with the help of abolitionist friends, to Massachusetts, and went on the Northern lecture circuit, telling of his perilous journey. Promptly displayed at each of his appearances was the famous box. Brown fled the United States after the passage of the Fugitive Slave Law of 1850. He went to England where he resumed his lecture tour for European audiences. After four years Brown mysteriously disappeared and was never heard from again.[18]

Political Compromises

Prior to the War Between the States, the United States had become increasingly fragmented along sectional lines. As much as the abolitionists had tried, they had not been successful in causing a strong public mandate in the North for ending slavery. Only a minority of Northerners actually supported the complete abolishment of slavery. The sectional conflicts between the North and the South related more to the expansion of slavery to the west, as well as a variety of other issues.

The expansion of slavery to the west had been a point of contention between the two sections for many years, but had, prior to the War Between the States, always been resolved through compromise. Most of the compromises are familiar to even the casual student of American history, but let us quickly review them. One of the first issues arose prior to 1819, as Thomas Jefferson put it, like "a fireball in the night." The crisis centered on the Territory of Missouri applying for statehood. The issue at hand, "would slavery be allowed west of the Mississippi River?" The Mississippi River along with the Mason Dixon line and the Ohio River had formed the generally accepted dividing lines between North and South and slave versus non-slave. Also in grave risk would be the United States political balance, as there were eleven slave states and eleven free states. Would Missouri be admitted into the United States as a slave state or a free state?

After much political debate and rancor, the Missouri Compromise of 1820 was reached. Missouri would be admitted as a slave state, Maine, which was carved away from Massachusetts, would be admitted as a free state, thus ensuring the political balance between the North and the South. In addition, an amendment to the bill prohibited slavery forever in the Louisiana Purchase Territory above a line of 36° 30′, roughly along a line of the northern border of the current states of Oklahoma and Arkansas.

During Andrew Jackson's term of office, 1829–1837 as United States president, again sectional flares ignited. The debate about states' rights, western lands, and tariffs became national issues. The State of South Carolina nullified the federally mandated trade tariffs in the state in 1832. Jackson directly confronted the state and warned that he would use troops if necessary to enforce the laws of the land. Calmer heads prevailed, and eventually another compromise was reached. Congress passed legislation which lowered the tariffs and South Carolina repealed its nullification ordinance. In 1836, Arkansas was admitted as a slave state, but the political balance, an equal number of slave states and free states, was restored the next year when Michigan was admitted as a free state.

Texas won its independence from Mexico in 1836 and formed its own government, the Republic of Texas. Texans overwhelmingly favored annexation into the United States, but again the issue of the

expansion of slavery and the political balance arose. Those supporting the annexation of Texas argued that Texas was not part of the
Louisiana Purchase, so slavery should be allowed. The issue was
not resolved until the presidential campaign of 1844. James Polk,
the Democratic Party candidate, supported Texas annexation, and
won a close election over the Whig Party candidate, Henry Clay.
Texas was admitted into the Union, as a slave state, in 1845. The
political balance was maintained as Iowa was admitted as a free
state in 1846. In addition, Florida was also admitted as a slave state
in 1845, but Wisconsin was admitted as a free state in 1848—the
political balance was preserved.

On April 25, 1846, near the Texas-Mexico border a small skir-
mish occurred between Mexican troops and United States troops,
on the Texas side. United States troops were forced to surrender to
the Mexicans and several American soldiers were killed in the brief
fight. This small encounter led President James K. Polk to ask Congress to declare war on Mexico, which they did. The war lasted
until United States troops captured Mexico City in September of
1847.

The war was formally ended by the Treaty of Guadalupe
Hidalgo in 1848. As a spoil of war, although the United States did
make a cash payment and assume some Mexican debt, the United
States gained a significant amount of new territory, including what
would eventually become the states of Arizona, California, New
Mexico, Nevada, Utah, and parts of the modern-day states of Colo-
rado, Kansas, and Wyoming. The land area of the United States was
increased by 66 percent as a result of the treaty.

With new virgin territory, the old issue of slave state versus
free state was once again re-ignited. Some Northerners viewed, incorrectly, the entire war as a Southern plot to expand slavery. In
1846 a Pennsylvanian congressman, David Wilmot, introduced an
amendment to an appropriations bill that enflamed Southern concerns and passions. The amendment would have totally prohibited
slavery in any of the new territory acquired from Mexico. The State
of Alabama threatened to secede if the amendment was passed. The
bill with the amendment passed the House of Representatives but

was never passed in the Senate. The Wilmot Proviso would become a principal plank in the emerging Republican Party.

Gold was discovered in the newly acquired territory of California in 1848. A year later some Texans arrived in California along with their slaves. The Texans used their slaves to begin panning for gold. The other gold miners were outraged over this development, not on moral grounds, but due to the fact that the use of slaves gave the Texans an unfair advantage in their mining efforts. The miners' complaints were strongly heard at a constitutional convention, three days later, and the new California Constitution forbade slavery in the territory. Later in the year, California applied for statehood. Once again the issue of slavery expansion was a national issue.

If California's application for statehood was approved by Congress, then the tilt of political power would swing towards the North. The South realized that there was no slave territory to pair with California statehood so as to maintain the political equilibrium. The Congress was in gridlock, North versus South. Several compromises were considered to no avail, such as the extension of the Missouri Compromise line, 36° 30', west to the Pacific Ocean; another approach was to just leave it up to those living in a territory to decide for themselves whether to allow slavery or not.

It was Senator Henry Clay, of Kentucky, that unstopped the logjam between the two sections. Clay proposed sweeping legislation that addressed the burning sectional issues. He proposed his plan in January of 1850, but eight months later no resolution had occurred. A series of events began that caused the Compromise of 1850 to succeed. First, Clay was able to get the support of an influential senator from Massachusetts, Daniel Webster. Webster made an eloquent appeal from the Senate floor supporting compromise, to the ire of many of his Northern colleagues. Secondly, President Zachary Taylor, who was opposed to Clay's compromise plan, unexpectedly died. His successor was Millard Fillmore, a fervent supporter of compromise. And finally, Stephen Douglas, a senator from Illinois, proposed to consider not one massive compromise bill, but rather to break the components of Clay's single bill into individual bills.

The Douglas approach worked, and the five components were considered individually. The first two acts were concessions to the North by the South: California was admitted to the Union as a free state, and slave trade was disallowed in the District of Columbia. The next three acts were concessions by the North to the South: A Fugitive Slave Law was enacted, which was a major concession by the North. The territory east of California would be divided into two territories, New Mexico, including present-day Arizona, and Utah. And finally, the State of Texas would be paid $10 million to settle boundary issues.

Fugitive Slave Laws

Of all the issues related to the Compromise of 1850, by far the most controversial was the Fugitive Slave Law of 1850. The law was of the utmost importance to the South. Fugitive slave laws were not entirely new. A clause in the Ordinance of 1787 allowed for fugitive slaves that had run away to the Northwest Territory, what is now the upper Midwest, to be returned to their owners. Even the United States Constitution made a vague reference to returning fugitive slaves, although slaves were not mentioned by name. The Constitution's intent seemed to be to support the right of slave owners to have runaway slaves returned to them. The Constitution stated, "No person held to service or labor in one State, under the laws thereof, escaping into another, shall, in consequence of any law or regulation therein, be discharged from such service or labor; but shall be delivered up on claim of the party, to whom such service or labor may be due."[19] However, the Constitution did not offer any specifics on how to accomplish the return of runaway slaves.

Until 1793 Southerners simply relied on the Constitution and the good faith effort of Northerners to return the runaway slaves.[20] The vagueness of the Constitutional wording, however, led to the Fugitive Slave Law of 1793. This law, which was passed by Congress, allowed either the slave owner or his or her agent to journey to any state or territory to recover a runaway slave. The slave owner or agent had to apply to a circuit or district judge to receive a certificate in order to take custody of the fugitive slave. From the slave owner's perspective this law had a number of shortcomings. The law did not allow for judges to issue arrest warrants and it did not authorize Federal marshals to assist in the recovery of the fugitive slaves.

There was an even greater concern to the slaveowners. In some Northern states, the laws were not uniformly enforced, and in some states not at all. Four individual Northern states also passed "personal liberty laws" which aided the runaway slave from being returned to the South. In spite of the Fugitive Slave Law of 1793, an 1840 law in Vermont made it illegal for its citizens to assist in the capture of a runaway slave.[21] Southern politicians found it unacceptable for Northern lawmakers to interfere with their right to a return of their personal property.

The Fugitive Slave Law of 1850 was an appeasement to the South. This law made it much easier for the slave owner to have a runaway slave returned to him. The law contained a number of provisions. First, control of the fugitive slave issue was removed from individual state control to Federal control. Commissioners, under Federal Court appointment, were authorized to adjudicate issues relating to alleged fugitive slaves. Federal marshals were required to assist in the capture of runaway slaves. An affidavit by the slave owner or their agent would be presented accusing an African American of being a fugitive slave. Those accused of being runaways were not allowed to testify in their own behalf and any who assisted or hid alleged fugitive slaves were subject to imprisonment, fines, and liable to the slave owner for civil damages.

To counteract predicted Northern non-compliance of the law, the Federal marshals were subject to a one thousand dollar fine, a massive amount in 1850, for dereliction of duty. A marshal could also be held liable for the value of the slave to the slave owner if the slave escaped while in the marshal's custody.

The law was highly unpopular in the North, and in some cases invoked angry responses. One Massachusetts factory owner wrote that he went to bed as an old-fashioned conservative and the next day he "waked up a stark mad Abolitionists." One part of the bill that some Northerners resented the most was the fact that the Commissioners, who heard the runaway slave's case, were paid five dollars if they ruled in favor of the slave, but were paid ten dollars if they ruled in favor of the slave owner.

Enforcement of the new law proved to be most difficult. Northern states responded by passing "personal liberty" laws. "Vigilance" groups were formed in an effort to protect fugitive slaves from those who were searching the Northern states for runaway slaves. Perhaps as many as 15,000 African Americans fled the North for Canada and other locations, in fear that they might be sent south. Mob violence did occur in Wisconsin and in Massachusetts when fugitive slaves were being apprehended in accordance with the law.

The Fugitive Slave Law of 1850 finally gave the abolitionists something they had searched for. For all their efforts they had really never caught the imagination of the Northern populace. Now, for the first time, they were beginning to make public opinion inroads, bringing the issue to the national forefront and seeing increased popular support, at least against the law. For Southerners, it was just another bit of evidence that the North did not want an equal union with them. The Southerners simply saw the North attempting to avoid national law and compliance with the United States Constitution.

Interestingly enough, the furor over the Fugitive Slave Law, other North-South differences, as well as other national issues, perhaps prevented the United States from having fifty-two states today. In 1853, the United States, under the direction of President Franklin Pierce, attempted to buy Cuba from Spain. Spain refused the offer. In 1854, the United States issued what is known as the Ostend Manifesto. This pronouncement stated that if Spain refused to sell Cuba to the United States then the United States should take Cuba by military force, ostentatiously to prevent the British or French from acquiring the island colony. Some in the North saw this only as an effort by the South to, yet again, attempt to expand slavery and eventually have Cuba enter the United States as a slave state. The effort went no further.

According to the 1860 Census, the number of slaves who escaped in 1860 was not only much less in proportion than according to the 1850 Census, but greatly reduced numerically. The greatest increase of slave escapes occurred in Mississippi, Missouri, and

Virginia, while there were fewer escapes in Delaware, Georgia, Louisiana, Maryland, and Tennessee.

The Kansas–Nebraska Act

The great compromise of 1850 lasted only four years. By 1854, new sectional issues had to be dealt with. Interestingly enough, the catalyst of the new debate was one of the politicians that helped get the Compromise of 1850 passed through the Congress: Stephen A. Douglas, the Democratic senator from Illinois. Douglas was interested in getting the Nebraska territory admitted into the United States as a new state. His motives were to help his home state in general and Chicago in particular, plus he stood to gain personally, based on some land holdings he owned. Douglas wanted a new western railroad, which would eventually be a transcontinental route, to be built from Chicago and not out of St. Louis.

His original proposal was that Nebraska enter as a state, "with or without slavery," in other words, slavery would be determined in Nebraska by popular sovereignty. There was a problem with that approach. If Nebraska was admitted with the possibility that it could become a slave state then its admission would have been in violation of the Missouri Compromise, which forbade slavery above the 36° 30' line. This required Douglas to amend his bill by adding a provision that would repeal the Missouri Compromise. This gained the support of Southern politicians, as it would create the opportunity to expand slavery in areas where heretofore slavery had been prohibited.

The bill passed through Congress, despite opposition, and was signed into law on May 30, 1854. The law did repeal the Missouri Compromise prohibition on slavery and allowed for two new states, Nebraska and Kansas, to eventually enter the Union. The slave question was to be decided by the exercise of popular sovereignty in each state. Nebraska was expected to join the United States as a free state, and Kansas was expected to enter the Union as a slave state.

Similar to the Fugitive Slave Law of 1850, the Kansas-Nebraska Act, as it would come to be called, created yet another national issue that inflamed passions in the North. However, it was more than just a single issue. Slavery at times was the focal point, but the North was beginning to see the South more and more as a political enemy. From the North's perspective the South was trying to expand slavery in every direction, northwest in Kansas, west of Texas, south to Cuba. But they also saw Southern politicians stopping new homestead laws, working to lower tariffs, and blocking internal improvements. From the Southern perspective, the South saw the North as a political foe. Her system of labor was potentially being threatened. How would the South, primarily an agrarian society, be able to produce its crops without the slave labor it had come to depend on? If slavery were ended, what would happen to the massive capital investment of the slave owners? Why wasn't the North willing to follow the laws of the land? Would the political balance between North and South be maintained?

Such concerns, on both sides, caused a massive change in the political landscape of the United States The Whig Party, one of the two major political parties, received its death knell over the issue. The Whig Party had won two out of the last three presidential elections, but it was no more. The Democratic Party, the other major political party, was split in several directions. And finally, a new political party emerged. The Republican Party was literally born out of the controversy surrounding the Kansas-Nebraska debate.

The Kansas-Nebraska Act created open warfare in Kansas. Since the act declared that the two territories would each determine its own fate on the slavery issue, outsiders attempted to influence the outcome of the slavery issue in Kansas. Both antislavery advocates and proslavery advocates entered the territory to influence the vote. Abolitionists formally organized efforts to promote antislavery immigration into the territory. Bordering Kansas was the slave state of Missouri, and proslavery advocates journeyed into Kansas to promote their agenda. The result was conflict and violence.

Settlers poured into the Kansas territory from all directions. Not only were there conflicts over their views related to slavery, but also numerous conflicts over land. Claim-jumping was common and much of the bloody violence was blamed on slavery, but may well have been rooted in land disputes. Lawrence and Topeka became antislavery strongholds, and Leavenworth and Atchison were proslavery strongholds.

The initial election was held in 1855. A proslavery legislature was selected. The antislavery advocates, called "Free Soilers," contested the election, blaming the result on illegal voters from Missouri. They held their own "Free State" convention and wrote a constitution that not only banned slavery, but also prohibited free African Americans from entering the future state.

The United States Congress had a dilemma when it convened in 1856. Two Kansas governments were requesting statehood, one antislavery and one proslavery. President Pierce recommended that the Congress accept the proslavery government and admit Kansas as a slave state. It would take five years for the issue to be resolved.

Meanwhile, back in Kansas, the year of 1856 proved to be a most violent year. It started in January when a Free Soiler was attacked by proslavery men in Leavenworth. Next, came the death of a proslavery sheriff after he had arrested several Free Soilers. The verbal war had become a deadly contest.

A proslavery grand jury indicted several members of the Free Soilers' government in May. A large militia of men went to Lawrence to arrest some of those indicted. When the conflict was over, several homes had been looted, antislavery printing presses had been destroyed; a hotel, The Free Soil Hotel, had been burned; and a man was killed.

In revenge, a few days later, John Brown, better known for his Harpers Ferry massacre, with four of his sons attacked a proslavery community on the Pottawatomie Creek. Brown said that the time had come to "fight fire with fire." He also promised to "strike terror in the hearts of pro-slavery men." Brown and his men lived up to Brown's terrorist threats as five proslavery men and boys were killed. The men and boys were hacked to death with axes, their skulls were split open, their hands cut off, and their stomachs were split open.

Open warfare soon reigned supreme. A semblance of order was not restored until September of 1856 when Federal troops were sent into the territory to attempt to prevent bloodshed. The troops eventually helped resolve the statehood issue as well. In 1856, proslavery supporters gathered in Lecompton to craft a proslavery constitution, known as the Lecompton constitution. An election was held, not to approve the proposed new constitution, but to ask the people of the Kansas territory to decide if they preferred: (1) "The constitution with slavery" or (2) "The constitution without slavery." Regardless of the vote, the constitution guaranteed the right to own slaves. If the Kansas voters voted "without slavery" it would mean that no new slaves could be brought in, but the right to own slaves already in the territory would be preserved. If they voted "with slavery" then they were supporting Kansas's entry into the Union as a slave state.

The Free Soilers boycotted the election. To no one's surprise the Lecompton constitution "with slavery" was overwhelmingly approved. United States President James Buchanan accepted the vote as a show of the will of the people, in compliance with the popular sovereignty requirement on the issue of slavery. Buchanan urged that Kansas be admitted into the Union as a slave state. The United States Senate approved the proslavery application for statehood, but it was rejected in the United States House of Representatives.

A compromise bill, in Congress related to Kansas statehood, came out of the statehood debate. The bill decided to let the people of the Kansas territory vote directly on the Lecompton constitution. There would be an incentive from the Federal government if they voted in favor of the Lecompton constitution: a large grant of public lands. Federal troops guarded the polls, but the incentive was not enough, and the Lecompton constitution was defeated.

With their victory the Free Soilers wasted no time. In July of 1859, a new constitution was written which forbade slavery in Kansas. Voters approved the new constitution in an October election. Slave owners, deprived of their legal rights to own slaves, for the most part left the state. According to the United States Census of 1860, only two slaves were left in the territory. The battle for Kansas was over. Kansas entered the Union as a free state, the thirty-fourth state, on the brink of the War Between the States in January of 1861.

The Dred Scott Case

Following the controversy and problems that occurred with the debate over slavery in Kansas, the election of 1856 was held, and it became one of the most contested and bitter elections in American history. The vote, as one might expect, was strictly down geographical section lines. The popular vote was very fragmented.

Around 1800, a slave named Dred Scott was born in Virginia. In 1830, Scott's owner moved to St. Louis and took Scott with him. He was sold the same year to an army officer and surgeon, John Emerson. Emerson, in 1837, was transferred to Fort Snelling in the Minnesota territory. The next year, Scott joined Emerson in Minnesota, a free territory, and lived there for two years.

They returned to Missouri in 1840. In 1846, Emerson died and Scott sued for his and his family's freedom. Scott claimed that he and his family had lived for two years in a free territory, thus making them free. A circuit court in St. Louis in 1850 found in favor of Scott and declared his freedom. In 1852, however, the Missouri Supreme Court ruled against Scott. The case worked its way up through the judicial system until it was heard by the United States Supreme Court in 1856.

A Supreme Court decision was not announced until 1857, well after the presidential elections of 1856. By a seven to two vote, the United States' highest court ruled that Scott had no right to sue because Scott was not a citizen of the United States. The court went further to say that the Missouri Compromise was unconstitutional, and that the United States Congress did not have the right to pass laws excluding slavery in any Federal territory.

Chief Justice Roger Taney's fifty-four-page majority opinion shocked many in the North. In his opinion, Taney argued, not only were slaves not United States citizens, but neither were the many free African Americans located in both the North and the South. Taney concluded that free African Americans could be citizens of their states, but not citizens of the United States. Taney stated that African Americans were "so far inferior, that they had no rights which the white man was bound to respect."

In Taney's opinion, any effort by the United States Congress to prohibit a slave owner taking his slave property to a territory was a violation of the slave owner's Fifth Amendment to the United States Constitution. The Fifth Amendment, which was part of the Bill of Rights, protects, among other things, personal property.

It is apparent that the Supreme Court ruling was designed to be an end-all ruling on the issues relating to slavery. In the South, all was clear—the highest court in the land had ruled. For many in the South it affirmed their right to own slaves and take them, as personal property, wherever they chose, and the Congress of the United States could do nothing about it. To those in the South, the slavery issue once and for all was resolved. To those in the North, it was anything but resolved. Some abolitionists called for the Northern states to secede from the Union. Abraham Lincoln called it a conspiracy to legalize slavery throughout the United States. Many in the North were outraged. Rather than close the sectional breach between the North and the South, the Supreme Court's decision may have made the breach much wider, and made future compromise more difficult, if not impossible.

A footnote to history, Scott still ended up a free man even after the Supreme Court's decision. The son of Scott's original owner purchased Scott and his family and freed them in May of 1857. Scott died less than a year later in February of 1858.

Sectional Issues Divide Denominations

The sectional issues, primarily slavery, between the North and the South made their way into divisions between the major Protestant denominations in the United States. A number of the church leaders were proslavery, including Carl F. W. Walther, founder and long-time president of what became known as the Missouri Synod Lutheran Church.[22] The Presbyterian Church was one of the first to experience division in the 1830s. Two separate factions within the Presbyterian Church formed in 1837. "Old School" churches mainly in the South and "New School" churches mainly in the North argued over slavery as well as a number of other issues.[23] By 1861, the Presbyterian Church had split in two, with a Northern branch and a Southern branch. The two churches did not formally reunite until 1983.

The Methodist Church experienced a number of schisms over race. Due to the segregationist policies of the Methodist Church, African Americans split from the denomination, as early as the eighteenth century. Both the African Methodist Episcopal Church, which was formed in Philadelphia in 1787, and the African Methodist Episcopal Zion Church, which was formed in 1820, were splintered off the Methodist Church. Although the Methodist Church had called slavery "a great evil," it had not gone as far as the abolitionist element in the church had wanted it to. In fact, at the church's 1836 General Assembly, the church rejected "any right, wish, or intention to interfere in the civil and political relation between master and slave." The Wesleyan Methodist Church was formed in 1840 when the abolitionist wing of the church broke away.

In 1844, the largest schism occurred when the General Conference of the Methodist Church could not resolve the slavery issue. The Southern delegates, of which nearly 85 percent owned slaves, demanded that the churches rescind its position that slavery was evil. When the issue could not be resolved, it led to the formation, in 1845, of the Methodist Episcopal Church, South, with about half a million members.[24] The two churches would not reunite until 1939.

The Baptist Church was more loosely organized than the Presbyterian and Methodist Churches. The slavery issue came to a head in the Baptist denomination in 1845 with a meeting of the Baptist Triennial Convention. That body supervised the Baptist foreign missionary work. At the convention, in an effort to prevent what had happened in other denominations, they passed a resolution stating that there would be no "sanction, either express or implied, whether of slavery or antislavery." It was not enough. Southerners formed their own church after the Board of Foreign Missions refused to agree to appoint slaveholding missionaries. In 1845, the Southern Baptist Convention was formed, and in the North, the American Baptist Missionary Union, opposed to slavery, was organized.[25] Unlike the Presbyterian and Methodist Churches, the two sectional Baptist churches have never reunited.

Proslavery sentiment was not confined to Protestant denominations. The leaders of two of the major segments of Jewish faith, Isaac M. Wise and Isaac Leeser, were proslavery rabbis.[26]

Other Sectional Issues

Slavery was certainly not the only factor to affect the polarization of the two sections, both politically and socially. Even taking away the slavery issue, the North and the South were two widely diverse regions. The South was primarily agricultural and the North far more industrialized. In spite of efforts to build cotton mills in the South, 75 percent of the South's cotton crop went abroad,[27] and much of what was not exported went north to mills in the Northeast. Such contrasts led to differences of opinions on tariffs, trade policies, internal improvements, and the like.

The primary funding for the United States government was through tariffs. The South had to import much of what it needed from either the North or from overseas, and obviously the South exported its agricultural products; for instance, by 1850 Southern cotton represented half of the United States' total exports. The South typically opposed high tariffs, but it was through tariffs that the nation's internal improvements were primarily funded. Internal improvements were of great concern to the growing and ever-industrializing North. Tariffs were the government's main source of revenues, in the days prior to personal and business income taxes. The North strongly favored internal improvements, such as roads and canals, to help its expansion.

There was also a major philosophical difference between the North and the South over what role a national government would play. Today, many Americans take for granted the power and dominance of our centralized federal government. In the first half of the nineteenth century the political thought was much different. Few historians would disagree over the fact that initially most people, in both the North and in the South, viewed the state government as the dominant government. The individual states' participation in the federal government was merely a voluntary relationship. Even New England threatened to secede from the Union over trade issues during the War of 1812.

Gradually the concept of a stronger national government began to take root in the North. The more the North became industrialized, the more the need arose for a stronger national government. To support its growth and financial interests, the North desired a number of things, issues like greater transportation capabilities, stronger control over imports, and a sound currency. More and more, politicians in the North saw these things being best accomplished by a national government and not by a variety of different state governments.

The South did not see things any differently than when the United States government was first formed by the founding fathers. In fact, they were willing to go to war to preserve what they thought was the governmental design of the founding fathers. The South desired most of the power to be vested in the state governments. One was a Virginian first or a South Carolinian first, and a citizen of the United States secondly. Unlike the North, the economic interests of the South were served well by the state governments being supreme.

The union that had lasted from 1776 would come crashing to an end after the election of 1860. The compromises that had saved the Union numerous times in the past would not be there in 1860 when South Carolina became the first Southern state to secede from the Union. The final catalyst was the 1860 election of the Republican Party's presidential candidate, Abraham Lincoln. Lincoln was certainly a regional candidate, as he received little support south of the Mason Dixon line. With the Democratic Party in a divided state, it opened the door for Lincoln to win the election with only 39.8 percent of the popular vote. It was more than the South could stand, as one by one the Southern states began to leave the Union and form their Southern confederation, the Confederate States of America.

Chapter Five
Snapshot of Slavery

The 1860 United States Census

One of the popular perceptions we want to explore is the prevalence of slavery prior to the outbreak of the War Between the States. How many slaves were there, where were they, who owned the slaves, were there really giant plantations with hundreds and hundreds of slaves? To answer these and other questions let us look at the demographics of slavery.

To accomplish this we draw on a highly valuable asset. Thanks to the United States government, we have various census records to peruse and actually have a United States census from the very eve of the War Between the States: the 1860 Census. The Constitution of the United States requires that a counting of people be done within three years of the first meeting of Congress, and then thereafter every ten years. The first United States census took place in 1790 and consisted of only six questions. By the 1860 Census, the number of questions had risen to 142 questions. With that many questions the 1860 Census would not be published before the next census took place.

The processing of the 1860 Census by hand counting obviously produced errors. The census data is not perfect; no census has been or ever will be. But the information from the 1860 Census provides us with objective, solid data which we can use to achieve a fairly accurate perspective of slavery in 1860.

According to the United States Census of 1860, the country had a total population of 31,443,321 from forty-two states and territories.[1]

Of the total population the vast majority were Whites—26,922,539, representing 85.6 percent. Slaves accounted for 3,953,760, or 12.6 percent of the total population; free African Americans, 488,070, 1.6 percent of the total populace. The balance of the people, 78,952, consisted of other ethnic groups. About 44,000 were listed as Native Americans (certainly an incomplete count); 458 were labeled as "Half-Breeds"; and nearly 35,000 people were of Asian descent, all of whom residing in California.

Listed below, in Table 5.1, is the population from the 1860 Census by state, territory, and District of Columbia.

Table 5.1—Population of the United States, 1860

State or Territory	Total Population	Whites	Slaves	Free Blacks	All Other*
Alabama	964,201	526,271	435,080	2,690	160
Arkansas	435,450	324,143	111,115	144	48
California	379,994	323,177	0	4,086	52,731
Connecticut	460,147	451,504	0	8,627	16
Colorado Territory	34,277	34,231	0	46	0
Dakota Territory	4,837	2,576	0	0	2,261
Delaware	112,216	90,589	1,798	19,829	0
District of Columbia	75,080	60,794	3,185	11,131	0
Florida	140,424	77,747	61,745	932	0
Georgia	1,057,286	591,550	462,198	3,500	38
Illinois	1,711,951	1,704,291	0	7,628	32
Indiana	1,350,428	1,338,710	0	11,428	290
Iowa	674,913	673,779	0	1,069	65
Kansas	107,206	106,390	2	625	189
Kentucky	1,155,684	919,484	225,483	10,684	33
Louisiana	708,002	357,456	331,726	18,647	173
Maine	628,279	626,947	0	1,327	5
Maryland	687,049	515,918	87,189	83,942	0
Massachusetts	1,231,066	1,221,432	0	9,602	32
Michigan	749,113	736,142	0	6,799	6,172
Minnesota	172,023	169,395	0	259	2,369
Mississippi	791,305	353,899	436,631	773	2
Missouri	1,182,012	1,063,489	114,931	3,572	20
Nebraska Territory	28,841	28,696	15	67	63
Nevada Territory	6,857	6,812	0	45	0
New Hampshire	326,073	325,579	0	494	0
New Jersey	672,035	646,699	18	25,318	0

* Note: In the "All Other" column all the numbers are listed as either Indian or "Half Breeds," except in California. In California the "All Other" is made up of 34,933 Asians and 17,798 Indians.

State or Territory	Total Population	Whites	Slaves	Free Blacks	All Other
New Mexico Territory	93,516	82,924	0	85	10,507
New York	3,880,735	3,831,590	0	49,005	140
North Carolina	992,622	629,942	331,059	30,463	1,158
Ohio	2,339,511	2,302,808	0	36,673	30
Oregon	52,465	52,160	0	128	177
Pennsylvania	2,906,215	2,849,259	0	56,949	7
Rhode Island	174,620	170,649	0	3,952	19
South Carolina	703,708	291,300	402,406	9,914	88
Tennessee	1,109,801	826,722	275,719	7,300	60
Texas	604,215	420,891	182,566	355	403
Utah Territory	40,273	40,125	29	30	89
Vermont	315,098	314,369	0	709	20
Virginia	1,596,318	1,047,299	490,865	58,042	112
Washington Territory	11,594	11,138	0	30	426
Wisconsin	775,881	773,693	0	1,171	1,017
Total	31,443,321	26,922,539	3,953,760	488,070	78,952

The numbers in Table 5.2 provide a regional perspective. For regional purposes, I included all free states and territories in the "North" numbers, and all states where slavery was allowed in the "South" numbers. The Southern numbers do include Delaware, which was a slave state but remained in the Union during the War Between the States. "South" also includes the slave states known as the "Border" states during the War Between the States: Maryland, Kentucky, and Missouri, and the District of Columbia, where slavery was allowed.

Table 5.2—Regional Population Comparison, North vs. South, 1860

Region	Total Population	Whites	Slaves	Free African Americans	Other
North	19,127,948	18,825,075	64	226,152	76,657
South	12,315,373	8,097,464	3,953,696	261,918	2,295
Total	31,443,321	26,922,539	3,953,760	488,070	78,952

As one can readily see, the North, with 60.8 percent of the population, certainly had a numerical advantage over the South. In terms of the white population, the North had well more than twice the population of the South. The South virtually had 100 percent of the slaves, but surprisingly also the majority of free African Americans, about a quarter of a million, lived in the South. There were about 15 percent more free African Americans in the South versus the North.

Next, let us look specifically at the slave numbers. Table 5.3 lists the number of slaves and the percentage increase of slaves from the first national census in 1790 to the 1860 Census. The number of slaves in the United States crossed the million number with the 1810 Census, hitting the two million mark in the 1830 Census and the three million level in the 1850 Census, falling just shy of the four million mark by 1860. A rather steady percentage increase—from 27 to 32 percent—in the slave population occurred during each decade from 1790 to 1830. The percentage increase began to slow, and by 1860 was less than 24 percent. The overall average increase per census from 1790 to 1860 was about 28 percent.

Table 5.3—Number of Slaves and the Percentage Increase by Census, 1790-1860

Year	Slaves	Percent Increase
1790	697,897	n/a
1800	893,041	27.97
1810	1,191,364	33.40
1820	1,538,038	28.79
1830	2,009,043	30.61
1840	2,487,455	23.81
1850	3,204,313	28.82
1860	3,953,760	23.39

There is a great deal of detailed information in the 1860 Census on the free population, but unfortunately the census does not have the same detail on the slave population. The census lists only the slave owner's name and county of residence and then the sex, age, and color, black or mulatto, of each slave. The slaves were not listed by name, as the free population was, nor were they grouped into family units. In spite of that we can still learn from the aggregate numbers.

Table 5.4 is a listing by state, territory, and district of the total number of slaves within each area, listed in order of the total number of slaves. The first percentage column is the percentage of the slave population compared to the total population in that state, territory, or district. The last percentage column is the percentage of slaves in that state, territory, or district of the entire United States slave population.

Table 5.4 —Number of Slaves by State, 1860

State or Territory	Slaves	Percentage Slave in State	Percent of Total U.S. Slave Population
Virginia	490,865	30.75%	12.42%
Georgia	462,198	43.72%	11.69%
Mississippi	436,631	55.18%	11.04%
Alabama	435,080	45.12%	11.00%
South Carolina	402,406	57.18%	10.18%
Louisiana	331,726	46.85%	8.39%
North Carolina	331,059	33.35%	8.37%
Tennessee	275,719	24.84%	6.97%
Kentucky	225,483	19.51%	5.70%
Texas	182,566	30.22%	4.62%
Missouri	114,931	9.72%	2.91%
Arkansas	111,115	25.52%	2.81%
Maryland	87,189	12.69%	2.21%
Florida	61,745	43.97%	1.56%
District of Columbia	3,185	4.24%	0.08%
Delaware	1,798	1.60%	0.05%
Utah Territory	29	0.07%	n/a
New Jersey	18	n/a	n/a
Nebraska Territory	15	0.05%	n/a
Kansas	2	n/a	n/a
Total	3,953,760		

Although Virginia was the state with the most slaves it is quite clear that many of the slaves were in the lower South. The states of Georgia, Mississippi, Alabama, and Louisiana accounted for over 42 percent of all the slaves.

It is interesting to look at slave ownership to test a popular modern perception that most whites in the South owned slaves. First let us look at slave ownership in the South versus the white population. Some modern pro-Southern supporters quote a very low percentage of white slave ownership. The number is obtained in the following way. According to the 1860 Census, there were 3,953,760 slaves in the South, a total white population of 8,097,464, and 393,967 slave owners. Under the assumption that all slaves were owned only by whites, then the percentage of whites owning slaves in the South would be only 4.9 percent, a rather astounding number. Using this calculation, the states with the highest percentage of ownership would be South Carolina, at 9.2 percent and Mississippi, at 8.7 percent and the states with the lowest percentage of ownership would be Delaware at only

.6 percent and Missouri, at 2.3 percent. Some people quote some variation of that calculation and claim that 95.1 percent of whites in the South did not own slaves. That number, however, is both flawed and misleading in at least a couple of ways.

First, not all slaves were owned by whites; for instance, both free African Americans and Native Americans owned slaves. Although it would make only a minor change in the percentages, those slave owners would have to be extracted from the calculation for it to be accurate. If these corrections were made, the results would be technically correct, but would not give us a truly accurate picture of the extent of slave ownership in the South. The major problem with the calculation is that if all whites are counted, including all children and adult females, it will unfairly skew the results and give us a less than candid picture of Southern slave ownership. Certainly children did not own slaves, nor did very many adult females in the South.

A more realistic view of the extent of slave ownership would be to look at the number of households that owned slaves. Looking at slave ownership from a household perspective would give us a better perspective on the extent of slave ownership. The following table, by state, shows the number of households, the number of slaveowners, and the percentage of households that owned slaves.

Table 5.5—Number of Southern Households and Slave Owners, 1860

State	Households	Slave Owners	Percentage
Alabama	96,603	33,730	34.9%
Arkansas	57,244	11,481	20.1%
Delaware	18,966	587	3.1%
Florida	15,090	5,152	34.1%
Georgia	109,919	41,084	37.4%
Kentucky	166,321	38,645	23.2%
Louisiana	74,725	22,033	29.5%
Maryland	110,278	13,783	12.5%
Mississippi	63,015	30,943	49.1%
Missouri	192,073	24,320	12.7%
North Carolina	125,090	34,658	27.7%
South Carolina	58,642	26,701	45.5%
Tennessee	149,335	36,844	24.7%
Texas	76,781	21,878	28.5%
Virginia	201,523	52,128	25.9%
Total	1,515,605	393,967	26.0%

This table gives us a much more accurate representation of how prevalent slave ownership was in the South in 1860. With over one and a half million households and nearly 400,000 slave owners we see that 26 percent of Southern households owned slaves. This number is less than 95.1 percent as we mentioned earlier, but will still astound most people. Simply put, about three quarters of the Southern families did not own slaves in the South in 1860.

The percentage variance is quite high when one compares the lowest state, Delaware at 3.1 percent, with the highest state, Mississippi, at 49.1 percent. But, no state, not even those in the lower South, had even half of the households owning slaves. The most typical state was the state that had the most slaves, Virginia, with a household slave ownership of 25.9 percent.

The majority of slave owners were males. He most likely was a native born, white Southerner. The median value of his land was under three thousand dollars. Females made up about 10 percent of the slave owners. Most of the

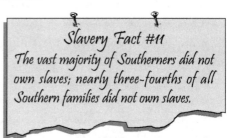

Slavery Fact #11

The vast majority of Southerners did not own slaves; nearly three-fourths of all Southern families did not own slaves.

females owned their slaves by way of inheriting them. For that reason the average female slave owner was fifty years old, while a male was only forty-four.[2]

The next table shows the number of slaves by state, the total number of slave owners by state, and the mean average.

Table 5.6—Number of Slaves and Slave Owners by State, 1860

State	Total No. of Slaves	Total No. of Slaveholders	Mean Average
Virginia	490,865	52,128	9.42
Georgia	462,198	41,084	11.25
Kentucky	225,483	38,645	5.83
Tennessee	275,719	36,844	7.48
North Carolina	331,059	34,658	9.55
Alabama	435,080	33,730	12.90
Mississippi	436,631	30,943	14.11
South Carolina	402,406	26,701	15.07
Missouri	114,931	24,320	4.73
Louisiana	331,726	22,033	15.06

(continued on next page)

Table 5.6 *(continued)*

State	Total No. of Slaves	Total No. of Slaveholders	Mean Average
Texas	182,566	21,878	8.34
Maryland	87,189	13,783	6.33
Arkansas	111,115	11,481	9.68
Florida	61,745	5,152	11.98
Delaware	1,798	587	3.06
Nebraska	15	6	2.5
Kansas	2	2	1.0
Total	3,950,528	393,975	10.03

Although a mean average is just that, an average, it gives us the first indication that one of the myths about slavery, that most slaves worked on plantations with at least hundreds and perhaps even thousands of other slaves, is false. With a total average of 10.03 slaves per slave owner, it is much lower than what most people expect. Most of the larger plantations were in the lower South, so one will observe that the average number of slaves owned is higher in states like Louisiana, at about 15, and Mississippi, at about 14, than in states like Delaware, at 3, and Kentucky at nearly 6. The numbers are higher in the lower South, but not dramatically so, when compared to the total regional average.

Fortunately for us today, the census takers asked the slave owners how many slaves each owned. With that data we are able to get a very good idea of just what were the typical holdings of slave owners in the South. The next series of tables explores the issue of what was the typical slave owner's number of slaves. Table 5.7 indicates slave ownership by state and the number of slaves owned by each slave owner from one slave to nineteen slaves, and the percentage of the total.

Table 5.7—Number of Slaves Owned from 1 to 19 by Slave Owners by State, 1860

State	1	%	2-5	%	6-9	%	10-19	%
Alabama	5,607	16.6%	10,783	32.0%	5,403	16.0%	5,906	17.5%
Arkansas	2,339	20.4%	4,197	36.6%	1,805	15.7%	1,777	15.5%
Delaware	237	40.4%	273	46.5%	52	8.9%	25	4.3%
Florida	863	16.8%	1,655	32.1%	850	16.5%	976	18.9%
Georgia	6,713	16.3%	13,364	32.5%	7,114	17.3%	7,530	18.3%
Kentucky	9,306	24.1%	15,414	39.9%	7,099	18.4%	5,271	13.6%
Louisiana	4,092	18.6%	7,453	33.8%	3,341	15.2%	3,222	14.6%

State	1	%	2-5	%	6-9	%	10-19	%
Maryland	4,119	29.9%	5,069	36.8%	2,015	14.6%	1,718	12.5%
Mississippi	4,856	15.7%	9,642	31.2%	5,061	16.4%	5,489	17.7%
Missouri	6,893	28.3%	10,456	43.0%	4,031	16.6%	1,332	5.5%
North Carolina	6,440	18.6%	11,876	34.3%	6,204	17.9%	6,073	17.5%
South Carolina	3,763	14.1%	7,795	29.2%	4,641	17.4%	5,210	19.5%
Tennessee	7,820	21.2%	13,895	37.7%	6,674	18.1%	5,523	15.0%
Texas	4,593	21.0%	8,188	37.4%	3,511	16.0%	3,423	15.6%
Virginia	11,085	21.3%	17,503	33.6%	8,989	17.2%	8,774	16.8%
Total	78,726	20.0%	137,563	34.9%	66,790	17.0%	62,249	15.8%

Table 5.7 reflects that 78,726 slave owners only owned one slave. Of all the slave owners in the South, 20 percent owned only one slave. This percentage again will probably surprise the casual student of history. About 55 percent of all slave owners owned five or fewer slaves. Slave ownership of less than ten slaves was 72 percent, nearly three quarters of all slave owners. Nearly 90 percent (87.7 percent) of all slave owners owned fewer than twenty slaves. Our myth of Tara and the hundreds or thousands of slaves is now crumpling!

The next table illustrates slave ownership of twenty or more slaves by state and the number of slaves owned by each slave owner, and the percentage of the total.

Our myth of the large plantation with many slaves is now, pardon the pun, gone with the wind! Total slave ownership of less than fifty slaves was an astounding 97 percent! Only 3 percent of slave owners owned more than fifty slaves. There were only fifteen slave own-

> ### Slavery Fact #12
> The vast majority of slave owners lived on small farms. The large plantations were a myth; only fifteen people in the entire South owned five hundred or more slaves.

ers in the entire South that owned more than five hundred slaves, according to the 1860 U.S. Census.

According to the 1860 Census, Native Americans also owned slaves. The Census reported that the Choctaw tribe held 2,297 slaves, owned by 385 slave owners; the Cherokees had 2,504 slaves, held by 384 slave owners; the Creeks 1,651 slaves, owned by 267 slave owners; and the Chickasaws held 917 slaves, by 118 slave owners.

Table 5.8 — Number of Slaves Owned from 20 to 1,000 Plus by Slave Owners by State, 1860

State	20-49	%	50-99	%	100-299	%	300-499	%	500-999	%	1,000 or more	%
Alabama	4,344	12.9%	1,341	4.0%	336	1.0%	10	0.030%	0	0.000%	0	0.000%
Arkansas	1,018	8.9%	279	2.4%	65	0.6%	1	0.009%	1	0.009%	0	0.000%
Delaware	0	0.0%	0	0.0%	0	0.0%	0	0.000%	0	0.000%	0	0.000%
Florida	603	11.7%	158	3.1%	47	0.9%	0	0.000%	0	0.000%	0	0.000%
Georgia	5,049	12.3%	1,102	2.7%	204	0.5%	8	0.019%	1	0.002%	0	0.000%
Kentucky	1,485	3.8%	63	0.2%	7	0.0%	0	0.000%	0	0.000%	0	0.000%
Louisiana	2,349	10.7%	1,029	4.7%	523	2.4%	24	0.109%	4	0.018%	0	0.000%
Maryland	747	5.4%	99	0.7%	15	0.1%	1	0.007%	0	0.000%	0	0.000%
Mississippi	4,220	13.6%	1,359	4.4%	307	1.0%	8	0.026%	1	0.003%	0	0.000%
Missouri	502	2.1%	34	0.1%	4	0.0%	0	0.000%	0	0.000%	0	0.000%
North Carolina	3,321	9.6%	611	1.8%	129	0.4%	4	0.012%	0	0.000%	0	0.000%
South Carolina	3,646	13.7%	1,197	4.5%	419	1.6%	29	0.109%	7	0.026%	1	0.004%
Tennessee	2,550	6.9%	335	0.9%	46	0.1%	1	0.003%	0	0.000%	0	0.000%
Texas	1,827	8.4%	282	1.3%	54	0.2%	0	0.000%	0	0.000%	0	0.000%
Virginia	4,917	9.4%	746	1.4%	113	0.2%	1	0.002%	0	0.000%	0	0.000%
Total	36,578	9.3%	8,635	2.2%	2,269	0.6%	87	0.000%	14	0.004%	1	0.000%

As with other slave owners, slave ownership among the Native Americans varied from owning a single slave to some with large numbers of slaves. One Choctaw tribe slave owner held 227 slaves, but the average was about six slaves to each owner of slaves in that tribe.[3]

Let us stop here and put into perspective what the 1860 Census has told us up to this point. First, the vast majority of white Southerners did not even own slaves. The minority of white Southerners that did own slaves were the owners of a small number of slaves—over half owned fewer than five slaves. This clearly refutes one of the myths of slavery that most white Southerners lived on large plantations with many hundreds or thousands of slaves. In round numbers in 1860, if you had twenty slave owners: four of them would own only one slave, seven of them would own from two to five slaves, three would own from six to nine slaves, three would own from ten to nineteen slaves, two would own twenty to forty-nine slaves, and only one would own more than fifty slaves.

However, what is not a myth is that the majority of slaves lived on plantations, if you accept the definition of most historians that one of the requirements to have a plantation versus a farm is slave ownership of twenty or more slaves. Of twenty slaves in 1860, twelve would live on plantations of twenty or more slaves and seven of the twelve slaves would live on plantations of fifty or more slaves.[4]

The 1860 Census also reflects a surprisingly large population of free African Americans in the United States. Table 5.9 lists the free African American population in the entire country, sorted by which state had the highest percentage of the state's overall population.

Table 5.9—Free African American Population by State, 1860

State	Total Population	Free African Americans	Percentage of State's Population
Delaware	112,216	19,829	17.67%
Maryland	687,049	83,942	12.22%
Virginia	1,596,318	58,042	3.64%
North Carolina	992,622	30,463	3.07%
Louisiana	708,002	18,647	2.63%
Rhode Island	174,611	3,952	2.26%
Pennsylvania	2,906,206	56,949	1.96%

(continued on next page)

Table 5.9 *(continued)*

State	Total Population	Free African Americans	Percentage of State's Population
Connecticut	460,138	8,627	1.87%
Ohio	2,339,502	36,673	1.57%
Total—USA	31,183,582	476,748	1.53%*
South Carolina	703,708	9,914	1.41%
New York	3,880,726	49,005	1.26%
California	379,985	4,086	1.08%
Kentucky	1,155,684	10,684	0.92%
Michigan	749,104	6,799	0.91%
Indiana	1,350,419	11,428	0.85%
Massachusetts	1,231,057	9,602	0.78%
Florida	140,424	932	0.66%
Tennessee	1,109,801	7,300	0.66%
Nevada	6,848	45	0.66%
Kansas	107,206	625	0.58%
Illinois	1,711,942	7,628	0.45%
Georgia	1,057,286	3,500	0.33%
Missouri	1,182,012	3,572	0.30%
Alabama	964,201	2,690	0.28%
Oregon	52,456	128	0.24%
Nebraska	28,841	67	0.23%
Vermont	315,089	709	0.23%
Maine	628,270	1,327	0.21%
Iowa	674,904	1,069	0.16%
New Hampshire	326,064	494	0.15%
Wisconsin	775,872	1,171	0.15%
Minnesota	172,014	259	0.15%
Mississippi	791,305	773	0.10%
New Jersey	672,035	25,318	0.07%
Texas	604,215	355	0.06%
Arkansas	435,450	144	0.03%

* Percentage of Free African Americans in total U.S. population

The states with the highest percentage of free African Americans were Delaware, at 17.7 percent and Maryland, with 12.2 percent, and the states with the lowest were Arkansas, at .03 percent, and Texas, with .06 percent. It is also interesting to note that of the top ten, in terms of the highest percentage of free African

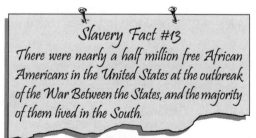

Slavery Fact #13

There were nearly a half million free African Americans in the United States at the outbreak of the War Between the States, and the majority of them lived in the South.

Americans in a state's population, the top five are Southern states: Delaware, Maryland, Virginia, North Carolina, and Louisiana.

Fortunately, the 1860 Census also recorded the gender and the ages of all slaves that were counted. Table 5.10 reflects the gender and age breakdown of the slave population. The percentage amount is the percentage of the total number of slaves, male and female, in each age category.

Table 5.10—Ages of Slaves by Gender, 1860

Ages	Male	Female	Total	% of Total
Under 1	55,221	58,360	113,581	2.89%
1–4	266,740	272,489	539,229	13.74%
5–9	287,135	288,449	575,584	14.66%
10–14	276,715	264,002	540,717	13.78%
15–19	220,215	228,178	448,393	11.42%
20–29	354,818	342,680	697,498	17.77%
30–39	218,234	220,299	438,533	11.17%
40–49	140,706	138,824	279,530	7.12%
50–59	79,720	75,789	155,509	3.96%
60–69	46,189	44,044	90,233	2.30%
70–79	15,415	15,694	31,109	0.79%
80–89	4,620	5,323	9,943	0.25%
90–99	1,317	1,714	3,031	0.08%
Over 100	671	899	1,570	0.04%
Unknown	318	379	697	0.02%
Total	1,968,034	1,957,123	3,925,157	100.00%

It is interesting to note that there were slightly more males slaves than female slaves, by a percentage of 50.14 percent to 49.86 percent. Looking at the data alone it is difficult to draw any conclusions, but let's compare it with both the white population data and the free African American data.

Table 5.11 indicates the gender and age breakdown of the white population. The percentage amount is the percentage of the total number of whites, male and female, in each age category.

Table 5.11—Ages of White Population by Gender, 1860

Ages	Male	Female	Total	% of Total
Under 1	406,372	394,098	800,470	3.00%
1–4	1,668,309	1,615,482	3,283,791	12.31%
5–9	1,775,151	1,726,176	3,501,327	13.13%
10–14	1,579,541	1,512,822	3,092,363	11.59%
15–19	1,391,402	1,442,207	2,833,609	10.62%

(continued on next page)

Table 5.11 *(continued)*

Ages	Male	Female	Total	% of Total
20–29	2,458,175	2,401,077	4,859,252	18.22%
30–39	1,841,125	1,623,867	3,464,992	12.99%
40–49	1,213,077	1,051,120	2,264,197	8.49%
50–59	735,441	655,200	1,390,641	5.21%
60–69	398,279	377,820	776,099	2.91%
70–79	152,844	155,829	308,673	1.16%
80–89	37,743	42,512	80,255	0.30%
90–99	4,068	5,563	9,631	0.04%
Over 100	368	534	902	0.00%
Unknown	4,000	2,730	6,730	0.03%
Total	13,665,895	13,007,037	26,672,932	100.00%

Table 5.12 shows the gender and age breakdown of the free African American population, North and South. The percentage amount is the percentage of the total number of free African Americans, male and female, in each age category.

Table 5.12—Ages of Free African American Population by Gender, 1860

Ages	Male	Female	Total	% of Total
Under 1	6,059	6,272	12,331	2.59%
1–4	26,116	26,121	52,237	10.96%
5–9	30,083	30,444	60,527	12.70%
10–14	29,807	29,226	59,033	12.39%
15–19	24,170	27,289	51,459	10.80%
20–29	38,380	45,191	83,571	17.53%
30–39	28,434	31,719	60,153	12.62%
40–49	20,974	22,693	43,667	9.16%
50–59	13,043	14,195	27,238	5.71%
60–69	7,566	8,214	15,780	3.31%
70–79	3,150	3,730	6,880	1.44%
80–89	986	1,528	2514	0.53%
90–99	320	510	830	0.17%
Over 100	126	236	362	0.08%
Unknown	31	34	65	0.01%
Total	229,245	247,402	476,647	100.00%

Table 5.13 is a comparison of the three classifications—slaves, whites, and free African Americans—comparing the percentages of the age classifications.

Table 5.13—Comparison of the Age Brackets for Slaves, Whites, and Free African Americans, 1860

Ages	Slaves	Whites	Free
Under 1	2.89%	3.00%	2.59%
1–4	13.74%	12.31%	10.96%

Ages	Slaves	Whites	Free
5–9	14.66%	13.13%	12.70%
10–14	13.78%	11.59%	12.39%
15–19	11.42%	10.62%	10.80%
20–29	17.77%	18.22%	17.53%
30–39	11.17%	12.99%	12.62%
40–49	7.12%	8.49%	9.16%
50–59	3.96%	5.21%	5.71%
60–69	2.30%	2.91%	3.31%
70–79	0.79%	1.16%	1.44%
80–89	0.25%	0.30%	0.53%
90–99	0.08%	0.04%	0.17%
Over 100	0.04%	0.00%	0.08%
Unknown	0.02%	0.03%	0.01%

By reviewing Table 5.13, one is able to get a glimpse of the population's age breakdown in 1860. All three categories are remarkably similar. Ages twenty to twenty-nine were the more prevalent ages for slaves, whites, and free African American, with only .69 percent separating the highest with the lowest. The second most common age bracket, again in all three categories, was ages five through nine.

The data would suggest that free African Americans had the better longevity. At least they had a greater percentage of their population in the upper ages. From age sixty on, free African Americans had 5.53 percent, whites 4.41 percent, and slaves 3.46 percent. If you look at the senior ages, from eighty on the free African Americans again prevail with almost twice as many as whites. Free African Americans had .78 percent of their population over the age of eighty, slaves had .37 percent, and whites trailed at .34 percent.

The data is not completely accurate, but it certainly gives us at least a very good indication of the population of slaves, free African Americans, and whites. What we see, as of 1860, is that free African Americans had the greatest chance of reaching age forty and beyond, and that both free African Americans and slaves had a greater percentage of their population reaching an advanced age than did the whites.

Slavery Fact #14
African Americans (slaves and freed men and women) in 1860 had a greater chance of reaching a senior age than whites.

Table 5.14 reflects basic Southern urban information. The table lists twenty selected Southern towns and cities reflecting total population, white population, slave population, and free African Americans. The cities and towns were selected to include the major Southern cities as well as the larger city or town in each Southern state. The table is in alphabetical order by state.

Table 5.14– Urban Population of Selected Southern Cities (Sorted by State), 1860

City or Town	Total	Whites	% of Total	Slaves	% of Total	Free African Americans	% of Total
Mobile, Ala.	29,258	20,854	71.3%	7,587	25.9%	817	2.8%
Little Rock, Ark.	3,727	2,874	77.1%	846	22.7%	7	0.2%
Pensacola, Fla.	2,876	1,789	62.2%	957	33.3%	130	4.5%
Savannah, Ga.	22,292	13,875	62.2%	7,712	34.6%	705	3.2%
Augusta, Ga.	12,493	8,444	67.6%	3,663	29.3%	386	3.1%
Atlanta, Ga.	9,554	7,615	79.7%	1,914	20.0%	25	0.3%
Louisville, Ky.	68,033	61,213	90.0%	4,903	7.2%	1,917	2.8%
New Orleans, La.	168,675	144,601	85.7%	13,385	7.9%	10,689	6.3%
Baltimore, Md.	212,418	184,520	86.9%	2,218	1.0%	25,680	12.1%
Natchez, Miss.	6,612	4,272	64.6%	2,132	32.2%	208	3.1%
St. Louis, Mo.	160,773	157,476	97.9%	1,542	1.0%	1,755	1.1%
Wilmington, N.C.	9,552	5,202	54.5%	3,777	39.5%	573	6.0%
Charleston, S.C.	40,522	23,376	57.7%	13,909	34.3%	3,237	8.0%
Memphis, Tenn.	22,623	18,741	82.8%	3,684	16.3%	198	0.9%
Nashville, Tenn.	16,988	13,043	76.8%	3,226	19.0%	719	4.2%
San Antonio, Tex.	8,235	7,643	92.8%	592	7.2%	0	0.0%
Galveston, Tex.	7,307	6,127	83.9%	1,178	16.1%	2	0.03%
Richmond, Va.	37,910	23,635	62.3%	11,699	30.9%	2,576	6.8%
Petersburg, Va.	18,266	9,342	51.1%	5,680	31.1%	3,244	17.8%
Norfolk, Va.	14,620	10,290	70.4%	3,284	22.5%	1,046	7.2%
Total	872,734	724,932	83.1%	93,888	10.8%	53,914	6.2%

The cities with the largest slave populations were Charleston, South Carolina; New Orleans, Louisiana; and Richmond, Virginia. Percentagewise, the largest slave urban populations were in Wilmington, North Carolina; Savannah, Georgia; and Charleston. The fewest urban slaves were in the west and in Florida. San Antonio, Texas, had the fewest, followed by Little Rock, Arkansas, and Pensacola, Florida. Percentagewise the fewest urban slaves were in the border state cities of Baltimore, Maryland, and St. Louis, Missouri, followed by San Antonio.

Chapter Six
The Lives of the Slaves (1831-1860)—Part 1

The Sources

The purpose of this chapter and the next one is to present a brief summary of the life of a slave, immediately prior to the War Between the States. This is a most difficult and daunting task. First of all, we don't know for sure what a slave's life was like; no one knows that with one hundred percent accuracy. All the slaves and all the slave owners are long since gone from this world. So, what do we do? We do the next best thing and scan, collect, and analyze what sources are out there to assist us in trying to piece together the life of the American slave.

In writing this chapter, it was difficult to keep from hopelessly falling into the same trap as most before me by stereotyping the slaves' lives. In reality, just as life is different for everyone in the world today, so was each slave's life. Some slaves were treated well, while others were treated horribly. Some slaves were well fed and clothed; others not well at all. What is presented, in this chapter and the next, is the best educated guess on what life may have been like for the "average" slave, knowing full well that there is no such thing as an "average" slave. But I think we are able to see at least a glimpse of what life may have been like.

This chapter and the next were written using a variety of sources. The goal was to accurately describe the life of the slave in the South. Although appendix A includes a discussion of the resources used to craft this image of slaves, four of the resources need to be specifically mentioned at this point. One of the earliest sources was by a chronicler who traveled throughout the South during the 1850s. Frederick Law Olmsted, a Northerner from New York, was hired by what is now known as the *New York Times*, to travel the South and to report back to their readers his observations about the South and about slavery. Some of his numerous observations, from his three Southern trips, are used in this chapter and the next.

Another source of firsthand accounts is from the former slaves themselves. During the Depression, the Federal Writers' Project (FWP), part of the Works Projects Administration, launched a project to interview as many of the still living former slaves as they could. Over two thousand two hundred interviews were done in seventeen states, by about three hundred interviewers. The interviews represented about 2 percent of the total slaves that were still alive in the 1930s.[1] The former slaves lived on farms and plantations that had from one slave to over a thousand slaves. What we have as a result of this effort is the story of slavery told by the slaves themselves through approximately three and a half million words.[2] I have included numerous of their accounts to give the reader the benefit of these firsthand recollections.

A variety of other books and resources were used, but I want to mention two books specifically that are landmark efforts in the study of slavery. The first was written by the pioneer researcher on American slavery, Ulrich B. Phillips. Phillips's book *American Negro Slavery*, published in 1918, was the standard on American slavery for nearly forty years. Phillips was the first to make a scientific investigation into slavery and although very dated, the book is very well researched. Phillips followed the first book with a subsequent effort about ten years later called *Life and Labor in the Old South*.

Another book that is important to the study of American slavery was published in 1974 by Robert William Fogel and Stanley L. Engerman. *Time on the Cross: The Economics of American Negro Slavery* is a controversial book that took a detailed economic look at slavery in America. The book, written by two highly distinguished and prominent economic historians, produced some startling facts and conclusions which are considered by many to be politically incorrect, yet presents strong historical evidence on the lives of slaves.

Many other sources were utilized, as evidenced by the footnotes. I encourage the reader to review the resource material discussion in appendix A for additional information on these resources as well as others.

Food, Clothing, and Shelter

A popular misconception about slave life is that the slaves were poorly fed. Evidence indicates that in fact there was an abundance of food for the slaves,[3] and there were even laws that demanded adequate food for the slaves. The Alabama slave code of 1852 required that the slave owner "must provide him with a sufficiency of healthy food."[4] Like for whites in the South, the staples of the American slave diet were corn and pork. Corn was easily stored, and pork, unlike beef and other types of meat, could also be stored over time. The typical ration was two pounds of corn and one and one-half pounds of pork for each slave adult per day[5] and a proportional amount for the slave children.

In what Olmsted called the "rice district," he described the doling out of rations on a plantation near Savannah, Georgia, "The provisions furnished, consisted mainly of meal, rice, vegetables, with salt and molasses, and occasionally bacon, fish, and coffee."[6] Olmsted reported, "the slaves were well provided for—always allowed a sufficient quantity of meal, and, generally, of pork—were permitted to raise pigs and poultry, and in summer could always grow as many vegetables as they wanted."[7]

But that was not all the food that the slaves received, as some historians infer. Southern farm records indicate that slaves commonly ate a variety of other foods including, beef, mutton, chickens, milk, turnips, peas, squash, sweet potatoes, apples, plums, oranges, pumpkins, and peaches, and as described by Olmsted, less commonly had molasses, fish, coffee, plus occasionally whiskey.[8] Potatoes were also very popular; typically the slaves would consume sweet potatoes, which actually have much more nutrients than the white or Irish potato. Many of the items consumed by the slaves were dependent on the season of the year and whether the product was produced on the farm or plantation.

Breakfast was almost always served, usually before the slaves left for any field work. If not eaten before leaving for work, the breakfast was usually brought to the fields early in the morning by about nine o'clock. Lunch was also a very important meal and it was usually taken to the fields in tin buckets. Perhaps this was the origin of our modern term "lunch bucket." The field workers were typically given ample time off to eat, anywhere from an hour to three hours. Supper would usually be made by the slaves themselves and eaten with the family, after the workday was done. Most slave owners were careful about ensuring regular hours for meals.[9]

Many slaves had their own patch of land to raise vegetables and other food items. Some slave owners would allow the slaves to have plots of land, as rewards or incentives for their work production. The slaves could independently use the land as they wished, and could either sell their crops or use them for their own consumption. Typically, the slaves would produce various vegetables, with corn being the most common, on their plots.

Slaves also had their own chickens and pigs, and less frequently their own cows.[10] It was a common practice for slaves to sell their eggs and chickens to the slave owner or to trade them in town and obtain money to buy luxury items. Slaves would also augment their food supplies through trapping rabbits, treed opossums, and fishing.[11] Campbell Davis, a slave in Harrison County, Texas, recalled how he had Friday afternoons and all day on Saturday off from work and that "mos' de man go huntin' of fishin'." He also had fond memories of the food back then, "Dey fed us beef and veg'tables—any kind, jus' name it—and 'low us sop bread in potlicker till de world look level. Dat good eatin' and all my life I ain't have no better."[12]

Lucinda Davis, a former slave from Oklahoma, told an FWP interviewer, "Dat was sho' good stuff to eat, and it make you fat too! Roast de green corn on de ears in de ashes, and scrape off some and fry it! Grind de dry corn or pound it up and make ash cake. Den bile de greens—all kinds of greens from out in de woods—and chip up de pork and deer meat, or de wild turkey meat; maybe all of dem, in de big pot at de same time! Fish too . . ."[13]

Another Oklahoma slave, Polly Colbert, speaking of her slave owner, "He allus had a smokehouse full of meat, lard, sausage, dried beans, peas, corn, potatoes, turnips and collards banked up for winter. He had plenty of milk and butter for all of us, too. Master Holmes allus say, 'A hungry man caint work.' And he allus saw to it that we had lots to eat."[14]

Did the slave get enough to eat? Some historians have said of the slave diet, "It did not provide adequate nutrition," and that the slave was abused because he or she was not adequately fed. Fogel and Engerman, in *In Time on the Cross*, took a specific look at the issue by examining the average amount consumed by slaves of the top eleven foods. They point out that the energy value of the food intake of slaves was substantial, and when compared to the food intake of free men in 1879, exceeded the 1879 amount by 10 percent. They also found that the slaves' diet actually exceeded twentieth-century daily levels of chief nutrients by substantial amounts.[15] Another independent study was done in 1976 which confirmed the Fogel and Engerman study with nearly identical results. The average daily caloric intake of slaves was determined to be 4,185 calories in the 1974 study and 4,206 calories in the 1976 study.[16] The later study estimated a higher meat consumption by slaves over the 1974 study by forty-six pounds. As Fogel said in his later book, *Without Consent or Contract*, "Quite clearly . . . the diet was substantial by the standards of the day for workers, and so contradicts abolitionist contentions that 'as a general thing' southern slaves 'suffer extremely for the want of food.'"[17]

Other studies have confirmed these findings, including archaeological investigations of four plantations in Georgia and Florida. Excavations of slave quarters have revealed that the remains of game and fish in the slave cabins were quite numerous. In addition to game animals, the bones of sheep, chicken, and cattle were also commonly found. Archaeologists have even compared the animal remains in the area of the slave cabins with those in the slave owner's quarters. The archaeologists found that the slaves generally received the "less preferable cuts of meat" which came from the "forequarters, head, and feet," rather than the more "desirable upper hind quarters."[18]

It should be pointed out that having a sufficient number of calories will help maintain a person's body weight and give them generally good health; however, a diet meeting the caloric needs does not

Slavery Fact #15

The vast majority of slaves were well fed and their nutrimental intake may well have exceeded modern-day standards.

necessarily mean a healthy diet. Receiving the proper level of vitamins and minerals is also important and not considered in the above research. Receiving the proper nutritional requirements is a challenge even today, and for inhabitants in the eighteenth and nineteenth century even a greater challenge, slave or free. One method that can at least partly help us determine if proper nutritional levels were met is the height of individuals. Fogel took a careful look at this by comparing the average heights of various nineteenth-century populations. He found that the height comparisons indicated that the nutritional status of slaves in the United States was better than that of most European workers, but not as good as that of native-born whites in the United States. For instance, the average height of a U.S. slave (1811–1860) was 66.4 inches versus a Northern born white (1863–65) of 67.5 inches. Others in the study included Frenchman-literate (1868) of 65.3, Frenchman-illiterate (1868) of 65.3 inches, British Royal Marine (1827–29) of 66.1 inches, Southern Italian (1874–75) of 63.0 inches, African imported into the United States of 64.2 inches, and Cuban-born slaves (1855–59) of 63.6 inches.[19]

The clothing of the slaves is difficult to determine. The best source of data relative to slave clothing has been found on the large plantations. The standard annual clothing allowance was likely similar to what is outlined in a South Carolina plantation manual, "Each man gets in the fall 2 shirts of cotton drilling, a pair of woolen pants and a woolen jacket. in the spring 2 shirts of cotton shirting and 2 pr. of cotton pants."[20] Robert Burns, a former slave from Tennessee, recalled, "We wore white cotton shirts and pants and shirts only during summer dat was weaved right dare on de plantation. I never seed any under-wear until I wuz bout 12 years of age. We all wore hats made from wheat straw."[21]

The adult slave would also receive annually either one or two pairs of shoes, although Phillips reports that shoes were only provided in the winter months.[22] Unfortunately for Burns and his fellow slaves, shoes were not provided. Burns told the FWP interviewer, "Dare wuz no shoes for de slaves a-tall. In winter de women would tie dar feet up in rags."[23] If shoes were only provided sometimes, socks were a different matter as they were almost never issued to the slaves. Very few resources indicate that the slaves were provided with any socks. With some exceptions, most plantation rules and regulations relating to clothing did not include socks.[24]

The adult female slaves were given either four dresses per year or the material needed to produce four dresses, about 24 yards of cloth, according to a South Carolina plantation manual. Much of the cloth was a special grade of cloth, rougher than normal, called "Negro cloth," produced in Northern mills especially for slaves in the South.[25] One former Mississippi slave, Martha Ann Ratliff, related, "In winter we wore jean underskirts made of wool and cotton top dresses. In summer we wore thin cotton goods. Master was a tailor and he would cut out de cloth himself for his slaves' clothing and de women did de sewing."[26]

The slaves liked to dress in their very best for Sunday morning worship service. A British traveler in the South during the War Between the States described the way that slaves dressed in their finest, "They had either just 'been to meetin,' or were just going; and, as we glided away, we could see black dress-coats, satin vests, and fancy 'pants' giving their arms to hooped muslins, bonnets a la Paris, fans and parasols, and strolling up the sandy road."[27] He was so impressed with the dress of the female slaves that he observed, "the negress, I think, as a rule, outdressed her mistress."[28]

Men also received hats, which were typically described as "woolen caps, straw hats, or camp hats."[29] Instead of hats, women usually received head kerchiefs. During winter, men were given jackets or overcoats.

Children were typically provided with a one-piece article of clothing which resembled an extra-long shirt. [30] Frederick Douglass described the children's clothes, from the days when he wore them, as a "coarse sack-cloth or tow-linen, made into a sort of shirt, reaching down to my knees. This I wore night and day, changing it once a week."[31] A former slave from Virginia recalled his youth as a slave, "I went in shirt tail all the time. Never had on no pants 'til I was 15 years old."[32] Fountain Hughes, born in 1848 and a slave from Virginia, laughingly called what slave male children wore "dresses." He told an interviewer, "wore a dress like a woman till I was, I [believe] ten, twelve, thirteen years old. Yes. I didn' wear -no pants, an' of course didn' make boys' pants. Boys wore dresses. Now only womens wearing the dresses an' the boys is going with the, with the womens wearing the pants . . ."[33]

Slaves were also issued blankets. Most typically, a blanket would be issued to each slave every other year. One slave owner complained about the high cost of providing "good" blankets, two dollars to two and one-half dollars every other year.[34]

What seems like rather a spartan collection of clothes is in reality very similar to what most Southern whites had. In all but the largest plantations, the Southern farmer had little or no improvement in their clothing. Some whites in the South would have gladly taken the slave allotment of clothing, one historian estimated, "In 1860 perhaps a third of all southern whites owned little more than the clothing they wore . . ."[35]

Of the basic essentials—food, clothing and shelter—slave housing probably varied the greatest. By using the 1860 Census data, we can, however, get a good indication that most slaves lived in single family dwellings. According to the census, there was an average of 5.2 slaves per dwelling on the large plantations. This compares to an average of 5.3 people per dwelling for free households. This data goes against that myth of families of slaves crowded into a single dwelling. There were some barracks-type slave quarters; in fact a well-preserved barracks example survives in the small Texas town in which I reside. However, barracks-style quarters were very much the exception to the rule.

It became standard to provide each slave family with a wood cabin that usually was sixteen by eighteen feet.[36] The cabins typically were one or two rooms, with raised plank flooring, perhaps a loft where the children would sleep, and some had either a stone or brick fireplace, front porches, and glazed windows.[37] Olmsted described some slave quarters on one Georgia plantation, "The cottages were framed buildings, boarded on the outside, with shingle roofs and brick chimneys; they stood fifty feet apart, with gardens and pig-yards, enclosed by palings, between them."[38] Olmsted described the slave quarter on one plantation as "neat frame houses, on brick pillars, . . . furnished with good bedding, mosquito bars, and all that is essential to health and comfort."[39]

The housing of the slaves compared very well to the vast majority of rural whites. Typically, their cabins were not much larger, or much improved, if any at all, compared to the slave dwellings. Olmsted described some rural whites' cabins in the Carolinas as "The cabins of the poor whites, much the largest in number, were of a meaner sort—being mere square pens of logs, roofed over, provided with a chimney, and usually with a shed of boards, supported by rough posts, before the door."[40]

Mary Reynolds was a slave in the lower South, from Louisiana. She described her slave dwelling to a FWP interviewer, "In the cabins it was nice and warm. They was built of pine boardin' and they was one long room of them up the hill back of the big house. Near one side of the cabins was a fireplace. They'd bring in two, three big logs and put on the fire and they'd last near a week. The beds was made out of puncheons fitted on holes bored in the wall, and planks laid cross them poles. We had tickin' mattresses filled with corn shucks. Sometimes the men build chairs at night."[41] Another former slave from Texas, Mary Ellen Johnson, recalled her slave quarters, "In them days we lived in a little, old log cabin in the backyard and there was just one room, but it was snug and we had plenty of livin.' My mammy had a nice cotton bed and she weren't no field nigger, but my pappy was."[42]

Fogel and Engerman point out that the slave quarters compared very well to the homes of urban workers in the North. Typically, the free urban dwellers lived in overcrowded and

Slavery Fact #16
Slave housing was typically one family to a cabin, similar to most rural white housing in the South.

filthy tenements. They compared the slave cabins of the South to a survey of workers in New York City in 1893, and found that the median number of square feet of sleeping space per person was considerably more in the slave cabins, half a century earlier.[43]

Work Life of the Slave

The South was primarily based on an agrarian society, and so most of the slaves, as well as the Southern whites, were engaged in agricultural work. That has led to a stereotype image of the slave at work that does not give proper justice to the slave. The image of Southern slave labor is that of the slave laboring in the cotton fields, either hoeing the cotton or picking the cotton when the crop matured. The work life of the slaves, both male and female, was far more than just monotonous, repetitive, and backbreaking labor.

Agricultural work was much more than hoeing and picking cotton. Cotton was by far the predominate crop in the South, but certainly not the only one raised by Southern planters. Fogel and Engerman estimated that efforts related to the cotton crop only accounted for about 34 percent of the slave's time. The work related to livestock, tending, including the production of feed for the livestock took about a quarter of the slave's time. The remainder of the slave work schedule included working the corn crop, about 6 percent of the time, and the balance, about 34 percent of the time, was spent on farm maintenance, building and repairing fences, barns and the like as well as time raising other, particularly seasonal crops, and domestic work.[44]

Most historians define the difference between a farm and a plantation based on the number of slaves, although in actuality many more factors must be considered. Nevertheless, most historians categorize a farm as having fewer than twenty slaves and a plantation as an operation with more than twenty slaves. Since the vast majority, almost 90 percent, of slave owners owned less than twenty slaves, many slaves had no a formal specialization of labor. Perhaps the only real specialization on Southern farms would be to assign a female slave cooking or household-type duties.[45] Only on the much larger plantations slaves had specific jobs as blacksmith, carpenter, etc. Slaves that had the talent to perform specialized skills would perform them as the need arose; otherwise they were involved in the typical needs of the farm.[46]

Some historians have portrayed the American slave as what Stanley Elkins referred to as a "Sambo" personality in his book *Slavery: A Problem in American Institutional and Intellectual Life*. By a "Sambo" image, Elkins referred to a docile, irresponsible person that was basically lazy. The slave was loyal to his master, but totally dependent on his owner, similar to the way a young child is to his or her parent. He blames this condition not on racial inferiority, as some historians over the years have actually implied, but rather on the slave society. According to Elkins, the slave society, over the years, stripped the slaves down to remold them to docile servants, similar to what the inmates of a Nazi concentration camp experienced.[47] Elkins was wrong, and his analogy was inaccurate and unfortunate. Contrary to Elkins' and others' portrayal of the slave, the evidence indicates that the American slave was anything but a "Sambo." The American slave was far more intelligent, talented, productive, and resourceful than the "Sambo" image. If anything, the American slave had more of a "Blue Collar" personality, the majority of the slaves being hard working and industrious.

What was the quality of slave labor? In *Time on the Cross*, calculations demonstrate that large plantations were 34 percent more efficient than free farms in the South. What were the reasons? The authors adjusted their calculations for greater efficiencies based on the size of the acreage, the greater availability of farm machinery and implements, and even a suspicion that the larger plantations had better land, and still there was a 34 percent greater efficiency. Some of the success can be attributed to plantation management, which we will see later is certainly not white only, but the authors give the majority of the credit to the African American slave labor force.[48]

When the slaves were in the fields on the larger farms and plantations, their work efforts were typically organized and well led. On the larger farms and plantation the worker's efforts were managed in two ways. One method was the gang system. The gang system, on farms with more than fifty slaves, typically consisted of two gangs, a plow-hands gang and a hoe gang. The plow-hands gang would include the more able-bodied younger men, and only infrequently included females. The plow-hands gang would be led by a driver, similar to a foreman. The driver was usually one of the slaves entrusted by the slave owner to manage the gang. The driver's job was to ensure that those in the gang worked in a steady fashion and that the goals of the gang's job assignment were met.

The hoe gang would include female slaves and males that were not up to the more strenuous work required of plow-hands. The method of management of the hoe gangs might not include a driver, like the other form of slave work management called the task system. In the task system, each worker was given a specific amount of work to complete for the day. The slave was expected to work until the tasks, as assigned, were accomplished. If the tasks were completed early then the slave was on his or her own time. Most tasks were assigned based on the production of the slower slaves, so an energetic worker would often be done by three or four o'clock in the afternoon.[49]

The gang system was the more common system, as it worked well with cotton production. In areas where rice farming was more common, the task system was preferred. Likely, however, slaves from time to time worked under both systems.[50]

Except at planting and harvesting times, in the fields the slaves' chief tool was the hoe. The slaves fought a never-ending battle against nature. If the fields were not properly tended to, the weeds and grasses could

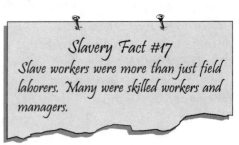

Slavery Fact #17
Slave workers were more than just field laborers. Many were skilled workers and managers.

completely take over a field and choke out the planted crop. The obvious goal of the field worker was to keep the weeds away from what had been planted. For instance, in the cotton fields the field slave's primary job was to chop the weeds and grasses away from the cotton stalk, but much had to be done before the plant grew to that stage.

Beginning in January or February the slaves would have to clear away the stalks and refuse of the previous crop. Following the·

clearing of the fields, the field would be plowed in March or April and the cotton seeds planted. Plowing rows straight and at the right depth required both skill and strength. It took only a week to ten days for the cotton plant to first sprout. Much hoeing was then needed to help the plant grow, keeping invading weeds and grasses away. The cotton plant will grow to become a shrubby plant with divided leaves producing, by mid summer, a "fruit" known as a "boll" that is the size of a golf ball which contains the cotton fiber along with cotton seeds.[51]

To keep a cotton field clear was hard and demanding work, particularly in the summers with high temperatures and sometimes oppressive humidity. The field work did require a degree of skill, a swing of a hoe too close could damage the cotton plant itself. The ideal single swing of the hoe would chop the grasses or weeds away as well as cultivate the soil, all without damaging the plant. The plow gang would keep the rows cleared, usually by using a cultivator plow. Finally, from July to December the cotton crop would be harvested, after the cotton bolls opened. "Picking" the cotton was extremely demanding and back-breaking work. Few would be spared from the harvest. Free or slave, domestic or field hand, young or old, male or female, all would be working during the harvest. The "picker," stooped over, would pull the cotton bolls away from the plant and dropped the picked boll into large bags. The bags would be dragged alongside the "picker." The adult slave was expected to pick anywhere from two hundred and fifty to three hundred pounds of cotton per day. The cotton would then be dumped and sent to the cotton gin to separate the cotton fibers from the seeds. The ginned cotton was then bound together in bales weighing nearly five hundred pounds.[52] The cotton was then ready to be transported for export. The cotton harvest process was always all over by Christmas, so everyone, slave and free, could take some time off, only to start the entire process anew in January.

A third category of slave workers was called the "trash gang" or "children's gang." This group was made up of older children and those male and female slaves incapable of any heavy labor. They would have rather minor tasks such as yard cleaning and weeding and worked under the task system.[53]

The workday most commonly stretched from dawn to dusk, particularly on the gang system. That seems excessive by modern standards, however it was the common standard in the 1800s, for both free and slave. In the summertime most slaves were given a two-hour lunch and rest period.[54] Most slaves would either have Saturday off, or work only a half day, again a very common practice for the entire population, slave or free. Rarely did anyone, slaves included, work on Sunday. Sometimes during harvesting season, duty would call for working on the Sabbath; however, the slave owner would usually pay the slaves or provide other incentives for the unusual times when Sunday work was required.

Additional time off would be granted to slaves. It was nearly a universal practice that slaves did not have to work the week between Christmas and New Year's Day. Also, after the planting had been done, and prior to the harvest, most slaves were given time off. One former Tennessee slave, Clayton Holbert, said in the FWP interviews, "We worked until Christmas Eve and from that time until New Year's we had a vacation. We had no such thing as Thanksgiving, we had never heard of such a thing."[55]

On the smaller farms, obviously, there usually were not enough slaves to have gangs. Normally, the slaves worked either under the direct supervision of the slave owner or on some sort of a task system. A day in the fields, typically, would find the slave(s), the slave owner, and more than likely the owner's family members working together, side by side.

There was another division of work by slaves that deserves to be mentioned. This was the work of the domestic servants. Typically, slave owners that had twenty or more slaves would have some that would primarily serve

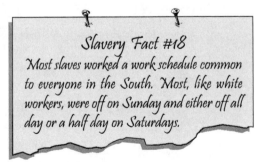

Slavery Fact #18
Most slaves worked a work schedule common to everyone in the South. Most, like white workers, were off on Sunday and either off all day or a half day on Saturdays.

in a domestic capacity. The larger the plantation the more slaves would be working in a domestic capacity. Having a higher level of slave status, when compared to the field hands, was one of the advantages of the slaves working as domestic servants. Even the term "servant," which had somewhat of a connotation of higher respect, would be more frequently applied to slaves employed as domestic workers than to field workers. Typically they would also receive better food, have a closer relationship with the slave owner and his or her family, and often were better dressed than the other slaves.

There were many disadvantages, primarily the amount of work that would be required of them. Most of them did work very hard, being at the beck and call of the slave owner and his family. Their quarters were typically close to or even attached to the primary residence of the slave owner. Most of the slaves were always in "shouting distance" of the slave owner or his or her family. Except on the very large plantations, they would be expected to move to the fields at special times of the year, such as at harvest time.

While performing domestic duties, the slave would be employed in typical household chores, from housecleaning, and doing laundry to cooking meals. On the handful of very large plantations the domestic workforce would also include valets, butlers, nursemaids, and coachmen. The relationship between these slaves and their owners was usually, certainly not always, a close one. A special feeling of kinship would often develop between the domestic servant and the slave owner.

Domestic work by slaves would also occur on the smaller farms. Often a female slave would be assigned for part of the day to help the white mistress with washing, ironing, cleaning, etc. Frequently the females would help in the meal preparation on the smaller farms. In the urban areas, female slaves would often be exclusively used for domestic work.

Overseers

Much has been written about the "plantation overseer." Stowe's *Uncle Tom's Cabin* has forever defined the overseer—the evil villain, Simon Legree—in most Americans' eyes. First, we must put the overseers' role in American history into proper prospective. Let us look at some of the myths. First, let us deal with the myth that basically all slaves worked under the auspices of an

Runaway slaves at Cumberland Landing, Virginia

Library of Congress

overseer. In fact, the exact opposite is true: the majority of slaves never worked under an overseer.[56] Rarely would an overseer be employed for a farm of less than thirty slaves. It has been estimated that the nearly 400,000 slave owners had only 3,800 overseers in 1860,[57] a rate of less than 1 percent. Although technically correct, that number is a somewhat unfair statistic since overseers were certainly not needed on farms with less than twenty slaves. However, even if you just count slave owners that owned twenty or more slaves, 47,584, the percentage increases only to about 8 percent.

Another myth is that because of the overseer position on the plantation hierarchy, the slave owner had little or no direct contact with his or her slaves. The fact is that even on the very largest plantations rarely would a slave owner let the overseer disrupt the paternalistic relationship of the owner with his slaves.[58] As we will determine later in this chapter, almost always a strong bond existed between the slave owner and the slaves.

A third major myth is that all overseers were white. Again, just the opposite is the case. Overseers were frequently not white. A slave driver was a slave that had earned the trust and confidence of the overseer or owner. He would be given duties to assist the overseer or owner in managing the slave work force. One that performed well would often be eventually promoted to the overseer position. Of small slave-holding farms, sixteen to fifty slaves, only 17 percent used a white overseer. On plantations having more than fifty slaves, only about 25 percent of the owners used white overseers. Even on the large plantation, with more than one hundred slaves, white overseers only made up about 30 percent of all overseers.[59] This meant that certain African American slaves were operating at the highest level of farm and plantation management. They would have been responsible directly to the owner for the basic day-to-day field operations.

> *Slavery Fact #19*
> The number of overseers in the South was quite small, and on those farms and plantations that had overseers, the majority were African American.

The overseer, in colonial times, was usually given a percentage of the crop as his compensation for services. Although the system motivated the overseer to join in with the manual labor it was also flawed due to the potential for abuse. An overseer, motivated by the potential for personal gain, might overwork the slaves. As a result of potential abuse, the percentage of crops approach was all but abandoned in the 1800s.[60] In the 1800s the overseer was hired by the slave owner on an annual basis, paid a modest salary, provided a place to live, given a ration of corn and pork, similar to the slave rations, and usually provided with a slave servant.[61] According to Olmsted, most overseers that he came in contact with were paid between $200 and $600 per year.[62] Many of the larger planters had written plans that the overseer had to follow, from both a production standpoint and a manual of slave treatment guidelines. An overseer was sometimes delegated the task of punishing the slaves, if the slave owner believed in corporal punishment.

Typically, the primary duty of an overseer was to supervise the slave work crews as well as to attend to any livestock. The overseer was also responsible to make sure that there was enough food on the farm or plantation for both the people and the livestock. If they produced the food themselves then he had to be sure the crops were cared for and harvested. He would have to plan to purchase the food stocks that they did not produce on the farm or plantation. Finally, the overseer had to produce whatever agricultural product the farm or plantation was primarily engaged in growing. Whether it was cotton or rice, or other crops, the overseer had to meet the production goals of the land owner and maintain good order and spirits in his slave work force. No small task for anyone.

The overseer then perhaps had the most demanding job of any on the farm or plantation. Typically, the overseer was charged with rising before dawn to blow the horn or ring the bell that called everyone to rise and prepare for the workday. Usually everyone was expected to be at their assigned work position by daybreak, and it was the overseer that had to ensure everyone was in place. During the day he had to supervise the work gang details and be sure the noon meal was delivered and served. The overseer called for the end of the work as the sun was setting. The overseer was responsible for getting all the slaves back to their quarters as well as being sure that all livestock were fed. Before going to bed, the overseer had to be certain that all the barns and stables were secured and would ring the bell or blow the horn at around nine or nine-thirty in the evening to signal curfew. He would then likely make the rounds to be sure all the slaves were accounted for before he could retire. The typical overseer would easily put in an eighteen-hour day.[63]

It was very helpful to have an overseer or driver that was physically powerful. African American overseers and drivers typically had an imposing physical presence, one that would produce great respect from the other slaves. Ex-slaves described the drivers as, for example, "a great, big cullud man," "a large tall, black man," "a burly fellow . . . severe in the extreme."[64] If he were armed with a whip and dressed in high leather boots and black greatcoat, the overseer or driver conveyed a strong sense of power and control.

The overseers seemed to be universally unliked, by both the slaves and by the planters. Even white society in general held the white overseers in very low regard. Perhaps the author of a book on overseers said it the best, "The overseer was not loved; as a rule he was not lovable."[65] Rarely would a white overseer stay on with the same slave owner more than a year or two. One Virginia planter, complaining about his long hours of work, was asked by Olmsted why he didn't employ an overseer. The planter replied, "Because I do not think it right to trust to such men as we have to use, if we use any, for overseers." He went on to explain his low regard for overseers, "They are the curse of this country, sir; the worst men in the community . . ."[66] George Washington complained about one overseer in that he had "no more authority over the slaves . . . than an old woman would have."[67]

In his book *The Plantation Overseer, As Shown in His Letters,* John Spencer Bassett has included a series of letters from overseers. One overseer, John Mairs, was employed on James K. Polk's plantation, Pleasant Grove, in western Tennessee. Polk had inherited the plantation and was busy serving as a congressman, governor, and later president; so he was an absentee landlord. Mairs completely ran the plantation and would write the owner, Mrs. James Polk, who inherited the plantation upon the death of her husband, with periodic reports. Mairs remained an overseer employee for at least fourteen years, far longer than the average. He was paid five hundred dollars a year initially, but that amount was raised to five hundred and fifty dollars. Much insight is gained into the life of the slave by looking at the letters.

In an April 12, 1850, letter, we get the idea that at least some of the slaves did have shoes. Mairs wrote, "I nough right you a few Lins youre people are all except colds the wether continues cold the spring is late we are planting coten And planting corn instead I had some 25 acres to plant over it was planted veary early making clothing for the negros clothes the Stock all Lucks as well as could be expected. All youre artickls has arrived you ordered from New orleans 10 pieces Baging about 103 yds in each peace or about [?] 8 coils of Rope 125 lbs or the rise in each coil 1 Bale Twine 2 Boxes of merchandis 1 Box have 4 dosin hats, 1 Box Box 3 dzin par shoes 10 Sacks of coars salt 2 sacks of fine salt."[68]

In August, Mairs writes the plantation owner giving her a report on the slaves and describing their efforts to produce slave clothing, "Yau- servents all behave vary well except Joe has left me wonst this year But Return home in a few days of his on actcord we have put up a coten press making the negro clothing . . ."[69]

Finally, in September, Mairs reports on the picking of the cotton crop, "I nough write you a few lins to inform you that your servents are all in Reasonable helth at present we are nough picking out coten the coten crop is a far crop for this year I think if the fall is favorable from this tim out we will mak as much as we made Last year and more I think we will make a plenty of corn to surply the plantation Your servents are all behaving well at this time the stock all Lucks as well as could be exspected Am in hops we will Ras enough Pork for the youse of the place I am a man [ag] ing to the best of my knowledge."[70]

Sexual Exploitation

A common overseer perception is that of the overseer having "his way" with the female slaves. For that matter, what about the slave owner or even the male children of the slave owner. It seems that this is the place to discuss this somewhat delicate topic. Is this a myth or reality?

Olmsted was told that the practice of slave miscegenation, the interbreeding of the races, had corrupted the "entire society" of the South.[71] Even the fabled diarist Mary Chesnut wrote, "we live surrounded by prostitutes." She wrote, "Like the patriarchs of old our men live all in one house with their wives and their concubines, and the mullattoes one sees in every family exactly resemble the white children—and every lady tells you who is the father of all the mulatto children in everybody's household, but those in her own she seems to think drop from the clouds . . ."[72] Such accounts have led many historians to believe that sexual relations between slave owners, overseers, and adult children of the slave owner with the slaves did occur and occurred on a regular basis.

In his book *The Peculiar Institution*, Kenneth Stampp spends eleven pages on the topic. Stampp concludes that based on the number of Southern "mulattoes," a person with one white and one African American parent, it was indeed a common practice.

Stampp says, "a large proportion of them (Southern white men), particularly in the cities and plantation districts, had one or more sexual contacts with slave women."[73] That it did occur is not the question, the question is the frequency of the occurrence and the effect that it had on the slaves.

In *Time on the Cross*, the authors looked not at just antidotal evidence but also at facts. First the authors looked at the 1860 Census data. They found that most of the mulattoes lived in the urban areas. Of the free African Americans in the towns and cities nearly 40 percent were mulatto. In fact, one out of every four urban African Americans, free or slave, was a mulatto. Where 95 percent of all the slaves resided, in the rural areas of the South, the mulatto population was much smaller, slightly less than 10 percent. For the nearly 240 years of slavery the mulatto average population was only 7.7 percent. They also pointed out that mulatto offspring was not just produced by a white parent, but could also be produced by the union of a mulatto and African American, either slave or free.[74]

Fogel and Engerman also looked at the FWP's slave interviews. They found that only 4.5 percent of those interviewed indicated a white parent. With this data analysis they suggest that the number of white fathers is exaggerated. They also have examined genetic studies of rural African Americans that would suggest that the number of children fathered by whites averaged only between 1 and 2 percent.[75]

Another issue that would prevent white male infringement on slave females was the basic plantation structure. Would a slave owner risk at least the consternation of his slaves and more likely the discipline problem his philandering would cause? With his substantial investment in slaves, would the slave owner risk damaging his plantation's production capabilities? There was also a severe social stigma associated with interracial sexual activities in the nineteenth century.

What of white women and male slaves? Much less has been written on this topic. Most miscegenation discussion centers on white males and female slaves. Did it happen the other way? The answer is yes, but almost certainly to a lesser degree. While traveling in the South, Olmsted was told, "There must always be women

of the lower class of whites, so poor that their favors can be purchased by slaves."[76] A Nansemond County, Virginia, white man accused his wife in 1840 of giving birth to a mulatto child that obviously
was not his. The man stated that she had "recently been engaged in
illicit intercourse with a negro man at my own house and on my
own bed."[77]

White female prostitutes would sell their favors regardless of
race or slave status. There are, however, recorded cases of non-pros-
titute white women having children fathered by slaves, in a non-
rape situation. The recorded numbers are very small.

Urban Slaves and Hiring Out

Not all the slaves lived on farms and plantations. Slaves lived
in towns and cities in both the North, before the slaves were freed,
and in the South. In the North, in the 1600s and 1700s urban slaves
were a common sight. In the eighteenth century, nearly one-quarter
of all the slaves in colonial New York lived in New York City. Other
Northern cities such as Portsmouth and Boston had approximately
one-third of all slaves in their state, and nearly half of Rhode Island's
slaves lived in Newport. Up until it was passed by Charleston, South
Carolina, and then New Orleans, Louisiana, in the middle part of
the 1700s, New York City had more slaves than any other American
city.[78]

Slaves in the urban North worked as domestics or as day-type
laborers, although, like in the South, many were skilled artisans.[79]
The African American influence was certainly felt in the Northern
cities. Various African American festivals were celebrated, perhaps
an offshoot of their African heritage. In New England, Election Day
was celebrated, and in New York and New Jersey, Pinkster Day was
the name of the festival. The celebrations varied, but in general each
was marked with the election of African American kings, gover-
nors, and judges. Many of the crownings or inaugurations were held
with great pomp and ceremonies, followed by much merrymaking.
Those elected to the various positions were typically the African
American leaders of the day. The festivals allowed for African Americans, slave and free, to provide tribute to their very own leaders.[80]

Southern slaves did live in an urban setting, although the use of the term "urban" is a bit of a misnomer when speaking of the pre-War Between the States South. Compared to the North, the South had much less urban development. There were only eight towns in the South that had twenty-two thousand or more people. The key Southern cities at the onset of the War Between the States included Baltimore, Charleston, Louisville, Mobile, New Orleans, Richmond, St. Louis, and Savannah. Five Southern states even lacked a town with as many as ten thousand people. About 6 percent of all the slaves lived in towns of one thousand or more.

Table 6.1 lists twenty selected Southern cities, including the largest town or city in each of the Southern states as well as other selected larger Southern cities, based on the 1860 Census.[81] These twenty towns and cities had over ninety thousand slaves, nearly 11 percent of the total population.

Three Southern cities had slave populations of over ten thousand: Charleston, South Carolina, with 13,909; New Orleans, Louisiana, with 13,385; and Richmond, Virginia, with 11,699. Seven Southern cities or towns had slave populations of about one-third of the total population. The highest percentages of slave populations were in Wilmington, North Carolina, at nearly 40 percent, and in Savannah, Georgia, and Charleston, South Carolina, each at about 34 percent. The smallest slave populations were in San Antonio, Texas, with 592, Little Rock, Arkansas, with 846, and Pensacola, Florida, with 957. From a percentage perspective, the cities and towns with the lowest slave percentages were, not surprisingly, all in the border states. Baltimore, Maryland, and St. Louis, Missouri, were each at 1 percent, and Louisville, Kentucky, at a little over 7 percent. San Antonio, in far away Texas, was also in the 7 percent range.

Table 6.1—Population of Selected Southern Cities and Towns (Sorted by State), 1860

City or Town	Total Population	Slave Population	Slave Percentage of Total
Mobile, Ala.	29,258	7,587	25.9%
Little Rock, Ark.	3,727	846	22.7%
Pensacola, Fla.	2,876	957	33.3%

(continued on next page)

Table 6.1 *(continued)*

City or Town	Total Population	Slave Population	Slave Percentage of Total
Savannah, Ga.	22,292	7,712	34.6%
Augusta, Ga.	12,493	3,663	29.3%
Atlanta, Ga.	9,554	1,914	20.0%
Louisville, Ky.	68,033	4,903	7.2%
New Orleans, La.	168,675	13,385	7.9%
Baltimore, Md.	212,418	2,218	1.0%
Natchez, Miss.	6,612	2,132	32.2%
St. Louis, Mo.	160,773	1,542	1.0%
Wilmington, N.C.	9,552	3,777	39.5%
Charleston, S.C.	40,522	13,909	34.3%
Memphis, Tenn.	22,623	3,684	16.3%
Nashville, Tenn.	16,988	3,226	19.0%
San Antonio, Tex.	8,235	592	7.2%
Galveston, Tex.	7,307	1,178	16.1%
Richmond, Va.	37,910	11,699	30.9%
Petersburg, Va.	18,266	5,680	31.1%
Norfolk, Va.	14,620	3,284	22.5%
Total	872,734	93,888	10.8%

Although many of these urban slaves were working as domestics and laborers, many were skilled artisans. For instance, in Charleston, South Carolina, about 27 percent of the all the adult male slaves were skilled artisans. These slaves would work as blacksmiths, carpenters, masons, machinists, and Olmsted describes meeting a slave engineer.

Slaves were also employed in workshops and mills. Although the South was overwhelmingly rural there were some burgeoning industries. Textile mills, mainly cotton, but some wool, had grown dramatically in the South. The production of cotton had gone from one and one-half million dollars in 1840 to a threefold increase of four and one-half million dollars by 1860.[82] Slaves were the majority of workers in most of the Southern cotton mills.

There were also iron mills, factories that processed smoking tobacco and hemp plants which produced cotton baling materials and rope. The majority of workers in the iron mills of the upper-South were slaves. The tobacco industry was also heavily dependent on slave labor. In Richmond, Virginia, alone three thousand four hundred slaves worked in the smoking and plug tobacco industry in the 1850s. In Kentucky, over three thousand slaves were employed in the state's hemp-processing plants in the 1850s.[83] Many of the slaves that worked in these industrial settings were slaves that were hired out by their owners to work in the mill or factory.

Slaves were used in an industrial setting because the cost to use slave labor was lower than using free labor, even taking into account the costs to feed, clothe, and provide shelter to the slaves. In his book *Industrial Slavery in the Old South*, Robert S. Starobin calculated that the annual cost to provide the basic essentials to slaves was about one hundred dollars per year. Since the typical white laborer averaged only one dollar per day and the typical skilled white laborer earned only three dollars per day, slave labor was very cost-effective for the mill or plant owner.[84]

Some slaves were actually owned by businesses. Corporate slaves can be found throughout the South. In Richmond prior to the War Between the States, at least fifty-four corporations owned at least ten slaves each. The Virginia Central Railroad had 274 slaves, and several other companies had 75 or more.[85]

In Southern towns, slave artisans usually could easily find jobs. Frequently, the urban slave lived a semi-independent existence, often living separately from the slave owner and determining where they would work. Skilled slave artisans could hire out their own time, pick whom they wanted to work for, and they could keep some of the wages they earned, giving the remainder to their slave owner. Charles Ball, a slave who was an undertaker in Savannah, was even able to hire other slaves to help with his jobs. Ball would pay his master $250 a year in monthly installments.[86]

Some Southern municipalities hired slaves for public service efforts. As early as 1822 New Orleans hired slaves to construct sewers and work with flood control. The city paid the slave owners between twenty-five and fifty cents a day for each slave used. The most common use of slaves by municipalities was as firemen. In Savannah, Georgia, a slave unit was the city's crack engine team; others were used as axe and bucket brigades. One official said, "We suppose that there are no more efficient or well managed fire companies in the United States." The city paid twelve and a half cents an hour to those on duty, and the first unit to arrive at a fire received a one dollar bonus.[87]

The hiring of slaves from the slave owner to someone who contracted for the slaves' services is often overlooked by historians, but
it was a fairly common practice. Based on the 1860 Census, one estimate is that around 31 percent of slaves in cities and towns were
hired out. In some cities, like Richmond, nearly half of all the slaves
in the city were hired out. But it wasn't just an urban phenomenon,
slaves on the farms and plantations were also hired out. It is estimated that, at any given time, 7.5 percent of all slaves were hired
out.[88]

Usually, a slave would be hired for a fifty-one-week period;
remember, most all slaves were off from work the week between
Christmas and New Year's Day. Sometimes the period of time might
be of a shorter duration, for a day, week, or month, but the fifty-one-
week arrangement was very common. The employer, who contracted
for the slave, was required to pay the slave owner, as well as provide food, clothing, shelter, and medical care for the slave.[89] In Virginia, a slave hired out for a year would bring about $120 to the
owner.[90] For a young male slave in his prime, that compensation
represented about a 10 percent return to the slave owner.

Most slaves did not like to be hired out, even though it involved
a "change of scenery" for them. It also posed some additional risk
to the hired-out slave. As is today, people have a tendency to take
better care of things they own over property that they rent. People
prior to the War Between the States were no different, and a slave
might not be treated as well on a hired-out basis. On the other hand,
slave owners were usually very careful to learn what type of work
his or her slave would be doing before they would agree to lease
out their slaves.

The slave owner would usually protect all slaves from hazard-
ous occupations. It was quite common for gangs of Irish laborers to
be used in dangerous work tasks. Phillips reports that in 1835 a British observer saw Irishmen working on a canal in Louisiana. He in-
quired why slaves were not being used on the project and wrote what
he was told, "Slave labour cannot be substituted to any extent, being
much too expensive; a good slave costs at this time two hundred
pounds sterling, and to have a thousand such swept off a line of
canal in one season would call for prompt consideration."[91] Fifteen

years later in Virginia, slaves hired out to dig the Blue Ridge Railroad tunnel were not allowed to be anywhere near any blasting so as to keep them out of harm's way.

Rather than using slaves, much of the perilous work, in the South as well as in the North, was done by gangs of Irish laborers. An overseer, on a Louisiana plantation, stated that slave owners usually employed Irishmen to clear swampy land, for such hard work was far too dangerous for slaves. Slave owners simply felt it was far smarter to hire Irishmen than exposing their slaves to dangerous and unhealthy jobs. To them the loss of an eighteen hundred dollar slave was far more serious than the death of an Irishman.[92]

Some historians assumed that the urban slave had an overall higher life style than the rural slave. In *Industrial Slavery in the Old South*, Starobin argues that assumption may be true for some house slaves and domestics, but it doesn't ring true for slaves employed in industries, over a third of the urban slaves.[93] Slaves were employed in industries such as cotton mills, tobacco-processing factories, sugar refineries, rice mills, iron mills, and hemp manufacturing. Many of these industries were located in rural areas or in very small towns. Starobin found, in general, that the living conditions of slaves employed in industries fared little better than the conditions of the slaves working on the farms and plantations of the South.[94]

Those slaves living in the cities typically lived in integrated neighborhoods, often in the same premises as the whites. They lived side by side with whites, obviously in frequent contact. In Savannah, slaves lived in every ward, and African Americans comprised between a quarter and a half of every neighborhood. A review of comparable data for the cities of Richmond and Mobile showed similar results: both cities were well integrated.[95]

Positive Rewards and Negative Punishment

Much has been written about the atrocities of American slavery. Who can forget the horrible images of slaves who were whipped, leaving awful scars or worse yet, those beaten to death? Did such unspeakable actions occur or was this just the propaganda of the abolitionists? Sadly for its victims such horrific treatment did take place. Unfortunately, even in today's "modern" society, mankind's inhumane treatment of others still happens. As I write this chapter, the United States is reeling and mourning the loss of around three thousand people—innocent men, women, and children killed in senseless terrorist attacks in New York City, Washington, D.C., and Pennsylvania in 2001. Also, a woman in Houston is on trial for brutally murdering her own five children. And in the South before the War Between the States, mankind's inhumanity to innocent men, women, and children did take place. We need to try to determine the extent of the cruelty to slaves. Was it widespread and an everyday occurrence or was it infrequent and isolated?

Modern management teaches a variety of ways to motivate workers. One of the most successful ways of motivation is through rewards and one of the least successful ways is by extreme punishment. Slave owners were well aware of the different approaches way back in the 1800s. For the institution of slavery, discipline and work production was maintained by a system of rewards and punishments. There was no common manual that outlined the degree of rewards and punishments, so it varied from slave owner to slave owner, although there were certainly economic, social, and moral constraints on the slave owner.

Let us examine the punishments first. The slave owner could inflict a variety of punishments on the slaves: the withdrawal of privileges, incarceration, and the threat of selling the slave, unless the slave "shaped up." In extreme cases the slave could be put to death.

The most common form of slave punishment was using the whip, although some slave owners, a distinct minority, forbade whippings. Whipping, in fact, has been the most common form of corporal punishment in the history of mankind. One did not even have to break the law to receive a whipping, dodging one's duties could warrant a whipping. In the 1800s, it was, in the North and South, a totally acceptable form of discipline for all races, slave and non-slave, but that was already beginning to change. Whippings began to decline outside the South as a modern American economy began to evolve. The need to whip began to diminish; a business owner or manager simply fired the lazy or insolent employee and replaced him or her with another. Even in my youth, in the middle of the twentieth century, I was whipped, by a switching from my mother and by a belt from my father. The old adage, "spare the rod and spoil the child," was taken seriously in my home as I was growing up.

The primary issue of whipping was its severity. The severity could range from a slight whipping to an abusive situation where the whipping could result in death. As a child, my punishments were minor, but what of the whipping administered to slaves? Historians recognize that most slave owners did not have a policy of brutality. By an overwhelming majority, the former slaves interviewed by the FWP reported that their owners were good people. One former slave from Alabama, Charity Anderson, described her owner in an FWP interview, "My old Marster was a good man, he treated all his slaves kind, and took care of dem, he wanted to leave dem hisn chillun."[96] Another FWP interviewee, Clayton Holbert, said, "Most of the slave owners were good to their slaves although some of them were brutish of course."[97]

There were certainly exceptions. Campbell Davis, the former Texas slave who had the fond recollections of slave food, recalled a specific whipping etched in his memory. It apparently was done by one of his relatives, who was the slave driver. Davis recalled, "I seed one of my sisters whip 'cause she didn't spin 'nough. Dey pull de clothes down to her waist and laid her down on de stomach and lash her with de rawhide quirt. I's in de field when dey whips my Uncle Lewis for not pickin 'nough cotton. De driver pull de clothes sown and make him lay on de groun'. He wasn't tied down, but he say he scart to move."[98] When the mistress of a plantation in Tennessee broke down crying over the death of one of her slaves, an African American woman gave her interpretation of why she was so grief-stricken, "Huh, crying because she didn't have nobody to whip no more."[99]

How extensive was whipping? There is not much in the way of solid historical data on whippings to examine. Some plantation records survive, some diaries survive that record whippings, and there are firsthand accounts from former slaves, but little else. Some conjecture is called for to determine the extent of whippings. The first consideration is the overall kind treatment indicated in the FWP interviews and the fond recollections those interviewed have of their lives under slavery. Would severe whippings allow those positive feelings to continue? Another fact is that each and every slave represented a substantial investment to the slave owner. As we have seen, the slave owner zealously guarded the health and safety of the slaves when they hired them out. Would they risk the potential physical harm by a severe whipping? There was also another harm that could befall the slave owner as a result of a severe beating of his slaves: lower slave labor production. Did not the slave owner want efficient and productive workers? Of course they did, and they found other ways to motivate slaves. A more common form of motivation was through a system of rewards.

Olmsted perhaps said it the best when he wrote prior to the War Between the States, "Men of sense have discovered that when they desire to get extraordinary exertions from their slaves, it is better to offer them rewards than to whip them, to encourage them, rather than to drive them."[100] There must have been many "men of sense," as many slave owners had reward programs as slave incentives. Rewards varied greatly as did the guidelines for issuing them. The awards typically were given for production met or exceeded. Most were short-term in nature, which slave gang picked the most cotton or hoed the most rows for a specific time frame. The reward itself could be many things: time off, alcohol, tobacco, additional clothing, a trip to town, and additional food supplies, such as coffee and sugar.

A popular reward was additional plots of land for the slave's personal use. The plots could be worked by the slave on his or her own time with the harvest of each plot sold in town or to the slave owner. One slave owner in Mississippi told Olmsted that his slaves bought a lot of personal items. When Olmsted asked how they got the money, the slave owner explained that they "earn it." When asked how they earned it, he explained, "By their owne work. I tell yoy my (slaves) have got more money 'n I hev."[101] Perhaps the most popular reward was cash. Usually cash was given for short-term performance, but some slave owners developed the forerunner of a modern corporate bonus plan by giving slaves a cash "bonus," often at the end of the year. Some cash "bonus" amounts paid to slaves were quite substantial.

One traveler from Britain during the War Between the States observed that the free enterprise system was alive and well among the slaves. While traveling by train in the South he wrote that he was able to get all the food he needed at train stops from slaves. "the negroes hawked round the cars at the depots . . . apples, molasses, cake, cracked corn, baked sweet potatoes, etc."[102]

Slavery Fact #20

Most slaves earned their own money from farming and craft production. Some were able to earn enough to buy their freedom.

Another factor that had at least some effect on the treatment of slaves by their owners was the religious conviction of the owner. Some slave owners saw a large contradiction between being a religious person, primarily a Protestant in the South, and the institution of slavery. Some slave owners freed slaves as a result of the religious dilemma. It also affected the form and intensity of slave punishment. Perhaps one Tennessee man wrote to his slave-owning children with advice,

> *Dear son and daughter may you ever mind*
> *And to your slaves be always very kind*
> *You soon with them on a level must meet*
> *When Christ doth call you to his judgment seat*
> *Christ will not ask if folks are black or white*
> *But judge the deeds and pass a sentence right*
> *The earth is not a place for our abode*
> *Prepare, prepare to meet a righteous God.*[103]

Perhaps the ultimate reward was promise of eventual freedom, in return for years of service, loyalty, and hard work. Manumission, the act of freeing a slave, was unfortunately not very common. According to census records, the manumission rate in 1860 was nearly double the rate reported in the 1850 census. The 1850 manumission rate was one manumission to every 2,181 slaves, but by 1860 it had increased to one manumission for every 1,309 slaves.[104] Compared to the 1850 Census, the 1860 Census reported greatly increased numbers of manumissions in Alabama, Georgia, Louisiana, Maryland, Mississippi, North Carolina, and Tennessee, while the number of manumissions decreased in Delaware and Florida, and remained about the same in the other Southern states.[105]

In spite of a rise in the manumission rate in 1860, a slave owner simply granting a slave freedom in return for the slaves' efforts was still not that common. More commonly, the slave owner would allow the slave to buy his freedom, at a reduced price, in recognition of the slave's faithful service. The money that the slave would use would be from money earned from his or her personal plots, credits given to the slave by the slave owner, or if the slave had a specific skill, from the results of his labor to outside purchasers of the skill or service. This would usually be a very lengthy process, for a rural slave it could be fifteen to twenty-five years, although a skilled urban slave might be able to accomplish the same feat in half the time.

The most common form of manumission was at the death of the slave owner. Owners would provide for the freeing of their slaves in their last wills and testaments. George Washington was perhaps the most famous slave owner to free his slaves in that fashion. One writer described it as a way for the slave owner to receive an emotional gain without suffering a financial loss.[106]

Chapter Seven
The Lives of the Slaves (1831–1860) — Part 2

Family Life

A slave's family was the core of the slave's social life. This was in spite of the various slave states having legal prohibition of slave marriages. Even though the laws were on the books, most slave owners encouraged slave marriages and promoted the bonds of slave families. In very rare occasions, a slave owner would assign an "unmarried" male to an "unmarried" female, but by far the vast majority of slave marriages were determined by the free will of the individual slaves. Slave owners usually would reserve the right to approve the marriage request, although it typically was a formality.

Usually, in spite of the state laws prohibiting slave marriage, there would be some type of formal marriage ceremony. Some marriage ceremonies were quite elaborate. In an FWP interview, a North Carolina slave, Tempe Durham, described her wedding to a slave, who belonged to a slave owner on a nearby plantation: "When I growed up I married Exter Durham. We had a big weddin'. We was married on de front po'ch of de big house. Marse George killed a shoat an' Mis' Betsy had Georgianna, de cook, to bake a big weddin' cake all iced up white as snow wid a bride an' groom standin' in de middle holdin' han's. De table was set out in de yard under de trees, an' you ain't never seed de like of eats. All de (slaves) come to de feas' an' Marse George had a for everybody. Dat was some weddin'. I had on a white dress, white shoes an' long white gloves dat come to my elbow, an' Mis' Betsy done made me a weddin' veil out of a white net window curtain. When she played de weddin' ma'ch on de piano, me an' Exter ma'ched down de walk an' up on de po'ch to de altar Mis' Betsy done fixed. Dat de pretties' altar I ever seed. Back 'gainst de rose vine dat was full or red roses, Mis' Betsy done put tables filled wid flowers an' white candles. She spread down a bed sheet, a sho nuff linen sheet, for us to stan' on, an' dey was a white pillow to kneel down on. Exter done made me a weddin' ring. He made it out of a big red button wid his pocket knife. He done cut it so roun' an' polished it so smooth dat it looked like a red satin ribbon tide 'roun' my finger. Dat sho was a pretty ring. I wore it 'bout fifty years, den it got so thin dat I lost it one day in de wash tub when I was washin' clothes."[1]

One custom in slave weddings was to "jump over the broom" to signify that the couple was officially married. Again, Durham describes the ceremony: "Marse George got to have his little fun: He say, 'Come on, Exter, you an' Tempie got to jump over de broom stick backwards; you got to do dat to see which one gwine be boss of your househol'.' Everybody come stan' 'roun to watch. Marse George hold de broom 'bout a foot high off de floor. De one dat jump over it backwards an' never touch de handle, gwine boss de house, an' if bof of dem jump over widout touchin' it, dey won't gwine be no bossin', dey jus' gwine be 'genial. I jumped fus', an' you ought to seed me. I sailed right over dat broom stick same as a cricket, but when Exter jump he done had a big dram an' his feets was so big an' clumsy dat dey got all tangled up in dat broom an' he fell head long. Marse George he laugh an' laugh, an' tole Exter he gwine be bossed 'twell he skeered to speak less'n I tole him to speak."[2]

Marriage ceremonies would usually be performed by the slave owner, an elder or well-respected slave, or a minister, either white or African American. White ministers commonly presided over slave marriages. One white South Carolina Episcopalian minister performed 139 slave marriages over a seven-year period, compared to only seven white marriages.[3] One slave owner, denying the slave couple a marriage performed by a minister, performed the ceremony himself, using an Almanac rather than a Bible.[4]

A slave married to another slave on a different farm, plantation, or town presented some unique problems. Sometimes such marriages were forbidden by the slave owners, but usually they were approved.[5] In some situations, one of the slaves would be allowed to stay with the other, as long as they were willing to make the journey back to their owners to work. Durham described her situation: "After de weddin' we went down to de cabin Mis' Betsy done all dressed up, but Exter couldn' stay no longer den dat night kaze he belonged to Marse Snipes Durham an' he had to go back home. He lef' de nex day for his plantation, but he come back every Saturday night an' stay 'twell Sunday night."[6] Olmsted describes a Mississippi slave whose wife lived on a plantation twenty miles away. The husband made the long journey on foot every weekend, leaving at noon on each Saturday and returning by noon each Monday.[7]

If a slave marriage did not work out, it was entirely up to the slave owner's discretion to grant a divorce. Different slave owners had different rules regarding divorce. One Louisiana slave owner granted a divorce only with one month's notice and prohibited remarriage unless the divorced slave agreed to receive twenty-five lashes.[8] One Florida slave owner, in his plantation records, reported marital discord with one of his slaves' husband, Renty, "Rose . . . ses that she don't want to Live with Renty on the account of his having so Many Children, and they were always Quarling so I let them separate."[9]

Slaves were even allowed to marry free African Americans. Permission for such would be required by the slave owner, but it was commonly granted. One review of church records in Maryland indicated that slave to free marriages was commonplace.[10] There was an inherent danger if the husband was free and the wife was a slave. Typically, any children of that marriage would automatically be slaves. One of the benefits of such a marriage was the potential that the free spouse would purchase their slave spouse.

That most slave owners encouraged both marriage and a strong family is not disputed by the majority of historians. Various historians have examined the motives of slave owners using different perspectives. It seems that there is little doubt that some slave owners felt a Christian obligation to treat their slaves in a way that would comply with biblical teachings. These owners would strongly encourage their slaves to take a mate for life and raise a family. It was, however, not always done for entirely benevolent reasons; it was also done to promote the best financial interests of the slave owner. Encouraging slaves to have a strong family unit would help preserve the slave owners' control by providing roots to help keep a slave from attempting to escape to freedom. It usually would also help with discipline on the farm or plantation. A strong family unit would also encourage having babies, and the more slaves the slave owner had the greater his or her financial worth would be.

Slave owners often provided incentives to their slaves to encourage matrimony. Slave owners ordinarily furnished the couple with their own cabin, and the slaves would have de facto ownership of furniture, farm animals, plots of land, and other property. Some slave owners gave a greater allotment of food, clothing, and other goods to married couples, so as to encourage other slave marriages.[11]

Unlike Durham's family, if indeed her husband was "skeered to speak less'n I tole him to speak," most slave families seemed to be led by the husband. Some historians have felt that the slave family was basically matriarchally driven. That perspective would appear to be incorrect. It was males that held virtually all the key farm and plantation management positions, from overseer to driver. It was the male slaves that were the craftsmen and artisans, not the females, and as they dominated the work life on the farm or plantation they also dominated the family life. Male domination was also very common in the white world in the South in the 1800s. All females played a more subservient role, black or white, than today.

Were slave husbands and wives loyal to each other? Some writers had either implied or stated that the slaves had a very high rate of promiscuity. Fogel and Engerman's research suggests otherwise, in fact they found just the opposite. In reviewing birth records and by looking at the ages of the mother and frequency of births, they found no demographic data to support such an allegation. Their findings would indicate a promiscuity rate among slaves that was no higher than that of whites. In looking at the data, they also found that slave mothers bore their young not in their early teens, as some abolitionist accounts state, but the average age of the mother at the birth of her firstborn was twenty-two and a half.[12]

One of the harshest aspects of slavery was the breakup of slave families due to the sale of one or more of the family members. Lula Chambers, a slave in Kentucky near the Virginia border, describes her parents to a FWP interviewer: "I don't know nothing at all about no kind of father. Course, I had one who he was I never knew. I ain't never even seen my mother enough to really know her, cause she was sold off the plantation where I was raised, when I was too young to remember her, and I just growed up in the house with the white folks. They sold my mother down de river . . ."[13]

That slave families were broken up is not questioned. But was it commonplace? One historian has estimated that one of three slave marriages was terminated by slave selling and that nearly half of the slave children were separated from at least one parent.[14] In *Time on the Cross*, the authors took a careful look at the most complete set of records still in existence related to the selling of slaves. The largest slave sale marketplace was in New Orleans, and they examined the New Orleans records for nearly forty years. What they found was that of those slaves over age fourteen, more than 84 percent of the slave sales involved unmarried people. Of the slaves that had been or were married, 6 percent were sold with their spouses. Taking into account that some of the slaves that had been or were married, were widowed or divorced from their spouse, leaves only a small percentage of marriages that were broken up.[15] The breakup of slave families was simply not that widespread.

> *Slavery Fact #21*
> *The sale of a slave(s) that resulted in the break up of a family was a very uncommon occurrence. Only rarely would slave families be split up.*

In the same study, the authors were also able to determine the extent of slave children being sold without their parents. They documented that such an event was extremely rare, with the exception of orphaned children. Their findings agreed with the previous findings of Phillips.[16]

One of the most common reasons for the sale of slaves and breakup of their family was due to the death of a slave owner, although sometimes a slave owner would have provisions in his or her will that would not allow families to be split up or at least not sold outside of the county in which they resided. Other reasons would usually relate to financial issues, either bankruptcy, foreclosure of property, or just generally "hard times." Some slave owners who had to sell their slaves due to a financial crisis would endeavor to re-purchase them during better times.

And what of the life of slave children? There are few harsh accounts of slavery as it relates to young children. With the exception of the sale of a young child, which we learned usually was as a result of the child's being orphaned, most accounts of young children as slaves, including the abolitionist-sponsored accounts, are positive. Even Douglass said, "it was a long time before I knew myself to be a slave. I knew many other things before I knew that." Young slave children often had free rein of the farm or plantation. Douglass described the early years of a "slave-boy's life" as "he is, for the most part of the first eight years of his life, a spirited, joyous, uproarious, and happy boy, upon whom troubles fall only like water on a duck's back."[17]

There was typically a close relationship between the slave children and the slave owner's children, if the ages were close. Many very close and long-lasting relationships were forged during childhood between white children and African American slave children. One former slave, Hanna Allen, who lived on a large Arkansas plantation, told the FWP interviewer about the close relationship her brother had with the slave owner's son. "De Bollinger boy, Billy Bollinger, would go to de cabin and sleep with George, my brother. Dey thought nothing of it. Old man Bollinger sent some colored folks up to his farm in Sabula and Billy cried to go long with dem. He let Billy go," Allen said.[18] Many of the relationships would manifest during the War Between the States when slaves offered and did accompany a slave owner's son into Confederate military service.

Some plantations would likely have a nursery for the small children and appoint a female slave to watch over the children during the day. As the slave child got older he or she was expected to go to work. Usually a child was working by the time he or she reached their teenage years, sometimes as early as ten or twelve years old.[19] Today this seems quite harsh, but Southern children of all races, free or slave, were expected to do agricultural work at very young ages.

The word "family" comes from a Latin word meaning all those included in a household. The Latin root word for family was inclusive of any and all slaves. It certainly was not universal, but for many, if not most, slave-owning families in the South a very special relationship developed between the slave family and the slave owner and his or her family. From the slaves' perspective, he or she had two families, his or her own personal family and the family of the slave's owner. From the slave owner's perspective, it was very much the same. A common term used by the slave owner in reference to his slaves was "my people." Journal diaries of slave owners frequently refer to the slaves in that manner.[20] As early as the colonial period, most slave owners considered for their slaves as more than just agricultural workers. Their concern was for the slaves' overall well-being. As time progressed, these feelings only grew, resulting in better treatment for most slaves.[21]

Some historians refer to the unique relationship as a paternalistic feeling by the slave owners for their slaves. What exactly is paternalism? The dictionary definition is "an approach to personal relationships, in which the desire to help, advise, and protect may neglect individual choice and personal responsibility." That is probably an accurate definition of the paternalism shown by the slave owner toward the slave.

There were two sides of paternalism. One side was a genuine display of love and affection on the part of many slave owners, certainly not all, toward their slaves.[22] The slave owner and member of the owner's family would know the slaves by name. Probably the the "mammy"had greatest effect on the slave owner's family. Often many of the slave owner's children might have been raised by a slave, a surrogate mother. The "mammy" was perhaps best described in John W. Blassingame's *The Slave Community: Plantation Life in the Antebellum South*, "Often the child formed a deep and abiding love for his mammy and as an adult deferred to her demands and wishes."[23] The "mammy" was a powerful figure on the larger plantations. She would raise the slave owner's children and managed the household, usually with a rather wide latitude in decision making, from the plantation's mistress. In Alabama a plantation mistress that had been away learned that the plantation's "mammy" had been whipped by an overseer during her absence. The mistress called for the overseer and as was described by one of the slaves, "When Miss Sarah comed back and found it out she was the maddest white lady I ever seed. She sent for the overseer and she say, 'Allen, what you mean by whipping Mammy? You know I don't allow you to touch my house servants. . . . I'd rather see them marks on my old shoulders than to see 'em on Mammy's. They wouldn't hurt me no worse.'"[24] The overseer was sent packing. The daughter of one plantation owner recalled how her father would consult with the plantation's "mammy" on all major plantation matters and usually took her advice. She recalled, in the middle of each day, when her father would return to the plantation home after touring his fields he and the "mammy" would sit, laugh, and talk in what appeared to have been among the more pleasurable moments in both of their lives.[25]

Another strong influence on the children of the slave owner as well as the slave children would be the childhood bonds which often formed between the slave child and the white child. Often as they were growing up slave children and the slave owner's children played together. When the War Between the States began, many male slaves refused to allow their lifelong childhood friend go to war alone. There are countless stories of slaves serving with either their owner or with the son of their owner in the Confederate army.

Older slaves were usually well respected by the slave owner and his or her family. They might be known to everyone as "uncle" or "auntie."[26] An example of this attitude is found in John Clark from South Carolina. When he died, childless and a widower, his last will instructed that his twelve slaves were to be kept together and remain on the Clark land, "without the society of white persons." The will further provided that proceeds from the slaves' agricultural production be used for their comfort and support. Clark's heirs contested the will, but the probate court upheld Clark's wishes.[27]

One British traveler in the South described the unique relationship as, "There is an hereditary regard and often attachment on both sides, more like that formerly existed between lords and their retainers in the old feudal times of Europe, than anything now to be found in America." A white preacher in Alabama described the African American slave as, "He is of all races the most gentle and kind. What other slaves would love their masters better than themselves?"[28]

The renowned Booker T. Washington was born in Virginia as a slave. In his book *Up From Slavery*, Washington wrote of the special relationship between the slaves and the slave owner's family during the War Between the States. Washington wrote, "During the Civil War one of my young masters was killed, and two were severely wounded. I recall the feeling of sorrow which existed among the slaves when they heard of the death of 'Mars' Billy.' It was no sham sorrow but real. Some of the slaves had nursed 'Mars' Billy'; others had played with him when he was a child." Washington said that there was as much sorrow in the slave quarters as there was in the "big house." Washington went on to say, "When the two young masters were brought home wounded, the sympathy of the slaves was shown in many ways. They were just as anxious to assist in the nursing as the family relatives of the wounded. Some of the slaves would even beg for the privilege of sitting up at night to nurse their wounded masters. This tenderness and sympathy on the part of those held in bondage was a result of their kindly and generous nature.[29]

Washington also showed that the special relationship survived both the war and the emancipation of the slaves. He wrote, "As a rule, not only did the members of my race entertain no feelings of bitterness against the whites before and during the war, but there are many instances of Negroes tenderly caring for their former masters and mistresses who for some reason have become poor and dependent since the war. I know of instances where the former masters of slaves have for years been supplied with money by their former slaves to keep them from suffering. I have known of still other cases in which the former slaves have assisted in the education of the descendants of their former owners."[30]

Phillips perhaps found the best expression of the love and concern of a slave located on the tombstone over a slave's grave. The marker was obviously erected by the slave owners and reflects the sentiment of the slave owner towards his now departed slave.

John:
A Faithful Servant
And True Friend:
Kindly, And Considerate:
Loyal, And Affectionate:
The Family He Served
Honours Him In Death:
But, In Life, They Gave Him Love:
For He Was One Of Them[31]

From the slaves' perspective theirs was a mutual feeling. One has to go no further than the FWP interviews to see the depth of love and fondness that slaves had for the slave owner and/or the owner's family. Listen to the words of Tempe Durham. "Freedom is all right, but de (slaves) was better off befo' (slavery ended), kaze den dey was looked after an' dey didn' get in no trouble fightin' an' killin' like dey do dese days. If he was sick, Marse an' Mistis looked after him, an' if he needed store medicine, it was bought an' give to him; he didn' have to pay nothin'. Dey didn' even have to think 'bout clothes nor nothin' like dat, dey was wove an' made an' give to dem. Maybe everybody's Marse and Mistis wuzn' good as Marse George and Mis' Betsy, but dey was de same as a mammy an' pappy to us . . ."[32] The overwhelming number of slaves interviewed, by the FWP, reflects a strong positive personal remembrance of the slave for his or her slave owners and families.

There was another side of paternalism, a darker side that was rooted in the racist perspective of the day, found in both the North and the South. This is in spite of a remarkable closeness of the races in the South, when compared to the North. Olmsted marveled at the frequent and close interaction of whites and African Americans. He marveled on a train ride as a white woman with her daughter sat with a African American woman and her daughter, and how they talked, laughed together, something he would not likely see in the North. He saw the children eating out of the same bag of candy, something that would have displeased many people in the North.[33]

There seems to be little doubt that many, if not most, of the slave owners felt that as children need to be protected so do the slaves, primarily due to their racial inferiority. Some nineteenth-century "scientists," such as Dr. Samuel Cartwright and Dr. Josiah Nott, had purportedly "proven" that the African American was inferior to the whites.[34] That helped some slave owners rationalize the need for slavery, and their needed obligation to take care of "their people."

The paternalism also created a dependency that many slaves had on their owners. This dependency, on the part of some slaves, did not serve them very well post War Between the States. Some of the FWP narratives cite the laments of the former slaves, rooted in dependency. One ex-slave, at age ninety-seven, told the interviewer, "I was born in slavery and I think them days was better for the niggers than the days we see now. One thing was, I never was cold and hungry when my old master lived, and I has been plenty hungry and cold a lot of times since he is gone. But sometimes I think Marse Goodman was the bestest man God made in a long time. . . . (the reason the slaves cried when told they were free) 'cause they don't know where to go, and they's always 'pend on old Marse to look after them."[35]

Many slaves were obviously not dependent and looked forward to the freedom that would come after the War Between the States. In spite of positive treatment received by many slaves, there was a strong craving for freedom. Perhaps one former Texas slave said it best, "I felt like it be Heaven here on earth to git freedom," proclaimed Green Cumby, "'spite de fac' I allus had de good marster. He sho' was good to us, but you knows dat ain't de same as bein' free."[36]

Medical Care

Medical care in the first half of the 1800s was, based on modern standards, primitive at its very best for any American, slave or free. Disease treatment for all Americans had not advanced a great deal. In Dr. James Ewell's popular book, *Planter's and Mariner's Medical Companion*, he prescribed treating cancer by "wearing a hare or rabbit skin over the part affected."[37] Bloodletting was still a common medical treatment, as was forced purging. Bleeding and purging were the standard treatments of the day for dysentery, cholera, and pleurisy.[38] Elixirs of all kinds were used to attempt to "cure" almost every ailment. Simply put, most Americans, including the nation's physicians, lacked the knowledge to successfully treat most diseases.

One Southern physician invented his own disease. Samuel Cartwright, the chairman of a Louisiana State Medical Convention committee whose task was to study the diseases of the slaves, found a disease labeled "Drapetomania." The word combined two Greek words meaning runaway slave and the other indicating madness. What were the symptoms? If a slave wanted to run away from the slave owner then the slave suffered from "Drapetomania."[39]

The most common diseases experienced by the slaves were frm cholera, pneumonia, dysentery, and certain dietary deficiency diseases, as well as some incidents of yellow fever and malaria. In the book *The Health of Slaves on Southern Plantations*, a list of the diseases afflicting the people in the District of Columbia in 1866 were basically the same as those afflicting the slaves. The most deadly were pneumonia and other pulmonary infections.[40]

The common perception is that most slaves received inferior medical care. That is yet another myth to correct. For the slave, his or her medical care actually exceeded the care that Southern whites received.[41] Few Southern whites ever even saw a physician, but the slave owners typically attempted to safeguard the health of their slaves as best they could. The slave owners had substantial dollars invested in each and every slave, and if for no other reason, the slave owner wanted to protect his or her slave investment. Slave owners' plantation records commonly reflect the provision and expenses of slave medical care. Slave owners' instructions to overseers usually contained wording to protect the health of the slaves that the overseer supervised.

Medical care varied greatly depending upon the size of the slave owner's farm or plantation and on the geographical area. Farms and plantations nearer to towns and cities would have better access to physician services. At times one of the slaves would serve as a nurse or care giver. A former Virginia slave, Elgie Davison, recalled, "Massa, he look after us slaves when us sick, 'cause us worth too much money to let die jus' like you do a mule. He git doctor or nigger mammy. She make tea out of weeds, better'n quinine. She put string round our neck for chills and fever, with camphor on it. That sho' keep off diseases."[42]

Farms and plantations that exceeded 150 slaves or so, usually had some type of a hospital or infirmary. The medical structures would range from brick two-story buildings to a cabin on the grounds reserved exclusively for the sick. Some very large plantations hired a full-time physician, but most farms and plantations in the South could not. At times, a slave owner would hire a physician, under an annual contract, to provide medical care for all that needed it, slave or white. Plantation records clearly reflect that the physician saw patients on the plantation regardless of race.[43] Sometimes the physician visits were for a fixed fee per visit. One South Carolina physician contracted for $2.50 per visit, "without reference to the number of sick prescribed for."[44] Perhaps this was an early form of pre-paid health care.

Occasionally, several farms or plantations would join together to hire a physician, who would travel between the various locations. Virtually every plantation of more than 150 slaves had a full time "nurse,"

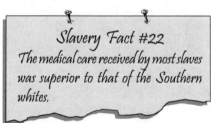

Slavery Fact #22
The medical care received by most slaves was superior to that of the Southern whites.

typically a slave. On smaller farms the slave owner would hire a physician as needed, if they could afford one.

One medical theory that had somewhat advanced prior to the War Between the States was that of hygiene. Physicians began to have some idea that unsanitary surroundings would produce disease and illness. One of the more common rules for overseers was that they were required to see to it that their slaves' quarters, clothing, and cabins were kept clean. Some slave owners even required weekly inspections to ensure cleanliness.[45]

Perhaps the highest level of health care was for slaves who were pregnant.[46] Lighter duty was a common prescription for any pregnant slave once it was learned of the pregnancy. The final month of her pregnancy the slave was assigned to little or no work duty. Delivery of the baby would be typically supervised by a midwife, normally another slave. The mother, post delivery, would in most cases be relieved of all work duties, a "lying-in" period, for approximately a month or more.[47] One study found an unusually large number of physician bills relating to obstetrical services for slaves. The physician fees ranged from ten to twenty-five dollars, and the fee was the same whether for slave or white females.[48]

In *Time on the Cross*, the authors examined the death rates of expectant slave mothers and the infant mortality rates of slave newborns. They found that the mortality rate among slave women during childbirth was actually lower than that of white females in the South. The infant mortality rate among slave children however was higher, when compared to the rate for whites in the United States. The slave infant mortality rate was approximately twenty-five percent higher than for whites. Some historians have assumed that the higher infant mortality rate among slaves is the result of parental infanticide, the desire of the slave mother or father to take the life of her infant child rather than have the child be subjected to a lifetime of slavery. There is absolutely no evidence to support that, and the most likely cause of the higher infant deaths is Sudden Infant Death Syndrome.[49] It is interesting to compare the infant mortality rates in the North with that of the South. It would appear that the higher slave infant mortality rate, when compared to the national average, is primarily due to a much lower infant mortality rate in the North. According to Fogel and Engerman, if you compare only the Southern white infant mortality rate to the slave infant mortality rate they are about the same.[50]

One way to judge the health of any group of people is to look at that group's life expectancy. Fogel and Engerman did just that. They examined the life expectancy of the slaves in the South. They found that the life expectancy of a slave, at birth in 1850, was thirty-six years. For a white, at birth in 1850 in the United States, the rate was forty years. According to their study, a white American would likely live about 12 percent longer than a slave born in 1850. The authors compared this to other life expectancies of France in 1854–58 at thirty-six years, Holland in 1850–59 at thirty-six years, Italy in 1885 at thirty-five years, and in Austria in 1875 at thirty-one years. They also pointed out that the slave life expectancy rate was longer than for the free industrial workers in the North.[51]

Antebellum Slave Codes

In chapter three, we discussed some of the early Slave Codes, laws that the slave states had that not only defined the legal status of the slave, but also gave legal governance over various aspects of the slave's life. The laws did vary from state to state, but most were quite similar. The statutes prohibited slaves from owning land, entering into contracts, and the ability to testify against any white people.[52] Other codes were in reaction to abolitionist propaganda, runaway slaves, and the fear of slave insurrection. There were edicts that limited the number of slaves that could congregate together, prohibitions on owning fire arms, and the right to travel without the slave owner's permission.

Enforcement of the slave codes varied across the South and with the mood of the people. To ensure that slaves were to remain on their owner's land, unless otherwise authorized, states mobilized local citizens to form "patrols" to look for slaves that were roaming without the authority of the slave owner. In Alabama all slave owners under age sixty and all non-slave owners under age forty-five were required to serve on local patrol duty.[53] The actual use of citizen patrols was sporadic and much more common in areas with a heavy concentration of slaves.

Slaves would certainly be granted the opportunity to travel to towns and villages, as well as visit friends and relatives on other slave owners' land, but they needed to have the slave owners' permission or risk being caught. A slave was considered to be "at large" if away from the slave owner and without a pass. A slave, in most states, was required to show to any white man who asked to see it his or her pass. If the slave forged a pass then they were subject to being guilty of a felony offense.[54]

The slave patrols, or "patrollers," were feared by many of the slaves. Members of the slave patrols had the right to detain a slave caught and actually punish a slave on the spot.[55] One of the popular slave songs about the slave patrols is mentioned in the FWP slave narratives. Although there were many variations of the song, one version was:

> *Run Nigger, run, De Patteroll git ye!*
> *Run Nigger, run, He's almost here!*
>
> *Please Mr. Patteroll, Don't ketch me!*
> *Jest take dat nigger What's behind dat tree.*[56]

Green Cumby, a former Texas slave, told a FWP interviewer about his personal experiences with the "patter rolls," the patrollers. It seems that Cumby's love of woman made the risk worthwhile. Cumby said, "De patter rolls dey chase me plenty times, but I's lucky, 'cause dey never cotched me. I slips off to see de gal on de nex' plantation and I has no pass and they chase me and was I scairt! You should have seed me run through dat bresh, 'cause I didn't dare go out on de road or de path. It near tore de clothes off me, but I goes on and gits home and slides under de house. But I'd go to see dat girl every time, patter rolls or not patter rolls, and I gits trained do's I could run 'most as fast as a rabbit."[57]

Education

A great shortcoming of slavery was the lack of education that most slaves received. Booker T. Washington's best recollection of school was, "I had no schooling whatever while I was a slave, though I remember on several occasions I went as far as the schoolhouse door with one of my young mistresses to carry her books. The picture of several dozen boys and girls in a schoolroom engaged in study made a deep impression upon me, and I had the feeling that to get into a schoolhouse and study in this way would be about the same as getting into paradise."[58]

As Phillips aptly called, "The plantation was a school,"[59] but what the slave learned, at their "school" was how to be a slave first, his or her job second, and lastly any general education. Allowing the slave to learn to read and write was at the total whim of the slave owner. Slave states, attempting to exert maximum control over the slave, passed laws that prohibited slaves from learning to read or write. Fortunately, some slave owners ignored these laws.

Certainly, slaves were eager to learn and many did so with or without the help of the slave owner. Olmsted describes a conversation that he had with a slave owner in Mississippi, who was telling him how his slaves could read, "I spose 'twill surprise you—there ent one of my (slaves) but that can read: read good too—better'n I can, at any rate." Olmsted asked how they learned to read. "Taught themselves. I b'lieve there was one on 'em that I bought that could read, and he taught all the rest. But (slaves) is mighty apt at larnin', a heap more 'n white folks is." The slave owner also described how many of his slaves would spend the money they earned by buying their own books, "Religious kind a books generally—these stories; and some of them will buy novels, I believe. They won't let on to that, but I expect they do it."[60]

It is interesting to note that the education of African Americans in the North was very limited. In 1865 the illiteracy rate for all African Americans in the United States was in the 90 percent range.[61] The number of African American children, of school age, attending school in the United States in 1860 was only 2 percent.[62] The lack of education of African Americans was a national problem, not just limited to one section of the country.

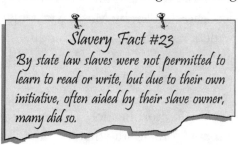

Slavery Fact #23
By state law slaves were not permitted to learn to read or write, but due to their own initiative, often aided by their slave owner, many did so.

Religion

There is no doubting that there was a massive slave conversion from their indigent religious beliefs to Christianity. Beginning in the late 1700s, organized religion grew rapidly in the South, as it did elsewhere in the United States. New Methodist and Baptist churches were a common sight. Likewise slave owners were caught up in the religious fervor that was sweeping much of the country. Some slave owners no doubt felt that adding religion to the life regimen of a slave would be a stabilizing force. Most slave owners seemed to encourage religion out of higher motives.

Some slave owners had difficulty with some of the basic tenants of Christianity relative to keeping a follower of Christ in bondage. A small number of slave owners actually freed their slaves when they could not satisfactorily square their Christian beliefs with slavery. The majority were able to deal with the issues; again we see it corresponding with the concept of a paternalistic attitude of the slave owner towards the slave. Charles Colcock Jones used Christianity as authority to justify slaves. He was a strong advocate of religious education for slaves. In his book *The Religious Instruction of the Negroes in the United States,* Jones encouraged religious education for slaves, and he claimed that Christianity could be used to help maintain order among slaves.[63] Jones called for African Americans and whites to worship at the same churches. Jones wrote, "This mingling of the two classes in churches creates a greater bond of union between them, and kinder feelings; tends to increase subordination; and promotes in a higher degree the improvement of the Negroes, in piety and morality."[64]

Another book, *Primary Platform of Methodism; Or, Exposition of the General Rules,* by Moses M. Henkle, offered instructions to slave owners regarding slaves attending church. Henkle wrote, "Whenever opportunity offers, servants should be encouraged to attend public worship. And a part of that encouragement should be, to provide them with such decent apparel, as shall not subject their feelings to mortification, in appearing in a public assembly of worshippers." To be sure that the slaves understood, slave owners were advised, "It is, also, a useful measure, to question them freely and plainly, on their return from public worship, about the discourse, and other religious exercises, and what they have not understood fully, explain to them; what they have understood, enforce, affectionately, on their minds and consciences. Let your whole course convince them, that you are deeply concerned for their eternal welfare. It will do for you to release yourself from these duties, on the ground that you have a missionary, whose special business it is, to attend to the religious concerns of servants."[65]

According to Olmsted, the slaves were very open to receiving the new religion. "The frequency with which the slaves use religious phrases of all kinds, the readiness with which they engage in what are deemed religious exercises, and fall into religious ecstasies . . . are striking and general characteristics," Olmsted wrote.[66]

Many of the church began deliberate efforts to provide the "Word" to slaves. Like the whites in the South, the most popular denominations among the slaves were the Baptist and the Methodist denominations. It has been estimated that somewhere between 20 and 40 percent of the Baptist congregations were African American. Typically, in Catholic churches, the slaves were permitted to worship side by side with whites, but in Protestant churches the general rule was for the slaves to be segregated.[67] They were normally relegated to the "slave gallery" of the church, either in the extreme front or back of the church or in a balcony. One Tennessee ex-slave, William Davis, recalled, "on Sunday us all go to church, and Massa John do de preachin'. Dey rides in de buggy and us follow in de wagon. De white folks sets in front de church and us in back."[68]

At some locations the slaves would hold their own church services; in fact there was what some historians call an "invisible" African American church for the slaves, with African American preachers and their own form of worship service. The Christian religion was well embraced by the slave population. The slaves made it their own, modifying worship services to suit their needs.

As is true with everyone else, accepting a religion was clearly a personal thing with slaves, although they could certainly be influenced by the slave owner and their fellow slaves. On the plantation of Leonidas Polk in Louisiana, slaves were strongly encouraged to engage in the Christian faith. Polk, who was an Episcopalian bishop, however was not tolerant of other denominations. His slaves could be Christians as long as it was of the Episcopalian faith.[69]

Hanna Allen described a religious "revival" of sorts while she was still a slave. "Several of dem got religion right out in de field and would kneel down in de cornfield. De boss went home and told his wife he thought de slaves was losin' their minds 'cause de yeas all kneeling down in de field," Allen told a FWP interviewer.[70] In Allen's situation it was the slaves that seem to bring religion to the slave owner and his family. In her interview she states, "De colored church finally made de boss and his whole family get religion. De old white mistress would sing and pray while she washed dishes, milked de cows, and made biscuits. So dey called de doctor and he come and said dat God had got a hold on her."

The famous period diarist Mary Chesnut described her visit to a slave church service, in October of 1861, "Methodist minister preached to a very large black congregation . . . they were well dressed—some very stylishly . . . (The minister) preached hell fire— so hot I felt singed . . . though I could not remember any of the world's sins worthy of an eternity in torment. Jim Nelson, the driver . . . was asked to 'lead in prayer.' He became widely excited. Though on his knees, facing us, with his eyes shut, he clapped his hands at the end of every sentence, and his voice rose to the pitch of a shrill shriek. I wept bitterly. The negroes sobbed and shouted and swayed backward and forward . . . 'Yes, my God! Jesus! Bless de Lord, amen!'"[71]

Some slaves did not completely forget their African religions. Voodoo survived in certain parts of the South, particularly in Louisiana. Curses would be put on one's enemies by the slaves' version of a shaman. In spite of this clearly the slaves forsook their old beliefs and accepted Christianity. Perhaps it was the nature of Christianity that appealed to the slaves. The idea that in God's eyes all were equal, regardless of skin color and that there would be a better life in paradise if one accepted the Christian teachings. The suffering Jesus, who had given His all for the world, was a figure that the slaves would find very appealing. They were also invited and welcomed. The idea that they were "sisters and brothers" in Christ no doubt made them feel like they belonged to something greater than what their slave owner provided. As one historian points out, no other "white" institution opened its doors to the African Americans like the Protestant churches of the 1800s. One estimate is that over a half million slaves were formal members of a church, and countless others attended church regularly.[72]

Social Life

The social life of the slave revolved primarily around three different areas for most slaves. First, the family was the cornerstone of the slave's life. As mentioned earlier, the slave had a strong family unit. Caring for the needs of the family members was time consuming and demanding for a slave couple.

Next, in terms of their social lives, was the effect of religion. Slave pastors and Sunday school teachers were held in high regard by the other slaves. The pastors may have been only field laborers during the work day but as "messengers of God," they held sway over many. Vibrant church services and church socials were common place. At an all-slave worship service it was a chance, however brief, for the slave to be free. There they would be free to express their feelings and their love for God. The services were usually loud and rambunctious, with men and women dressed in their finest. Chesnut described the dress of the women in attendance at a slave service, "they were well dressed—some very stylishly gotten up. The house women in white aprons and white turbans were the nicest looking. But the youthful sisters flaunted in pink and sky blue bonnets which tried their complexions."[73]

There was social stratification, by occupation, on the larger farms and plantations. We must keep in mind however that social stratification would occur only on the larger farms and plantations. Most of the Southern farms, with slaves, were far too small to have such stratification. On the larger farms and plantations, the type of job that the slave had gave social status and prestige. The result was a rather complex social hierarchy that roughly paralleled the occupational and supervisory structure of the farm or plantation.[74] Those slaves that had earned the confidence of the slave owner to be leaders, drivers or overseers, were at the top of the social pyramid. Following closely behind were domestic servants and the artisans, if there were any. These slaves usually had a closer association with the slave owner and family, which gave them a higher social status. They might well be fed a little better, and particularly the domestics were more than likely dressed better than the other slaves.

At the bottom of the slavery social pyramid were the majority, the common field laborers. But even the field laborers had bragging rights. Often the slaves would boast of the price that the slave owner had paid for them or what their current marketplace value might be. A healthy and strong young male slave might have cost or be worth twelve hundred dollars versus an older male's cost or value of seven hundred and fifty dollars.

Slaves also took some social distinctions from their slave owners. If they belonged to a wealthy plantation owner often they would look with disdain at other slaves belonging to lesser plantations. Almost universally slaves looked down on non-slave owners, and in particular the people at the bottom of the white social scale in the South, the poor whites.[75] Frederick Douglass perhaps said it the best, "To be a slave, was thought to be bad enough; but to be a poor man's slave, was deemed a disgrace indeed."[76]

One of the big social events of the year for the slaves occurred after the corn harvest each year. One former slave, Robert Shepherd from Kentucky, told a FWP interviewer, "Dem corn shuckin's was sure 'nough big times." Throughout the FWP narratives the corn shucking event is a common theme. Shepherd went on to describe the event, "When us got all de corn gathered up and put in great long piles, den de gettin' ready started. Why, dem womans cooked for days, and de mens would get de shoats ready to barbecue. Master would send us out to get de slaves from de farms round about dere. De place was all lit up with light-wood knot torches and bonfires, and dere was 'citement aplenty when all niggers get to singin' and shoutin' as dey made de shucks fly."[77] It was a big event that lasted through the night and would include slaves from nearby plantations. Every slave would join in, regardless of their social rank on the plantation. The "gala" event would include much singing, dancing, socializing, some drinking, and shucked corn.

Crime

For the most part, any act of minor criminal behavior, by slaves, was dealt with by the slave owner. From the perspective of the slave owner the most common crime was petty thievery.[78] Slaves would, on occasion, kill one of the farm animals, take liquor, steal part of the harvested crop, or pick up personal items from the slave owner's home.

For more serious crimes, state laws would have to be followed. In many states the laws relating to crimes committed by either slaves or free African Americans were more severe than for whites. What might be a felony charge for a slave or free African American might not be for a white. Often also the penalties were more severe for slaves and free African Americans than for whites. A death penalty might be ordered at the conviction of a slave or free African American for murder or rape, but also for the offenses of attempted murder, manslaughter, attempted rape, or attempted rebellion.[79] The courts hearing slave cases were typically not at the same level as those for whites. Many times they would be presided over by a justice of the peace rather than the regular judge.[80]

A Virginia law provided public compensation for losses as a result of slave actions in serious offenses. Consequently, we do have a public record of serious slave crime in that state from 1780 to 1864. There were nearly fifteen hundred offenses during that time period. Most of the convicted offenders were male, 94 percent. Of the convicted crimes, 346 were convictions for murder, 56 for either poisoning or attempting to poison, 73 for rape, 32 for attempted rape, 91 for insurrection or conspiracy to insurrect, 119 for arson, 257 for burglary, 15 for highway robbery, 20 for horse-stealing, 111 for miscellaneous assault, 301 for unspecified felonies, and finally there were 2 convictions for administering medicine to white people.[81] It is interesting to note that out of the 346 murder convictions, 56 were for the murder of the slave owner and 11 were for the murder of the slave owner's wife.[82]

Did the laws in the Southern states afford the slave any protection? For instance, if a slave was savagely attacked by a slave owner could he or she defend his or herself? The laws did vary by state, but surprisingly there was protection for the slave. Basically, if a slave was attacked by a white man he or she could kill the attacker in self-defense if the slave's life was clearly at peril.[83] A Virginia slave, in the late 1700s, killed his overseer, claiming that his life was in jeopardy. In spite of a strong outcry from the white community, the courts ruled that the slave was justified in his actions.[84] Early on in American slavery, in most Southern states, it was legal for a slave owner to kill one of his slaves without suffering criminal punishment. By the 1800s, the Southern states had changed that archaic position, causing the slave owner to be subject to possible criminal punishment if the owner killed one of his or her slaves. In 1851 the Virginia Supreme Court ruled on the conviction of a slave owner for killing a slave by excessive whipping. The court ruled, "But in so inflicting punishment for the sake of punishment, the owner of the slave acts at his peril; and if death ensues in consequence of such punishment, the relation of master and slave affords no ground or excuse or palliation."[85]

Slave Prices

Slaves were expensive, as evidenced by the very small percentage of Southerners that could afford to own slaves. Slave prices varied over the years, based on a variety of factors as indicated below, but even with price fluctuations slaves always remained costly. To get a general idea of the cost of a slave, a $1,500 slave, during the War Between the States, would be the equivalent of $16,500 in 2002 dollars.

The monetary value of slaves depended on a number of things. First it depended on the political and economic conditions at any given time. The War of 1812 brought a decline in slave prices, likewise when the economic Panic of 1837 occurred slave prices dropped. Like any commodity, as distasteful as it is today to refer to a person as a commodity, the value fluctuated with market conditions. Prices varied based on the supply or demand of slave labor. There was a relationship of slave prices to free wages.

The price of the crops that the slave would be hired to work had some effect. Some maintain that the price of the slave directly related to the price of cotton. One old rule of thumb was to multiply the per pound price of cotton times ten thousand to determine the value of a prime field hand, a male between the ages of eighteen to twenty-five years old. This certainly did not hold true as there were simply too many other factors affecting the price other than just the price of the cotton crop. Crop prices certainly influenced the slave price, but crop prices did not control the price of slaves. One New Orleans writer wrote in 1860, "The theory that the price of negroes is ruled by the price of cotton is not good, for it does not account for the present aspect of the slave market. . . ."[86]

Other major factors affecting the individual price of a slave were age, gender, health, and skill sets. Also playing a role was the attitude and the demeanor of the slave. Slave owners were simply not interested in buying a slave that had a history of running away or one that was surly or overtly aggressive.

Phillips in his *American Negro Slavery* charted slave prices. Generally speaking, a slave's value peaked in their mid- to late-twenties. Slave owners would discount the value based on the estimated number of productive years left. In the prime years a female was worth about 20 percent of the value of the male. Slave owners would pay a premium; however, any slave with a specific skill set, for instance a blacksmith, might bring an additional 50 percent.[87]

With the increasing importance of the cotton crop and its labor-intensive aspect, the price of slaves, for the most part, rose during the 1800s. A prime field worker would have brought nearly three hundred dollars on the open market in 1830 in Virginia or South Carolina. By 1860, however, the same slave would have been worth twelve hundred and fifty dollars in Virginia and eighteen hundred dollars on the New Orleans slave market.[88] The very peak of slave prices occurred just prior to the War Between the States.

In Phillips' book he describes the values of the slaves on a Virginia plantation in Powhatan County in 1854. Phillips points out that these were probably conservative values placed on each slave and that because the artisans were not valued any greater than what they were, they were probably not very good at their trades and may well have worked in the fields as well.[89]

All the slaves listed were under age sixty except for five of them. Only one of the five older slaves had any value, a male worth only three hundred dollars. The other four were a shepherd, a dairy maid, and two spinners. The highest value, eight hundred dollars, was given to a twenty-eight-year-old male ox driver. The next highest in value, seven hundred dollars, were all males, including six plowmen, five field hands, three other ox drivers, two wagoners, two blacksmiths, a carriage driver, four stone masons and a carpenter.

Interestingly enough, a twenty-eight-year-old male invalid named Ned was also worth seven hundred dollars. Phillips speculates that Ned's infirmities must have not been too chronic. The remaining male slaves ranged between two hundred and fifty dollars and five hundred dollars, except for two shoemakers whose value was listed at only two hundred dollars each. None of the women were valued above four hundred dollars. There were two twelve- and thirteen-year-old boys, who were valued at four hundred dollars each. All the younger children were valued at one hundred dollars each. The fact that the ox driver had the highest value in the appraisal would indicate that the skilled artisans were without much skill. In addition to their artisan work they were more than likely used in the fields from time to time. Phillips speculates that these slave prices were relatively conservative for that time period.[90] The slaves would likely have had a higher value in the "Deep South" versus Virginia.

Chapter Eight
Free African Americans in the South

The Numbers

Although somewhat beyond the original scope of this book, I have included this chapter to summarize the story of the free African Americans in the United States in general, but in particular in the South. Most of the free African Americans were originally slaves, so we do not deviate too far from our subject concentration.

In 1790, the free African American population in the United States totaled 59,466. Only ten years later that number had nearly doubled to 108,395. By the time of the 1810 Census, the number of free African Americans in the United States had risen to 186,446, a growth rate of 72 percent. According to the 1810 Census, free African Americans in the South, over 108,265, represented the fastest growing segment of that region's population.

What was responsible for the large growth? There were a number of factors. First some slaves had exchanged their slave status for freedom as a result of their military service during the Revolutionary War. There was also a minor influx of free African Americans emigrating from the West Indies. The major reason, however, was the dramatic increase in the number of manumissions. A good example is Virginia. Virginia in 1782 legalized manumissions. That same year, only about two thousand or less free African Americans lived in the state. The Virginia numbers dramatically increase to 12,766 in 1790 and to 30,570 by 1810, a total increase of more than fourteen fold. Also adding to the increased numbers was the emancipation movement in the North following the Revolutionary War, as discussed in chapter three. Finally, the overall national numbers of free African Americans was also increased by the United States' territorial expansion, in particular the Louisiana Purchase of 1803.

The free African American population continued to increase rather briskly after 1810, but not at the astronomical rates of growth of 1800 and 1810. The next highest growth decade was 1820 to 1830 with a percentage increase, on a national basis, of almost 40 percent. Table 8.1 reflects the free African American population growth by decade and the percentage increase.

Table 8.1—U.S. Free African American Population by Census Year & Percentage Increase over Previous Census

Year	Free African Americans	Percentage Increase
1790	59,466	N/A
1800	108,395	82.3%
1810	186,446	72.0%
1820	233,524	25.2%
1830	319,599	36.9%
1840	386,303	20.9%
1850	434,449	12.5%
1860	487,970	12.3%

Some may wonder how many of the free African Americans were the result of abolitionist efforts—after all the abolitionists in the North worked hard to try to liberate Southern slaves. Their efforts were never very successful; likely well less than a thousand a year fled the South. Yet, very surprising to some, there were already many free African Americans in the South.

As we saw in chapter five, by 1860 and the eve of the War Between the States nearly a half million free African Americans resided in the United States. The majority of them, nearly a quarter of a million, were found in the Southern slave states. They made up 1.3 percent of the total United States population. There may well have been more free African Americans than indicated by the 1860 Census. One historian argues that his review of the 1860 Census indicates that free African Americans were typically undercounted.[1]

Table 5.8 lists the free African Americans by state. The three states that had the most free African American population were

Maryland, with 83,942, Virginia with 58,042, and Pennsylvania with 56,949. Table 8.2, below, shows the Southern states' population of free African Americans by size and the percentage of free American Americans in each state's total population. In the South, the free African Americans made up a little over 2 percent of the total population and about 3 percent of the total free population.

Table 8.2—Free African American Population by Southern States and Percentage of Total Population, 1860

State	Free African Americans	Total Population	Free African Americans % of Total
Maryland	83,942	687,049	12.22%
Virginia	58,042	1,596,318	3.64%
North Carolina	30,463	992,622	3.07%
Delaware	19,829	112,216	17.67%
Louisiana	18,647	708,002	2.63%
Kentucky	10,684	1,155,684	0.92%
South Carolina	9,914	703,708	1.41%
Tennessee	7,300	1,109,801	0.66%
Missouri	3,572	1,182,012	0.30%
Georgia	3,500	1,057,286	0.33%
Alabama	2,690	964,201	0.28%
Florida	932	140,424	0.66%
Mississippi	773	791,305	0.10%
Texas	355	604,215	0.06%
Arkansas	144	435,450	0.03%
Total	250,787	12,240,293	2.05%

A significant number of the free African Americans lived in the cities of both the North and the South. According to the 1860 United States Census, over 61 percent of the free African Americans lived in Northern towns and cities, and in the South slightly over 35 percent lived in towns and cities.

Freedom

Many slaves undoubtedly yearned for freedom. One exceptional man was a slave named Bacchus. Bacchus was a house servant in Williamsburg, Virginia, just prior to the American Revolutionary War. He worked for a physician and was described as "a cunning, artful, sensible fellow." He no doubt learned that the British had decreed that any slave reaching English soil would be free. Bacchus saw this as his chance for freedom. Using an assumed name, John Christian, Bacchus forged a pass and ran away. He had hoped to make it to the coast and catch a boat bound for England. Unfortunately for Bacchus he was captured before he made it. Bacchus apparently never found his elusive dream of freedom.[2]

But for some slaves freedom did become a reality. In the United States, the free African American population began to grow dramatically after the Revolutionary War. Prior to the war the free African Americans were mainly the remnants of the earliest African slave trade. These were slaves that had been brought to the colonies before slavery had really taken hold. Some of the first "slaves" were treated more like indentured servants, and after a while were freed by their "owners" and allowed to go out on their on. Others had been treated as traditional slaves, but had been freed by their slave owners.[3]

In the book *Slaves without Masters,* Ira Berlin expresses his perspective on how many of the first African Americans became free. He states that many were of mixed race, mulattoes. Berlin theorizes that most of the mulatto children were born as a result of sexual relations between African Americans and white indentured servants. Most were thought to be the result of sexual relations between white indentured servant males and African American women. Many of the mulattoes, according to Berlin, however were the offspring of African American males and white indentured servant women. Why this pairing? Berlin thinks that part of that answer lies with the employer of the indentured servants. There was an economic incentive for the indentured servant's employer to encourage sexual relations between the African American men and the white women. If the white indentured servant woman gave birth, it would tie the interracial child to the employer for thirty-one years and also extend the indentured period for the mother.[4]

Life for the Free African Americans

To understand the life that free African Americans led in the United States we need to look back at our earlier comments about the racial perceptions of the American people in the nineteenth century. With most white Americans holding racist opinions—and it was nearly universal—all free African Americans led a shaky existence in both the North and the South. It may be surprising to some that early on a free African American, in many ways, was better off in the South than in the North. The South, however, with somewhat of a knee-jerk reaction to several slave insurrections, responses to abolitionist literature, and Northern efforts to encourage slaves to escape via the Underground Railroad, would become as uncomfortable a place to live as the North, immediately prior to the War Between the States.

The North was not the haven for black-skinned people as many today might imagine it was. They were clearly treated as second class citizens in the North. The main advantage they had, north of the Mason-Dixon Line, was that they were usually spared the threat of re-enslavement. In some states in the South the breaking of a law, by a free African American, could possibly cause him or her to be re-enslaved.

Four Northern states—Indiana, Iowa, Illinois, and Oregon—at times actually forbade free African Americans from even entering their territory.[5] It seems rather ironic today that the state, Illinois that claims Abraham Lincoln (Lincoln was actually born in Kentucky) at one time barred free African Americans. If a free African American did indeed break the Illinois law barring their entrance and stayed more than ten days, then he or she was guilty of a "high misdemeanor."[6]

In ten Northern states, a free African American was not given the right to vote, also in ten Northern states they were not allowed to testify in a court; they were barred from assembling in two Northern states, as well as being relegated to segregated public transportation, and not being allowed to have their children educated in public schools.[7]

Even the churches in the North were widely segregated. The Free African Society was formed in Philadelphia in 1787 after the white members of a Methodist church decided not to allow African Americans in their worship service. Like the Free African Society, hundreds of aid and charitable groups, fraternal groups, and churches were formed in Northern cities to assist needy free African Americans, when white charitable groups would not, due to race discrimination.

Some white workers in the North viewed the free African Americans as competitors in tight labor markets. There were a number of anti-free African Americans riots in Northern cities. Riots, where white mobs attacked and killed free African Americans, occurred in Philadelphia in 1829 and 1849, Boston in 1843, Providence, Rhode Island, in 1831, New York City in 1834, and in Washington, D.C., in 1835.

In *Time on the Cross*, the authors concluded that free African Americans were at least financially better off in the South than in the North. Relegated to menial jobs and crowded living conditions in the North, the authors used 1850 Census data to compare life in New York City and New Orleans. They found that the free African Americans in New York City lived in more crowded housing, had a lower proportion of skilled craftsmen, and overall had less wealth on a per capita basis.[8]

What of life for the free African American in the South? His or her life depended a great deal on where they lived and got more restrictive as we approached the War Between the

> *Slavery Fact #24*
> *Period data suggests that, at least from a financial sense, free Africans were better off in the South versus the North.*

States. For the many free African Americans in Southern cities life could be relatively good. Some were skilled craftsmen, such as carpenters, masons, as well as working as mechanics and tailors. These free African Americans could earn a decent wage. Other urban free African Americans worked more menial jobs such as day laborers or domestics.

One occupation that free African Americans had a near monopoly on was the barber profession. Just prior to the War Between the States, in virtually every Southern city, if you wanted a haircut, you went to a barber who was a free African American. Free African Americans were so closely identified with barbering that one English writer wrote that it was the free African American's "birthright."[9]

Baltimore and New Orleans had, by far, the largest free African American urban population. In 1860, Baltimore had a free African American population of over twenty-five thousand and New Orleans over ten thousand. Table 8.3 lists selected Southern cities, including the largest town or city in each of the Southern states, plus selected other larger Southern cities, based on the 1860 Census.[10] There were nearly fifty-four thousand free African Americans living in these towns and cities, making up over 6 percent of the cities' total population. From a percentage perspective, the cities and towns with the highest slave percentages were in either Virginia or Maryland. The highest percentage of free African American population was in Petersburg, Virginia, at nearly 18 percent, followed by Baltimore, Maryland, at 12 percent, and Charleston, South Carolina, at 8 percent.

The smallest free African urban populations were in Texas. San Antonio had no free African Americans, and Galveston only had two. Little Rock, Arkansas, had the next smallest number at seven. From a percentage perspective, these same three cities prevailed. The lowest percentage of the total population was in San Antonio with 0 percent, Galveston with not much more than 0 percent, and Little Rock with less than 0.25 of a percent.

Table 8.3—Population of Selected Southern Cities and Towns (Sorted by State), 1860

City or Town	Total Population	Free African Americans	Percentage of Total
Mobile, Ala.	29,258	817	2.79%
Little Rock, Ark.	3,727	7	0.19%
Pensacola, Fla.	2,876	130	4.52%
Savannah, Ga.	22,292	705	3.16%
Augusta, Ga.	12,493	386	3.09%
Atlanta, Ga.	9,554	25	0.26%
Louisville, Ky.	68,033	1,917	2.82%
New Orleans, La.	168,675	10,689	6.34%
Baltimore, Md.	212,418	25,680	12.09%
Natchez, Miss.	6,612	208	3.15%
St. Louis, Mo.	160,773	1,755	1.09%
Wilmington, N.C.	9,552	573	6.00%
Charleston, S.C.	40,522	3,237	7.99%
Memphis, Tenn.	22,623	198	0.88%
Nashville, Tenn.	16,988	719	4.23%

(continued on next page)

Table 8.3 *(continued)*

City or Town	Total Population	Free African Americans	Percentage of Total
San Antonio, Tex.	8,235	0	0.00%
Galveston, Tex.	7,307	2	0.03%
Richmond, Va.	37,910	2,576	6.80%
Petersburg, Va.	18,266	3,244	17.76%
Norfolk, Va.	14,620	1,046	7.15%
Total	872,734	53,914	6.18%

Free African Americans made up over 6 percent of the total New Orleans population. In New Orleans there was a large number of light-skinned free African Americans. Many were of mixed blood, offspring of the early French and Spanish settlers and the slaves or free African Americans. These mulattoes were better accepted by the white citizens than darker-skinned free African Americans. The Creoles were originally French-speaking mulattoes and many were quite socially prominent in Louisiana. Since they were lighter skinned, one author called them "neither physically nor mentally black," a people who set themselves apart from and above the other free African Americans and the African American slaves.[11]

In the rural areas of the South, the free African Americans, for the most part, lived a marginal existence. They worked as farm hands or day laborers, although many had small farms. Economically, their lives were not much different than the poor whites' that lived in rural areas of the South—many were just trying to survive day by day. The rural free African Americans were relatively isolated. Due to the racial mores of the time, white people had little to do with them, and they were mainly cut off from other African Americans who were slaves.

Certainly not all free African Americans were poor. Some did very well both in an urban setting and in the rural areas. In the rural areas some free African Americans were quite successful planters. One glimpse of South through the eyes of a free African American is from Hiram Revels. Revels was born in 1822 to free African American parents in Fayetteville, North Carolina. After the War Between the States, Revels would become the first African American to become a United States Senator. According to his brief autobiography, he indicated that despite the increased restrictions that followed the Nat Turner slave insurrection, "so much of the former friendly generous feeling toward the free people of color remained that in many parts of the state, especially in the cities, colored schools were tolerated through the sympathy of the better class of the white people." He wrote that there were two "fine" schools in Fayetteville for African Americans, one which was taught by a white woman and the one, which he attended, taught by a free African American.[12] Revels, in 1870, was elected as a United States Senator from Mississippi, and later served as the president of Alcorn A&M College in Aberdeen, Mississippi.

Another glimpse of the life of a free African American in the South comes from the diary of William Johnson of Natchez, Mississippi. Johnson kept a diary from 1835 until his death in 1851. Johnson started out working as a barber. By the 1830s, he was making excellent profits from his barber shop and had accumulated an estate worth $25,000. He speculated in land, including two stores, which he rented out, and he was a moneylender, making loans to whites and African Americans. As most of the well-to-do people in Natchez, he purchased a large farm outside of town, which he named "Hardscrabble." He worked the land with fifteen slaves, some free African Americans, and some white tenant farmers. He had a white overseer to manage his farm interests. Johnson concluded that "the key to happiness" in life was to own land. Today, Johnson's Natchez townhouse, built in about 1841, is part of the Natchez National Historical Park and is open for public tours.

In 1835, the editor of the *Charleston Courier* stated that free African Americans' conduct in Charleston "has been for the most part so correct, evincing so much civility, subordination, industry and propriety, that unless their conduct should change for the worse, or some stern necessity demand it, we are unwilling to see them deprived of those immunities which they have enjoyed for centuries without the slightest detriment to the commonwealth."[13]

Free African Americans Owning Slaves

That William Johnson owned slaves is not unique as owning slaves it started early on in our history. It perhaps first began in the colony of Virginia. In 1694, a Virginia court ruled that John Casor's suit for freedom against his owner, Anthony Johnson of Northampton County, would be denied. Johnson claimed that Casor, an African American who had run away from Johnson, was a "servant" for life. The court would find for Johnson, requiring Casor to become in effect Johnson's slave. And who was this Anthony Johnson? Recall, back in chapter two, the first twenty slaves brought into Jamestown by the Dutch in 1619. Johnson was one of the original twenty slaves brought into the English colonies of America.[14]

Tradition has it that Johnson had won his freedom by 1623 and by 1651 owned land and five "servants" of his own, four whites and one African American. Johnson certainly may have set a lot of firsts in American history. He could well have been the first African American to set foot in Virginia, at least one of the first twenty; he perhaps was the first African American to become a free man, and he was the first African American to own slaves.

The court's decision against Casor set a precedent that would be followed by other colonies and later states. First it helped determine that a "servant" with African ancestry could be a "servant" for life, unlike the specified time periods for indentured servants. Secondly, it helped determine that any free person, regardless of race, could indeed own slaves, although it would be laws passed in Virginia and Maryland in the 1660s that would codify the lifetime servitude of African American slaves. Throughout the South free African Americans would begin to own their own slaves. Eventually in Arkansas and in Delaware, the courts would rule that free African Americans could not own slaves.

In the Arkansas' decision, the Arkansas Supreme Court ruled that slavery had its establishment "in an inferiority of race." It further ruled that for one African American to own another it would lack, "this solid foundation to rest upon."[15] Arkansas, by the way, in 1859 ordered the expulsion of all free African Americans from the state.[16] That perhaps helps explain why, according to the 1860 Census, the state had the lowest percentage of free African Americans of any state. Only .03 percent of the state's population were free African Americans, compared to the national average of over 1.5

percent. By 1860, only 144 free African Americans were left in the state.

The majority of free African Americans did not own slaves. But the fact that some free African Americans did own slaves is not disputed. According to the 1830 United States Census, just in the states of Louisiana, Maryland, South Carolina, and Virginia, free African Americans owned more than ten thousand slaves.[17] In South Carolina alone there were 171 free African American slave owners that owned 766 slaves in 1860. Like free African Americans in general, Larry Koger in his book *Black Slaveowners: Free Black Slave Masters in South Carolina, 1790–1860*, envisions that perhaps as many as 50 percent of the free African Americans that owned slaves in Charleston, South Carolina, were not included in the 1860 Census. He cites confusion in the census data when a free African American had whites in the household; for example, a free African American employing a white overseer. In such situations this might be listed as a white slave owner rather than a free African American slave owner.[18]

Free African Americans owning slaves was a common urban situation. In Charleston, the majority of the free African American heads of households owned slaves from 1820 to 1850, although the percentage was in a decline. Between 1820 and 1840 about three-quarters of all free African Americans owned slaves in Charleston. The percentage had fallen to under 50 percent by 1850.[19]

Some of the free African Americans that owned slaves had simply purchased wives, children, parents, and the like. Others were less noble in their slave purchases. It seems surprising to Americans today that some free African Americans owned slaves. It was even surprising to Northerners in the nineteenth century. Union soldiers that invaded the South would write home about coming across a plantation where all the residents were black, free and slave. One Union soldier wrote, "Some of the richest planters, men of really great wealth, are of mixed descent." He added that these free African Americans would gather to stare at the Union troops as they passed, and he added, "These are not the former slaves, observe, but the former Masters."[20]

Many historians claim that the vast majority of slaves owned by free African Americans were simply their family members, spouses, children, and parents, as well as friends that they had bought out of slavery.[21] Koger looked carefully at the slave ownership of free African Americans in South Carolina. He did find that some free African Americans did purchase family members from the bonds of slavery. He also found that many times free African Americans did not stop there. Koger found at times that South Carolina's free African Americans would own two sets of slaves, one set of family members, but another set that clearly appeared to be for labor only purposes. James Brown, a butcher, in Charleston Neck, purchased his wife, but also purchased four other slaves from a slave trader. The four other slaves were used as domestics and to work in his butcher shop.[22]

A war report gives the account of an incident, in Alexandria, Louisiana, when Union troops came across an African American woman in a well furnished home. They demanded to know where her "mas-

> *Slavery Fact #25*
> *Thousands of Free African Americans in the South owned their own slaves.*

ter" was. When she informed them that she had no "master" that she was free woman, they mocked her and continued to demand to know where her owner was hiding. Not believing her, they stole or destroyed most of her personal property. As she pleaded with them to stop, she was told that she was a liar because everyone knew that African Americans "could not own property in the South."[23]

Being a successful planter in the South, regardless of race, meant the likelihood that one would own slaves. By 1830, the number of free African Americans that owned slaves had reached 3,600.[24] It has been estimated that the 3,600 free African Americans that owned slaves in 1830 owned approximately 13,000 slaves. This number would only grow as the nation approached the War Between the States. By 1860, collectively free African Americans in the South owned an estimated nine million dollars worth of property. That was more than nine times as much as Northern free African Americans.[25]

A number of large slave owners were among the free African American population. One of the most prosperous free African Americans in the South was found in South Carolina: William Ellison, perhaps the wealthiest free African American in the South. Ellison, who was originally named April, was a born as a slave around 1790. At a young age April was sold to a white slave owner, William Ellison. The owner found that, with April, he had purchased a very bright and a very ambitious young man. The elder Ellison taught April to read and write as well as basic carpentering skills. About 1816, the elder Ellison, freed April who was twenty-six years old. In April of 1820, April petitioned the South Carolina courts to change his name to William Ellison in honor of the slave owner that had freed him.

A year after earning his freedom, April was hired to build his first cotton gin. He became one of the premier cotton gin builders in the region, and would also offer a cotton gin repair service. He advertised across the state selling his cotton gins. April, now known as Ellison, began acquiring slaves to help him meet the demand for his booming business. In 1830, he had four slaves working for him. In 1849, Ellison made fifteen cotton gins, with each gin selling for one thousand dollars.[26] Most of Ellison's labor force, needed to construct the gins, were slaves, numbering twelve at that time.

By that time Ellison had joined a Charleston Episcopal Church. At first, he was only permitted to worship from the balcony, but before long he was granted worship rights from the main floor. By 1860, Ellison had bought a plantation of nine hundred acres and owned sixty-three slaves—he was one of the richest men in the county. Ellison was a supporter of the Confederacy, but died in December of 1861, long before the outcome of the war was determined.

Speaking of Charleston, the city had its own elite free African American social club, the Brown Fellowship Society. It was formed in 1790 by a group of five free African Americans, all members of St. Philip's Episcopal Church. Because St. Philip's refused African American worshippers burial plots in their churchyard, the society was formed to provide a cemetery for members. The membership was limited by color restrictions, although slaves were excluded from membership,[27] and a $50 membership fee. The Brown Fellowship Society provided numerous services for its members, including an aristocratic place for its members to meet and socialize. It also provided for some philanthropic services such as education, medical care, and financial support for widows and orphans, but never to slaves. The Brown Fellowship Society was renamed the Century Fellowship Society well after the War Between the States, and actually lasted into the twentieth century.[28]

Another wealthy free African American was Andrew Durnford, who owned a large sugar plantation in Louisiana. Durnford had as many as seventy-five slaves and complained at times about his slaves' work effort, calling them "rascally negroes." He perhaps made as much money in slave trade as he did from his sugar plantation. In 1835 he traveled to Virginia to buy slaves for himself and a wealthy New Orleans white friend.

Letters from Durnford, while in Virginia, reflected his nearly complete disassociation from his race. He complained about the high prices of slaves, pondered the transportation problems of getting purchased slaves back home, and he noticed the poor opinion that white Southerners had towards those that bought and sold slaves, regardless of the race of the buyer or seller. Durnford purchased twenty-five slaves on his trip, and during his life never showed any inclination to free his slaves, save one personal body servant.[29]

It was in New Orleans that some very strong support came from free African Americans in favor of the South's seceding from the Union. Their mindset was decidedly more pro slave owner than pro slave. In a New Orleans newspaper, before the War Between the States, a group of "free colored population" stated their readiness to shed blood for their state because they "own slaves, and they are dearly attached to their native land."[30]

To be a free African American in the United States prior to the War Between the States was to be free, but it was not without its price. Some like Andrew Durnford lived nearly the same life as a well-to-do white man, but he was certainly the exception not the rule. Most free African Americans lived a hard life, not that life in the mid-nineteenth century was not extremely hard for most Americans, black or white. But for the free African American is was all the more complicated and difficult due to racial discrimination, North and South. From a social, legal, and even a religious perspective the free African American simply was not treated on equal terms as white citizens were. The cards were definitely stacked against him, but many free African Americans did thrive and they made the best they could out of the lot that was cast to them.

Chapter Nine
The War Between the States, 1861 to 1865

Slavery, the Cause of the War?

In 1858 Senator William Henry Seward, in a keynote speech in Rochester, New York, perhaps predicted the upcoming war between the North and the South when he called it the "Irrepressible Conflict."[1] Seward said in his talk: "It is an irrepressible conflict between opposing and enduring forces, and it means that the United States must and will, sooner or later, become either entirely a slaveholding nation, or entirely a free-labor nation. Either the cotton and rice-fields of South Carolina and the sugar plantations of Louisiana will ultimately be tilled by free labor, and Charleston and New Orleans become marts for legitimate merchandise alone, or else the rye-fields and wheat-fields of Massachusetts and New York must again be surrendered by their farmers to slave culture and to the production of slaves, and Boston and New York become once more markets for trade in the bodies and souls of men."[2]

Seward's prediction came true. The nation did eventually become entirely a free-labor nation, but there was a huge price to pay. The North-South conflict of words soon turned to the sword and the gun, resulting in the bloodiest war in American history. Over six hundred thousand soldiers lost their lives in a war that literally was brother against brother, family against family, and was clearly the most horrific event in the American experience. It certainly had more to do with shaping the course of American history than any other single event in American history. Was all this carnage due to an effort to end slavery in the United States? Was this what it took to end the American institution of slavery?

I took a most unscientific poll of everyday people. I simply asked the question, "If you had to narrow it down to a single cause, what was the cause of the American Civil War, also known as the War Between the States?" I gave no possible answers to chose from. I did avoid giving the poll to students of the war, professional historians, War Between the States re-enactors, and the like. What I hoped to find was the general population's perception of the cause of the War Between the States.

My simple poll's results will probably not surprise anyone. Again, this was just an unscientific random poll, in one geographic region, Texas, so only limited conclusions can be drawn. The overwhelming answer was not very astounding: "slavery," a one-word answer to a most difficult question. Eighty-four percent of the respondents said slavery, followed by no answer or unknown as the second most common answer, at 11 percent. The next highest answer was "The firing on Fort Sumter," a remarkably interesting answer. Of course the firing on Fort Sumter, by Confederate forces, was the actual start of the war, so perhaps these respondents were answering the question only from a strictly Union perspective.

What exactly was the cause of the War Between the States? That is a question that professional historians and writers have debated since the war began in 1861. Was slavery the sole cause of the war, or was it primarily fought over states' rights? Was it a series of events that occurred, with states' rights and slavery just two of many reasons? On the exam given by the Immigration and Naturalization Service (INS), prospective American citizens are asked the question, The War Between the States was fought over what important issue? Does the INS then provide us with the answer that we seek? According to INS officials either "slavery" or "states' rights" will be counted as correct.[3] It appears that even the United States government is unsure of the answer. We perhaps could write an entire book just trying to answer that simple question. Let us, at least, take a very brief look at some ideas on why a war started in 1861.

First of all, it has always been my opinion that the actual cause of the fighting that broke out between the North and the South, i.e., the firing on Fort Sumter and subsequent military action, was due to only one reason, that of secession. I do not think fighting would have erupted between the two regions without the Southern states' having disavowed their voluntary union with the other states that made up the United States. I use the term, voluntary, from the Southern perspective. Some in the North had a perspective that the United States was not a voluntary union of states. Many in the government of the newly elected president, Abraham Lincoln, were bound and determined to prevent the withdrawal of the Southern states. Thus we had a powder keg situation in the Charleston Harbor. As the Southern states withdrew, they seized federal properties. In Charleston Harbor, Lincoln "drew the line in the sand" and said to the South, you will not take this federal property. This then caused the leaders of the newly formed Confederate States of America to fire on the Union fort, and the result was four long years of warfare between the Confederacy and the United States.

No, I have not skirted the question on a technicality; it simply leads us to ask yet another question, What caused secession? That answer, I think, is also rather obvious. It indeed was the election of Abraham Lincoln as the United States' president. What exactly happened in the election of 1860? Perhaps the election of 1860 could be labeled a national election with strictly regional candidates. The Democrat Party, the party with the incumbent president Franklin Pierce, was badly fractured along sectional lines. Stephen A. Douglas, from Illinois, was the candidate for the Northern branch of the party, and John C. Breckinridge, of Kentucky, was the Southern Democrat Party candidate. The non Democrat Party candidates for president were John Bell, from Tennessee, from the newly formed and short-lived Constitutional Union Party, and Lincoln, from Illinois, as the Republican Party candidate.

In a vote, strictly along geographical lines, Lincoln won the election with less than 40 percent of the popular vote, although he clearly won the electoral vote. Lincoln carried the Northern states, which was basically a contest between him and Douglas. Douglas got nearly 30 percent of the popular vote, yet he only received twelve electoral votes. Breckinridge carried most of the Southern states, and Bell carried three states in the middle of the country: his home state of Tennessee, plus Kentucky and Virginia. Lincoln did not come close to carrying the electoral vote of any Southern state. In fact in nine Southern states—Alabama, Arkansas, Georgia, Florida, Louisiana, Mississippi, North Carolina, Tennessee, and Texas—Lincoln did not even receive a single recorded vote.[4] Breckinridge did not come close to carrying the electoral vote of any Northern state.

Table 9.1—Presidential Election of 1860

Candidate	Party	Popular Vote	% of Popular	Electoral Vote	% of Electoral
Abraham Lincoln	Republican	1,865,593	39.78%	180	59.41%
John C. Breckinridge	Southern Democratic	848,356	18.09%	72	23.76%
John Bell	Constitutional Union	592,906	12.64%	39	12.87%
Stephen A. Douglas	Northern Democratic	1,382,713	29.48%	12	3.96%
Total		4,689,568		303	

In spite of Lincoln's comments that Southerners "have too much good sense and good temper to attempt the ruin of the government," his election was simply more than what the South could tolerate. The South didn't see it that way. One Southern paper, the *New Orleans Daily Crescent*, ran an obituary of the Union, saying, "The soul of the Union is dead, and now let its body be buried."[5] Beginning with South Carolina in December of 1860, one by one the Southern states began to leave the Union. In January of 1861, five Southern states left the Union—Georgia, Florida, Alabama, Mississippi, and Louisiana—followed by Texas, which put the question of slavery to a popular vote in February. After the firing on Fort Sumter, four more states—Virginia, North Carolina, Tennessee, and Arkansas—left the Union.

The next question in our backward chain of questions is, What caused the election of Lincoln? Lincoln was elected due to the sectional issues that had ripped the nation apart, of which slavery was the

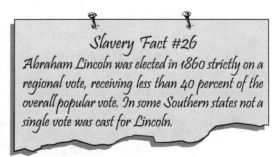

Slavery Fact #26

Abraham Lincoln was elected in 1860 strictly on a regional vote, receiving less than 40 percent of the overall popular vote. In some Southern states not a single vote was cast for Lincoln.

leading issue. Slavery was the most emotionally laden issue of all, and it was the one issue that transcended everything. It touched every aspect of life, economic, social, political, and religious. Yes, there were various other key sectional issues: an agrarian way of life versus an urban way of life, various trade and tariff issues, political power issues, such as who would control the national government, the North or the South, and finally an important key issue, a governmental ideological issue, Where would the seat of governmental power be, at the state level or at the

Abraham Lincoln
Library of Congress

national level? On each of these sectional issues the matter of slavery permeated each topic.

The bottom line, slavery was an issue but not an absolute cause. If you read Southern correspondence during the war there is no question why Southerners were fighting. In the thousands of soldiers' letters that I have read there is a very strong theme and it certainly is not the defense of slavery. Perhaps one Alabama Confederate said it the best, "when a Southeron's home is threatened the spirit of resistance is irrepressible."[6] Clearly many, if not the vast majority of Southerners, were fighting not in the defense of slavery but rather to defend their homes from invaders.

And what of the Union soldiers? For what were they fighting? Was it the noble and grand crusade to free forever the bonds of slavery of African Americans? Just as reading Southern soldiers' letters answers the question for the South, so does Union correspondence root out the Northern reasons to fight. The Union soldier was clearly fighting to "Save the Union," or as one Union soldier said to put down "this infernal rebellion." Union soldiers felt strongly compelled to not allow the Union to be splintered into two separate nations. It was Lincoln himself that set the tone and the reason for the fight. In his first inaugural address he said, "I hold that . . . the Union of these States is perpetual, . . . The Union is unbroken, and to the extent of my ability I shall take care, as the Constitution itself expressly enjoins upon me, that the laws of the Union be faithfully executed in all States."[7]

The sentiment in the North prior to the outbreak of war was clearly not to fight a war over slavery. Editorials in papers across the North echoed a similar theme, "leave slavery alone." Papers such as the *New York Times*, which called slavery "a very tolerable system," and the *New York Herald*, the largest paper in the country, mentioned the "contented lot of the slaves," and how they were "comfortably fed, housed, clothed, and seldom or never overworked."[8]

Some have called the War Between the States the result of a failure of democracy. It was, however, not democracy that failed the people; it was the people that failed democracy. In summary, slavery was not the direct single cause of the war—we have to look at too many other events to determine that—but slavery was the leading issue in the sectional strife that caused the North and the South to settle its differences in a most bloody and horrible fashion. Other historians, such as Avery Craven, have stated that the "war was the product, not so much of sectional differences as of emotions developed about differences, which by 1861 made it impossible longer to reason, to trust, or to compromise,"[9] in effect the failure of reason. My opinion, contrary to Craven's, is that the war erupted primarily due to the sectional division of the United States. The sectional division was due to a number of different issues, of which the most important were the issues of states' rights and slavery. Had the war not occurred or had the South won the war, would slavery have continued on? It is extremely doubtful that slavery would have survived, but we will look at that question in chapter ten.

Lincoln, the Sectional Crisis, and the Slaves

As some Southern states left the Union even before Lincoln was inaugurated, he was faced with a major dilemma, could he retain the slave border states that had not left the Union—Arkansas, Delaware, Kentucky, Maryland, Missouri, North Carolina, Tennessee, and

Virginia—and was there any way to get those states that had seceded back in the fold?

People in the United States were divided on what to do about
Southern secession. Some, like *New York Tribune* publisher Horace
Greeley wanted the South to go its separate way. Greeley said that
the "erring sisters," the Southern states, should be allowed to "go in
peace."[10] Others wanted compromise. Senator John Crittenden suggested compromise, one that would allow slavery where it already
existed with no future restrictions. Lincoln did not like either course
of action, and Lincoln's Republican Congressional committee members voted against the compromise.

In his inaugural address, delivered on March 4, 1861, Lincoln
indicated his staunch desire that the Union should not be split apart.
His position was clear, he compared secession to anarchy, and he
said, ". . . no State upon its own mere motion can lawfully get out of
the Union; that resolves and ordinances to that effect are legally
void, and that acts of violence within any State or States against the
authority of the United States are insurrectionary or revolutionary,
according to circumstances."[11] Lincoln further alluded to the fact
that he would "hold, occupy, and possess" the property and places
belonging to the federal government in the South.

Regarding slavery, Lincoln said, "I have no purpose, directly
or indirectly, to interfere with the institution of slavery in the States
where it exists. I believe I have no lawful right to do so, and I have
no inclination to do so."[12] Clearly Lincoln was telling the South, and
in particular those slave states that had not left the Union, that he
would not interfere with existing slavery. Also very clear in his address was Lincoln's desire to see that slavery was not expanded
into any of the additional territories.

In a direct appeal to the South, Lincoln, in his address, further
promised enforcement of the Fugitive Slave Laws. Lincoln noted
that the Constitution required the return of fugitive slaves and said,
"All members of Congress swear their support to the whole Constitution—to this provision as much as to any other. To the proposi-
tion, then, that slaves whose cases come within the terms of this
clause 'shall be delivered up' their oaths are unanimous."[13]

Some scholars are questioning the traditional views of Lincoln as the "Great Emancipator." In his 2002 book, *The Real Lincoln*, author Thomas J. DiLorenzo maintains that Lincoln rarely even spoke about slavery prior to 1854.[14] In his twenty-three years of trial work in Illinois, he never represented a fugitive slave, but did represent a slave owner trying to recover his slaves, in a case that Lincoln lost.[15] Lincoln said in his eulogy to Henry Clay, "[Clay] did not perceive, as I think no wise man has perceived, how [slavery] could be at once eradicated, without producing a greater evil, even to the cause of human liberty itself,"[16] and called the elimination of all African Americans from the United States "a glorious consummation."[17]

With Lincoln's clear challenge to the right of a state to leave the Union, most in the South interpreted the speech to mean that war was unavoidable. The *Richmond Dispatch* said of Lincoln's address, "it inaugurates civil war."[18]

In February of 1861, representatives from the seven states that had seceded met in Montgomery, Alabama, and formed the Confederate States of America. They elected Jefferson Davis of Mississippi as their president, and went about the arduous task of creating a brand-new government. The Confederate Constitution was modeled after that of the United States, except that it stressed individual states' rights. The Confederate Constitution did allow for slavery but had a prohibition on slave trade. All across the Confederacy, Federal property was seized. By April, only two major United States fortifications had not been seized by Confederate forces: Fort Sumter in the harbor of Charleston, South Carolina, and Fort Pickens at Pensacola, Florida.

Lincoln received a report from the Union commander at Fort Sumter, Major Robert Anderson, that he had to be resupplied within six weeks, or he would be forced to abandon the fort. Lincoln now was in a position to determine whether war would occur. He knew that if he sent his navy to resupply Fort Sumter, Confederate forces would fire on them. Lincoln ordered that supplies be sent. He did inform the governor of South Carolina that the naval resupply effort was going to be made, and he made a promise that no additional "men, arms or ammunition" would be brought in, if the

Confederates would allow the United States Navy to reach Fort Sumter. The governor notified Davis of the Lincoln communication. The Confederate government issued orders that Confederate General Pierre Gustave Toutant Beauregard demand the fort's surrender. Anderson refused to surrender. At 4:30 A.M. on April 12, 1861, Confederate guns opened fire on Fort Sumter. The naval resupply effort failed, and two days later Anderson surrendered the fort.

Lincoln immediately responded by asking for 75,000 troops to put down the "insurrection." This move caused the remaining four Southern states to leave the Union. The War Between the States was now a reality. Maryland was a deeply divided state. Lincoln could not afford to lose the state of Maryland, which would in effect endanger the capital city of Washington, D.C. One of the earliest episodes of bloodshed occurred in Maryland just days after the firing on Fort Sumter. In Baltimore a group of sympathizers to the Confederacy attacked Massachusetts troops, the Sixth Massachusetts Regiment, as they moved between railway stations. Lincoln reacted forcibly. He suspended the writ of habeas corpus, which allowed him to jail pro-Confederate supporters and hold them indefinitely without the right of indictment or trial by jury.

One such Confederate supporter who was arrested, John Merryman, actually had the Chief Justice of the Supreme Court, Roger Taney, who had administered the oath of office to Lincoln, issue a writ of habeas corpus ordering that Merryman either be tried or released. Lincoln refused to obey the Supreme Court order. After the war, the Supreme Court found that Lincoln was incorrect and that a president does not have the right to suspend the writ of habeas corpus without Congressional approval. During the war it has been estimated that as many as 14,000 dissidents were jailed without the benefit of a trial.

Lincoln further secured Maryland for the Union through brute military force. As soon as he had Washington, D.C., militarily secured, Lincoln ordered troops to Baltimore. Baltimore remained an occupied city for the rest of the war and was perhaps the most heavily fortified city in the country, next to Washington, D.C.[19] In the governor's election in 1861, Lincoln had pro-Confederate politicians arrested in an effort to ensure that a pro-Union candidate would be elected. Maryland remained in the Union.

Following the first major battle of the war, a Confederate victory at the First Battle of Manassas Junction (Bull Run) on July 21, 1861, the United States Congress passed, almost unanimously, a resolution that declared the intention of the war. The joint Senate and House resolution declared that "this war is not waged . . . for the purpose of conquest or subjugation, nor purpose of overthrowing . . . established institutions . . . but to defend . . . the Constitution and to preserve the Union.[20] By "established institutions" Congress clearly was referring to the institution of slavery. Just where did slavery fit in with Northern war aims?

Also following the battle several Republican leaders, including Lincoln's vice president, Hannibal Hamlin, met with the president to urge that the aim of the war be changed from one of preserving the Union to one of freeing the slaves. The Republicans felt that to not take the antislavery approach was going against the very basic ideology of the Republican Party. They also suggested that if Lincoln made the move to free the slaves in the South it would create pandemonium in the region, and the possible immediate collapse of the Confederacy. Lincoln refused to grant their requests. He felt that their ideas were not in the mainstream of the general public's opinions.[21]

In the summer of 1861, the United States Congress did pass the first Confiscation Act. This act stated that a slave owner would lose his or her slaves if those slaves were used to assist the Confederate military. Such confiscation would be subject to a judicial determination.

In August of 1861, Lincoln had yet another slavery issue to deal with. His Union army commander in the west, John C. Fremont, proclaimed martial law in Missouri and proclaimed that any slaves of people who aided the Confederate war effort would be freed. Fremont had done this unilaterally without consulting the Lincoln administration. Lincoln was most upset at Fremont's actions, which also allowed for the shooting of armed captured civilians. Lincoln rebuked Fremont, reminding him that his freeing of the slaves proclamation would "alarm our Southern Union friends, and turn them against us." Lincoln also pointed out that Fremont's proclamation would violate the terms of the Confiscation Act. Lincoln's rejection of Fremont's proclamation was widely criticized in the North, including several influential newspapers of the day.[22]

The United States Congress did move, in March of 1862, to end the Fugitive Slave Law. Prior to the elimination of this law some Union field commanders allowed the slave owners to search Union army camps for runaway slaves. One Federal commander who did not was General Benjamin F. Butler from Massachusetts. Butler, a staunch antislavery man, refused to send any runaway slaves that made it to his camps back to the slave owners. Lincoln concurred that runaway slaves should not be returned.[23]

As David Herbert Donald points out in his Pulitzer Prize-winning book *Lincoln*, Lincoln constantly struggled with what to do with the African Americans if they were freed. According to Donald this issue goes all the way back to Lincoln's Illinois days. As early as 1852, Lincoln made speeches favoring colonization of the African American. Lincoln appointed his brother-in-law to look into the idea of a colony for runaway slaves somewhere in the Caribbean or Central America.

What started as a plan to look at colonization, slowly evolved into an emancipation program, one that preceded what we now know as the Emancipation Proclamation. Lincoln first began to look at a plan whereby slaves would be freed in the border states. That plan evolved into a message from Lincoln to the Congress, on March 6, 1862, where Lincoln proposed that any state could voluntarily adopt a program of gradual emancipation of slaves along with a payment by the Federal government to be used by the states as compensation for the freeing of the slaves.

Although the plan received some popular support it seemed that it was too "middle of the road." The border state representatives were not enthralled with the idea, and many felt that it was unconstitutional. For the hard-line abolitionists, it certainly didn't go far enough; it was a voluntary plan, and a state did not have to participate if it did not want to. The resulting legislation did not resemble Lincoln's original proposal. All that was passed was a bill that provided for compensation of the slaves in the District of Columbia. Yes, up until 1862 slavery was allowed in the nation's capital.

The District of Columbia bill, which was approved on April 16, 1862, did have some of the features in Lincoln's national plan. The bill provided for the payment of three hundred dollars per slave eman-

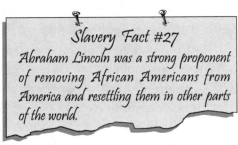

Slavery Fact #27

Abraham Lincoln was a strong proponent of removing African Americans from America and resettling them in other parts of the world.

cipated to the slave owner loyal to the Union. The bill set prison terms for anyone convicted of taking an emancipated slave outside the District of Columbia with the intention of re-enslaving them. The United States government paid nearly one million dollars to free about thirty-one hundred slaves. It also provided for up to a total of $100,000 for the effort of colonization for those freed slaves that wanted to look at the possibility of leaving the country, specifically for Haiti or Liberia.[24]

It is interesting to note that Lincoln made a much earlier effort to free the slaves in the District of Columbia, as a young member of the House of Representatives in 1849. He introduced a bill that would have provided for the gradual emancipation of slaves in the district. The legislation, had it passed, would have allowed slave owners the option to free their slaves and then to be compensated by the Federal government. Children born after January 1, 1850, would have been eventually freed after serving as an apprentice to the slave owner. The bill would also have required that the voters of Washington, D.C., approve the plan. No action was ever taken on Lincoln's controversial legislation.[25]

By the summer of 1862, the United States Congress passed a second Confiscation Act. This version of the act defined that those slave owners in the South fighting against the United States were traitors and allowed for the confiscation of their property including their slaves, thus allowing the slaves to be freed. Initially, Lincoln vetoed the bill, feeling that Congress had gone too far. After some revisions were made to the bill, Lincoln did sign the legislation, but took the unusual step of issuing a statement of objections to the bill that he had just signed. The Confiscation Acts are sometimes known as the Contraband Laws, and frequent period references will be made to freed slaves as "contraband."

Lincoln was still not done with the idea of colonization of African Americans outside the United States. In August of 1862, he met with a group of African American leaders. He solicited their support for colonization. He told them, "We have between us a broader difference than exists between almost any two races. It is better for both, therefore, to be separated."[26] Lincoln's request for their support fell on "deaf ears."

Perhaps the best summary of Lincoln's position on slavery vis-à-vis the War Between the States comes in August of 1862 from a public statement that Lincoln made in the *New York Tribune*. Lincoln was responding to an earlier editorial by Horace Greeley. In the editorial Greeley was criticizing Lincoln for not proclaiming the freeing of the slaves. Lincoln responded to Greeley: "My paramount objective in this struggle is to save the Union, and is not either to save or to destroy slavery. If I could save the Union without freeing any slave I would do it, and if I could save it by freeing all the slaves I would do it; and if I could save it by freeing some and leaving others alone I would also do that. What I do about slavery and the colored race, I do because I believe it helps to save the Union; and what I forbear, I forbear because I do not believe it would help to save the Union."[27]

Lincoln was not the only one that looked for a way to separate African Americans from the white population. In January of 1863, Senator James Henry Lane, an antislavery advocate, introduced a bill in the United States Congress that called "to set apart a portion

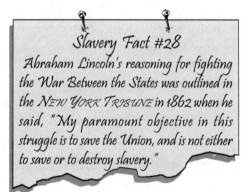

Slavery Fact #28
Abraham Lincoln's reasoning for fighting the War Between the States was outlined in the NEW YORK TRIBUNE in 1862 when he said, "My paramount objective in this struggle is to save the Union, and is not either to save or to destroy slavery."

of the state of Texas for use of persons of African descent." The bill would have split Texas in half, with the southwestern half to be an all-African American territory called The Territory of the Rio Grande. The bill's purpose was to provide a separate home for the "four million of blacks to be thrown upon us for protection and direction." The bill never made it for a vote, dying when the Senate postponed consideration of the legislation.[28]

The Emancipation Proclamation

When Lincoln wrote the *New York Tribune* response he already had a draft version of the Emancipation Proclamation. Lincoln's *Tribune* public pronouncement was likely some political jockeying. He wanted to assure the Northern general public, and in particular those in the slave border states, that he was still fighting a war to preserve the Union. There was, however, a strong message for the slave owners in the Confederacy, as if he were saying, "I will do what is necessary to save the Union, including the freeing of your slaves."

By the summer of 1862, Lincoln had decided that the time had come to issue the Emancipation Proclamation. There were several factors that were incentives for him to do so. First, many in Lincoln's own party were strongly in favor of it. He would receive intense lobbying efforts from his fellow Republicans. The Republicans in Congress had many fervent advocates of the abolishment of slavery, including Charles Sumner and Benjamin Wade in the Senate and Thaddeus Stevens in the House.

Another reason for the proclamation was the concern that Lincoln had over the possible recognition and/or support of the Confederacy by European powers. The Europeans, who perhaps saw greater self-interest in the South over the North, might support the Confederacy, since the war was one over preserving the Union and not one to end slavery.[29] By freeing the slaves Lincoln would certainly gain the moral advantage and make it all the more difficult for Europeans to enter the war to help "save slavery."

The Emancipation Proclamation also had the potential to disrupt the agricultural production in the South. If the proclamation caused Southern slaves to leave their slave owners then the vast agricultural production of the South could be harmed and thus its ability to feed and equip its soldiers.

In the summer of 1862, Lincoln was ready to issue the Emancipation Proclamation, although the timing was not good from his perspective. At the suggestion of his secretary of state, William H. Seward, Lincoln delayed the issuance of the proclamation for political reasons. Seward recommended that the proclamation not be issued until after a Union victory in battle. The issuance of the proclamation, on the heels of several Confederate battlefield victories, would make it appear to be a move of desperation.

Confederate General Robert E. Lee's Army of Northern Virginia, in September of 1862, moved north into the border state of Maryland. At a small stream called Antietam Creek near Sharpsburg, on September 17, Lee encountered Union forces commanded by General George B. McClellan. Lee was outnumbered and although tactically the battle was a draw, Lee did withdraw back into Virginia. It was considered a Northern victory, and Lincoln finally had his opportunity. Five days after the battle, on September 22, 1862, Lincoln issued a preliminary version of the Emancipation Proclamation.[30]

Lincoln issued his preliminary proclamation under his war powers authority as president, a rather dubious claim. The proclamation called for the freeing of all slaves if Southerners did not end the armed conflict and the states return to the Union by the end of 1862. Lincoln however did promise to continue to work for compensation to slave owners and for colonization of African Americans outside the United States.[31]

The initial reaction to the proclamation was mixed. In the North, the abolitionists were obviously pleased, and in the South the response was overwhelmingly negative. In November, the governor of South Carolina, Francis W. Pickens, stated that "the infamous proclamation" would "produce none of the effects intended by its vulgar author."[32] The mayor of Savannah, Georgia, called it "a direct bid for insurrection," and an "infamous attempt to incite flight, murder, and rapine on the part of our slave population."[33]

As January 1, 1863, rolled around, Lincoln's proclamation had failed to produce the return of any Southern state. Lincoln held a

New Year's Day reception at the White House. Around noon he retired to his office where he signed the Emancipation Proclamation. Lincoln said that signing the proclamation was the right thing to do, "I never, in my life, felt more certain that I was doing right, than I do in signing this paper."[34]

The Emancipation Proclamation declared, "that all persons held as slaves within said designated States, and parts of States, are, and henceforward shall be free; and that the Executive government of the United States, including the military and naval authorities thereof, will recognize and maintain the freedom of said persons." The specific areas were, "Arkansas, Texas, Louisiana, (except the Parishes of St. Bernard, Plaquemines, Jefferson, St. John, St. Charles, St. James Ascension, Assumption, Terrebonne, Lafourche, St. Mary, St. Martin, and Orleans, including the City of New Orleans) Mississippi, Alabama, Florida, Georgia, South Carolina, North Carolina, and Virginia, (except the forty-eight counties designated as West Virginia, and also the counties of Berkley, Accomac, Northampton, Elizabeth City, York, Princess Ann, and Norfolk, including the cities of Norfolk and Portsmout)." Interestingly enough specifically excluded was the Confederate state of Tennessee and all the border states.[35]

In effect the Emancipation Proclamation, as of its effective date, freed only a small number of slaves. One historian wrote of the effectiveness of the proclamation, "Lincoln issued his proclamation and nothing happened in the immediate or prompt freeing of slaves."[36] Secretary Seward saw the incongruity of the effect of the proclamation when he said, "We show our sympathy with slavery by emancipating slaves where we cannot reach them and holding them in bondage where we can set them free."[37] It did cause some fear in the South, fear of a slave revolt at worse, or they feared the massive flight of slaves from their owners. South Carolina Governor Pickens ordered, "to protect ourselves from any effort instigated by the deluded or ignorant I would urge the immediate organization of a large State Police Guard under the direct command of the Governor, to be ordered out at such times and in such Districts as he may think proper, to be kept at least for some months in actual daily duty to give a feeling of safety to the helpless."[38]

The fear, for the most part, was unwarranted. In actuality, as of January 1, 1863, the Emancipation Proclamation only freed some slaves in far northern Virginia, parts of coastal North Carolina, a sliver of northern Mississippi and Alabama, a small area of coastal Florida, the far northern portion of Arkansas, and the Sea Islands of Georgia and South Carolina, perhaps as many as 20,000 slaves.[39] The vast majority of slaves remained where they were in bondage. Emancipation came very slowly for the slaves. Even Lincoln, near the end of the war in February of 1865, said that only two hundred thousand slaves had been freed.[40] Only until invading Union troops were close at hand, was there any exodus of slaves, and even then most slaves remained loyal to their slave owners.

The Emancipation Proclamation also allowed for military service for the freed slaves. The proclamation said, ". . . further declare and make known, that such persons of suitable condition, will be received into the armed service of the United States to garrison forts, positions, stations, and other places, and to man vessels of all sorts in said service."[41]

One response to the proclamation was from Frederick Douglass. Speaking to a church audience in Rochester, New York, only three days before the proclamation went into effect, Douglass said, "Among the first questions that tried the strength of my childhood mind—was first why are colored people slaves, and the next was will

> *Slavery Fact #29*
> The Emancipation Proclamation when issued on January 1, 1863, freed virtually no slaves, and the slaves that could have been freed in the border states were specifically excluded from being freed.

their slavery last forever. From that day onward, the cry that has reached the most silent chambers of my soul, by day and by night has been How long! How long oh! Eternal Power of the Universe, how long shall these things be. This inquiry is to be answered on the first of January 1863."[42] From Douglass's perspective the Emancipation Proclamation changed the perspective of the war. In the same speech Douglass said, "That this war is to abolish slavery I have no manner of doubt. The process may be long and tedious but that that result must at last be reached is among the undoubted certainties of the future!"[43]

Confederate President Davis, in a speech before the Confederate Congress, said of the Emancipation Proclamation: "The people of this Confederacy, then, cannot fail to receive this proclamation as the fullest vindication of their own sagacity in foreseeing the uses to which the dominant party in the United States intended from the beginning to apply their power, nor can they cease to remember with devout thankfulness that it is to their own vigilance in resisting the first stealthy progress of approaching despotism that they owe their escape from consequences now apparent to the most skeptical. This proclamation will have another salutary effect in calming the fears of those who have constantly evinced the apprehension that this war might end by some reconstruction of the old Union or some renewal of close political relations with the United States."[44]

Draft and Race Riots

In an effort to satisfy its manpower needs for the Union army, the United States Congress in January of 1863 passed the Draft Act of 1863, also known as the Conscription Act. The law applied to all males between the ages of twenty and thirty-five and to all unmarried males between thirty-five and forty-five and required them to register with a Provost Marshal's Bureau in the War Department, so that they would be eligible for forced conscription into the military. There were some loopholes in the law, whereby one could legally evade the draft by one of two ways. The draftee could either find a substitute to replace him, or he could pay three hundred dollars to have his name removed from the current draft, although he might be called again in any subsequent draft.[45]

The right to buy your way out of the draft produced a firestorm of controversy. Many in the North labeled the draft "a rich man's war and a poor man's fight," and the loopholes were repealed in July of 1864. Prior to its repeal, draft riots broke out across the North, from Boston to Milwaukee, protesting the draft, the war, and then turning and taking a very ugly racial turn. The worst riot, usually referred to by historians as only a "draft" riot, omitting the racial aspects of it, was in New York City in the summer of 1863.

In New York City on Saturday, July 11, draft officials drew the first batch of draftee names. After mulling over the prospect of being drafted, men had time for the emotions to fester over the remainder of the weekend. By Monday, July 13, hundreds of angry draft aged men attacked the offices where the draft was being conducted. It was the start of violence which reigned in New York City until July 17. Total mob violence ruled. Symbols of the Federal government were attacked, prominent abolitionists and Republicans had their homes ransacked, and African Americans were a main target. According to one eyewitness the mob was after "three objects—the badge of a defender of the law, the uniform of the Union army, the skin of a helpless and outraged race."[46] Martha Perry, who observed what was happening from her Lexington Avenue home, wrote, "Men, both colored and white, were murdered within two blocks of us, some being hung to the nearest lamppost, and others shot. An army officer was walking in the street near our house, when a rioter was seen to kneel on the sidewalk, take aim, fire, and kill him."[47]

To be an African American on the streets of New York City during the mob violence was as close as you could get to a death sentence. As one observer put it, "the African race in this city were literally hunted down like wild beasts."[48] Many were beaten, at least six African Americans were lynched, and many of their homes were looted or destroyed. Unimaginable brutality was inflicted on some of the city's African Americans. Various attacks on African Americans occurred, such as, "A child of 3 years of age was thrown from a 4th story window and instantly killed. A woman one hour after her confinement was set upon and beaten with her tender babe in her arms. . . . Children were torn from their mother's embrace and their brains blown out in the very face of the afflicted mother. Men were burnt by slow fires."[49] The rioters even sacked and burned to the ground the Colored Orphan Asylum, which housed nearly eight hundred African American children.

At one time the rioters virtually had control of the city. The draft and race riot was not ended until Union troops, fresh from the Battle of Gettysburg, arrived to end it, but not before combat between the rioters and the army regulars raged on the streets of New York. Union troops fired point blank into the mob. Casualty estimates ran as low as several hundred to over one thousand. One historian wondered, how could the North, a society in which racial hatred ran so deep, secure justice for the emancipated slaves?[50]

African Americans in the Union Army

African Americans, both free and former slave, proudly served in the Union war effort, although originally it was a struggle for them to even be accepted into the military service. The National Archives has about 185,000 compiled military service records of men who served in what was known as the United States Colored Troops.[51] That number does include their white officers, as African Americans were not allowed to serve as combat officers. Of that number, it has been estimated that two-thirds came from the South, predominately slaves, but some free African Americans as well.[52]

When the war began, free African Americans in the North quickly wanted to offer their services to the Union military, but their effort to volunteer went unheeded. After the Confederates captured Fort Sumter, a free African American employee in the United States Senate, Jacob Dodson, wrote the War Department. He offered his services in defense of Washington, D.C., and said he knew three hundred more African Americans who would sign up with him for military service. He received a rather terse reply from Lincoln's secretary of war. Simon Cameron wrote, "This Department has no intention at present to call into the service of the Government any colored soldiers."[53]

In spite of honorable service during the Revolutionary War and the War of 1812, African Americans were not seemingly welcomed in the United States Army. When the War Between the States opened no African Americans were in the army, in fact the regular army had never enlisted an African American soldier. Since 1792, even the state militias had barred African Americans.[54]

Lincoln had pronounced that the war was not a war to end slavery, but a war to preserve the Union. Lincoln feared that he might lose key border states, such as Missouri and Kentucky, both slave states, if he pursued a war to abolish slavery. So Lincoln, for political reasons, initially would not allow African American enlistments.

It is interesting to note that the United States Navy did not have the same limited vision as the army. The navy had accepted African Americans nearly from the start. Secretary of the Navy Gideon Welles wrote in September of 1861, "The Department finds it necessary to adopt a regulation with respect to the large number of persons of color, commonly known as contrabands, now subsisted at the navy yard and on board ships of war." Rather than sending them away, Welles logically reasoned, "nor can they be maintained unemployed, and it is not proper that they should be compelled to render necessary and regular services without a standard compensation. You are therefore authorized, when their service can be made useful, to enlist them for the naval service, under the same forms and regulations as apply to other enlistments. They will be allowed, however, no higher rating than 'boys,' at a compensation of $10 per month and one ration per day."[55] The African American sailors were typically restricted to lesser roles, such as stewards, cooks, firemen, and coal shovelers, and they were paid less wages, but they were accepted as sailors.[56] During the war some did assume more combat type positions, but these were isolated situations.

The earliest effort to recruit African American soldiers into the Union army was in Union-occupied territory, along the coastal areas of South Carolina and Georgia. Union forces, in late 1861, had captured a number of the islands off the coast of South Carolina, Georgia, and northern Florida. In March of 1862, Union General David Hunter was assigned command of the Union forces in the occupied area. In assessing his new command situation, he realized the immediate need to hold the captured territory, but felt that he lacked sufficient manpower to do so. Hunter, who was an abolitionist, saw a natural way to solve his manpower shortage. On April 13, 1862, Hunter declared that all the slaves on the islands were "confiscated and declared free." He then began to promptly "recruit" slaves, although some were forced into joining. By May 4, he had gone even further, declaring that all slaves in the states of South Carolina, Georgia, and Florida were free.[57]

In June, when Lincoln learned of Hunter's actions, he sharply rebuked Hunter. Lincoln said, "Neither General Hunter nor any other commander or person has been authorized by the Government of the United States to make proclamations declaring the slaves of any State free." Lincoln later refused to authorize pay for the African American soldiers and Hunter disbanded the unit. That only delayed the inevitable as a new African American unit was formed in November of 1862 and even saw action along the coast. This group would eventually become the Thirty-third United States Colored Infantry.[58]

The earliest formal formation of African American regiments occurred in Union-captured territory in the South and in Kansas. At about the same time, in the fall of 1862, African American units were being formed in New Orleans and in Kansas. New Orleans, a key port for the Confederacy, fell to Union control, early on in the war, after a United States naval fleet captured the city in April of 1862. Once Union troops were firmly in command of the city, free African Americans quickly volunteered for Union military service. What was initially called the First, Second, and Third Louisiana Native Guard was formed, mainly made up of free African Americans. Five days after Lincoln issued the Emancipation Proclamation, the Union commander in New Orleans, General Benjamin Butler, formally mustered the First Louisiana Native Guard into the Union army, on September 27, 1862.[59] This made the unit the first African American unit formally accepted into the Union army. The three regiments were known as the First, Second, and Third Infantry, Corps d'Afrique, but these units would ultimately become the Seventy-third, Seventy-fourth, and Seventy-fifth United States Colored Infantry.[60]

Even though the First Kansas Colored Infantry was not formally mustered into service until January 1863, the regiment had already seen action at Island Mound, Missouri, on October 27, 1862.[61] Kansas Senator James H. Lane, who gave up his Senate seat, recruited and organized this regiment of African Americans in Leavenworth, Kansas. Many members of the regiment were escaped slaves. The unit would eventually become the Seventy-ninth United States Colored Infantry and has the distinction of being the first formal Northern African American regiment to be accepted into the Union army.[62]

There was support in the United States Congress for enlisting African Americans into the Union army. Two bills that went into law on the same day are evidence of that. The Second Confiscation Act, passed in the summer of 1862, authorized the president "to employ as many persons of African descent as he may deem necessary and proper for the suppression of this rebellion," as well as to "organize and use them in such manner as he may judge best for the public welfare."[63] The other bill was the Militia Act of 1862 which authorized the employment of African Americans as soldiers. The bill also allowed for the emancipation of each African American soldier and their families, providing that their slave owners were supporting the Confederacy. The bill however authorized pay at a lesser rate than what was paid for white soldiers.[64] The Congress had squarely put the burden of African American service into the lap of Lincoln. Lincoln moved cautiously, still fearing the political results of such action in the border states.

The issuance of the Emancipation Proclamation caused a new wave of interest in African American military recruitment. The proclamation formally called for the enlistment of freed slaves, although Lincoln's continued reluctance to use African American troops is perhaps uncovered in the official wording, "such persons of suitable condition will be received into the armed service of the United States to garrison forts, positions, stations, and other places and to man vessels of all sorts in said service."[65] Nevertheless, with the Emancipation Proclamation, the Union army began to make plans for forming regiments of African American soldiers, although many skeptics in the army questioned whether African Americans would make good combat soldiers. The earliest men recruited for the African American troops ironically were not African Americans. The War Department ruled from the onset that the African American units would be in segregated units and would have to have white officers. The War Department went about the task of selecting white men to lead the African Americans soldiers.[66]

Massachusetts Governor John Andrew was one of the first to actively support the enlistment of African Americans for military service. In the fall of 1861, Andrew stated, "It is not my opinion that our generals, when any man comes to the standard and desires to defend the flag will find it important to light a candle, and see what his complexion is, or to consult the family Bible to ascertain whether his grandfather came from the banks of the Thames or the banks of the Senegal."[67]

After the Emancipation Proclamation was issued, Andrew, who was a fervent abolitionist, began to raise an African American brigade. Massachusetts did not have the African American population to support a brigade, so he sent recruiters thoughout the North to recruit African American men. Eventually, they were able to raise two regiments, the Fifty-fourth and the Fifty-fifth Massachusetts Volunteer Infantry Regiments.

The War Department, on May 22, 1863, created a bureau to oversee the African American units, the Bureau of Colored Troops. The chief of the bureau was Major Charles W. Foster who was given the title of Assistant Adjutant General.[68] On the day before the first day of fighting at the Battle of Gettysburg, June 30, 1863, the first African American regiment under the new bureau, the First U.S. Colored Troops, were mustered into the Union army in Washington, D.C.

Most of the African American troops raised to this point had gone under various state names, like the Fifty-fourth Massachusetts, or some in the western theater of the war as Corps d'Afrique. They attempted to standardize the names of the African American units, naming them all "The United States Colored Troops," although some state regiments, like the Fifth-fourth Massachusetts, continued to use their original names.[69]

Although most of the African American troops were initially raised in the Northern states, eventually the bulk of the men came from the South, many of them former slaves. Lincoln actively encouraged his military commanders in the South to recruit former slaves. In 1863, Lincoln sent his adjutant general, Lorenzo Thomas, south to recruit African American men. Lincoln said of the potential African American soldiers, "the colored the great available and yet unavailed of, force for restoring the Union."[70] By the end of the year Thomas had recruited twenty regiments, almost all of them former slaves.[71]

Nearly two-thirds of all the men in the United States Colored Troops were from the South. Men from the states of Louisiana, Kentucky, and Tennessee contributed over one-third of all the enlistments.

African American troops (Company E., 4th United States Colored)

The Northern state with the largest number of enlistments was Pennsylvania with almost twice as many as the next highest state, Ohio. Texas had the fewest of any state or territory with only forty-seven enlistments. Table 9.2 lists the number of men by state, from the free states, and what percent each state made up of all the United States Colored Troops. Table 9.3 shows the same information for enlistments from the slave states.

Table 9.2—United States Colored Troops Enlistments from Free States Sorted by Number of Enlistments.

Free State	Enlistments	% of Total
Pennsylvania	8,612	4.63%
Ohio	5,092	2.74%
New York	4,125	2.22%
Massachusetts	3,966	2.13%
District of Columbia	3,269	1.76%
Kansas	2,080	1.12%
Rhode Island	1,837	0.99%
Illinois	1,811	0.97%
Connecticut	1,764	0.95%
Indiana	1,537	0.83%
Michigan	1,387	0.75%
New Jersey	1,185	0.64%
Iowa	440	0.24%
West Virginia	196	0.11%
Wisconsin	165	0.09%

Free State	Enlistments	% of Total
New Hampshire	125	0.07%
Vermont	120	0.06%
Minnesota	104	0.06%
Maine	104	0.06%
Colorado Territory	95	0.05%
Unknown	5,896	3.17%
Officers	7,122	3.83%
Total	51,032	27.42%

Table 9.3—United States Colored Troops Enlistments from Slave States Sorted by Number of Enlistments.

Slave State	Enlistments	% of Total
Louisiana	24,052	12.92%
Kentucky	23,703	12.74%
Tennessee	20,133	10.82%
Mississippi	17,869	9.60%
Maryland	8,718	4.68%
Missouri	8,344	4.48%
Virginia	5,723	3.08%
Arkansas	5,526	2.97%
South Carolina	5,462	2.94%
North Carolina	5,035	2.71%
Alabama	4,969	2.67%
Georgia	3,486	1.87%
Florida	1,044	0.56%
Delaware	954	0.51%
Texas	47	0.03%
Total	135,065	72.58%

In his excellent book, *Eagles on Their Buttons: A Black Infantry Regiment in the Civil War*, which is an account of the Fifth United States Colored Troops Regiment from Ohio, the author, Versalle F. Washington, looked at the makeup of that regiment. He found that the men ranged in age from fifteen to fifty-five years old. The average was a little over age twenty-four. He found that the height of the men ranged from four foot ten inches to six foot four inches with the average being about five foot seven inches. Most of the men that joined the Fifth were farmers, 53 percent, with the category of laborer the next most common at 22 percent, followed by barbers at 4 percent, and blacksmiths at 3 percent.[72]

How well were the African American soldiers received in the Union army? One must examine that question in the framework of the times. Most Northerners, even the staunch abolitionists, did not believe in the equality of the African American and the white person. For the African Americans to serve in integrated units was never seriously considered. To allow African American officers to lead men of their own race was unthinkable. Many questioned if they could even serve in combat situations. One Union colonel wrote of the African Americans in the Union blue uniform, "makes a good enough soldier for garrison and guard duty but for Field service a Hundred (white) men is worth a thousand of them."[73] Such was a common sentiment. A Union sergeant writing from the front lines in Virginia said that he did not want to fight side by side with them, suggesting rather that the African American soldiers "be sent here to use the pick and shovel in the broiling sun as we are doing now, and we will take a soldier's tool—the gun and Bayonet."[74]

Some white Union soldiers felt that the African American troops were given special treatment. One wrote, "Some of the Boys say that the Army Motto is First the Negro, then the mule, then the white man."[75] A sergeant from Minnesota complained about the special treatment received by an African American aide on the headquarters staff. He wrote, "Their has been moore sympathy lavished on him than I ever saw on 20 white men. I guess the day is not distant when a white man will be as good as a Nigar."[76]

If would take the actions of the African Americans in combat to overcome some of the racial stereotyping and prejudice by white Union soldiers. Many African Americans, in combat situations, were equal to the task and performed well under fire. Examples of such are listed later in this chapter. Even the Union colonel, who had pigeon-holed African Americans for only noncombat roles such as garrison and guard duty, changed his opinion. He wrote in 1864, after observing United States Colored Troops under fire, "In this great war even the nigger has justified himself . . . while in the field he has proven himself a man."[77] In addition to their becoming "brothers in combat" to their white counterparts, the fact that by the later part of the war they were also becoming a common sight in the Union army helped break down at least some of the barriers of white soldier acceptance.

The first African American recruits were enlisted with the understanding that they would be paid the same rate of pay as white Union soldiers. The War Department in June of 1863 changed its policy. The normal rate for a white Union enlisted man was $13.00 per month for privates and $21.00 per month for sergeants. The rate for African American enlisted men was only $10.00 per month of which $3.00 per month was a clothing allowance. The reduced rate was the same rate that the Union army paid to day laborers.[78]

Many African American units refused to be treated in that manner. Members of the Fifty-fourth Massachusetts refused to accept their reduced pay. Several African Americans were charged with insubordination and at least one African American, Sergeant William Walker, was executed when he refused to work for less than what he had been promised. It took a public campaign to correct the inequity, and then only partially so. Realizing the increasingly important role that the African American soldier was playing in the Union army, the War Department in June of 1864 finally acted. They allowed for equal pay and back pay for African American soldiers, provided, however, that they had been free on April 19, 1861. The soldiers had to swear an oath that they were free in 1861 and had to be able to substantiate their claim. For the bulk of African American soldiers this would not apply, since most had been slaves in 1861. It was not until March of 1865, the year the war ended, that equal pay was granted to the former slaves who were Union soldiers.[79] In fact most of the former slave soldiers would not actually receive their back pay until after the war was over.[80]

The issue of African Americans not being allowed to serve as combat officers did not cause quite the fury that the pay issue did. The War Department decided early on that African American regiments would only have white officers. In fact they may well have had, proportionally, better officers than the white regiments did. The War Department did not want their African American "experiment" to fail, so they attempted to find the very best white officers.

An examining board was established to help determine the officers. Applicants to serve as officers for the United States Colored Troops were required to furnish a letter of recommendation from their commanding officer if they were existing military and if civilian a letter from a prominent citizen. They would then be subjected to a verbal examination which tested the applicants on such diverse topics as military tactics, mathematics, history, and geography.[81]

The majority of the white officers that commanded African American troops were good men and good soldiers, but not all of them. The Fourth Louisiana Native Guard, unlike the other New Orleans units that were primarily made up of free African Americans, was made up primarily of former slaves. The Fourth, later re-designated the Seventy-Sixth United States Colored Troops, was a very undisciplined unit. The Union army command felt in order to instill stronger discipline they needed to appoint a new and stronger commander. Lieutenant Colonel Augustus Benedict, of New York, was given the task of remolding the regiment into a disciplined unit. Benedict was a tough disciplinarian and ended up whipping two men in the unit, whom Benedict had accused of lying. The use of a rawhide whip on former slaves did not sit well with the other men in the Fourth. Soon Benedict was facing an angry regiment of men and was nearly executed by his own solders. Calm finally prevailed and Benedict was eventually dishonorably discharged for his actions.[82]

Just before the War Between the States was over, African Americans were allowed to serve as noncombat commissioned officers. African American physicians and chaplains were appointed as commissioned officers. The very first African American Union officer was Martin R. Delany. Delany was a Virginian, born in 1812, to a free African American mother and slave father. He attended Harvard, where he studied medicine, and was active with Frederick Douglass in abolitionists' activities.

Delany began to embrace African American colonization in the 1850s and became the leading African American supporter of the effort. In his 1852 book, *The Condition, Elevation, Emigration, and Destiny of the Colored People of the United States, Politically Considered*, Delany explains why his race should relocate, "Every people should be the originators of their own designs, the projector of their own schemes, and creators of the events that lead to their destiny—the consummation of their desires."[83]

A few months before the war ended in 1865, Delany was commissioned as an army surgeon with the One Hundred and Tenth United States Colored Troops, with the rank of major.[84] He was the highest ranking African American officer during the war. A total of about one hundred African American men were officers by the end of the war.[85]

African Americans units fought in approximately forty major battles and over four hundred skirmishes during the War Between the States. They played important roles in fighting at Port Hudson, Millikens Bend, Fort Wagner, Brice's Crossroads, Nashville, and at Petersburg. The concern that many Union military authorities had, that African Americans would not make good soldiers, was, for the most part, proven wrong. They suffered over three thousand battle deaths and approximately thirty-three thousand more deaths due to disease.[86] Renowned War Between the States historian Bell I. Wiley in his book *The Life of Billy Yank*, notes that like white Union troops the African American troops had those in combat that were brave and bold, but there were also those men that retreated and ran under fire. His assessment is that the African American Union troops compared favorably to white troops with comparable background and training. He noted an edge in performance of those African American troops that were primarily recruited in the North versus those made up of recently freed or runaway slaves.[87]

Several of the African American regiments are well known in the annals of War Between the States history, such as the Fifty-fourth Massachusetts and the 1st South Carolina Volunteer Infantry Regiment. The Fifty-fourth Massachusetts perhaps had the greatest effect on the United States. What the Fifty-fourth accomplished helped change Northern perceptions about African American soldiers. The Fifty-fourth was a pet project of the Massachusetts governor. The governor appointed the unit's white commander, Robert Gould Shaw. He was the twenty-five-year-old son of a prominent abolitionist family. Other white officers were from prominent Massachusetts families, and two of Frederick Douglass's sons served in the unit.

After training in May and June of 1863, the Fifty-fourth Massachusetts was sent to South Carolina, near Charleston harbor. Charleston was still firmly in the hands of Confederate forces and was guarded by Confederate troops on barrier islands near the harbor. One of those islands was Morris Island, which contained an earthen Confederate fort called Fort Wagner. The Fifty-fourth Massachusetts was selected to lead an attack against the fort. There was only one route to reach the fort as the ocean was to one side and wetlands to the other side. To take the fort would require a frontal assault.

On July 18, 1863, the approximately 650 men of the Fifty-fourth Massachusetts launched the infantry attack. The Confederate forces were ready for them and unleashed round after round of vicious artillery and musket fire from the fort. The Fifty-fourth Massachusetts leading the advancing Union forces towards the fort received heavy casualties. Shaw was killed in the assault, shot through the heart, while leading his men. The men reached the fort's parapet, before being forced to withdraw, along with the other attacking Union forces. The Fifty-fourth Massachusetts suffered 50 percent either killed or wounded. The flag bearer of the Fifty-fourth Massachusetts, William H. Carney, in spite of several wounds, was able to drag himself to safety with the colors aloft. He was honored as the first black recipient of the Medal of Honor, although it took thirty-seven years for him to receive it. He was given the medal in May of 1900.[88]

Even though the attack failed, the efforts of the Fifty-fourth Massachusetts were well publicized in the Northern press. An *Atlantic Monthly* article perhaps best summed up the Northern public perception after the attack, "the manhood of the colored race shines before many eyes that would not see."[89] The very popular perception that an African American could not fight as a combat soldier had now become completely unraveled. After the exploits of the Fifty-fourth Massachusetts proved that African Americans could fight, the number of United States Colored Troops regiments increased from thirty in July of 1863 to sixty by the end of the year.[90]

The African American soldiers greatly assisted the Union victory over the Confederacy. What was the legacy of the African American Union soldier? Perhaps it was best summed up by a Medal of

Honor winner, Christian A. Fleetwood, sergeant major Fourth Colored United States Troops. In a speech given in Atlanta, Georgia, in 1895 he summed up their war record: "Never again while time lasts will the doubt arise as in 1861, 'Will the Negro fight?' As a problem it has been solved, as a question it has been answered, and as a fact it is as established as the eternal hills. It was they who rang up the curtain upon the last act of the bloody tragedy at Petersburg, Va., June 15, 1864, and they who rang it down at Clover Hill, Va., April 9, 1865. They were one of the strong fingers upon the mighty hand that grasped the giant's throat at Petersburg and never flexed until the breath went out at Appomattox. In this period it would take page on page to recount their deeds of valor and their glorious victories. . . ."[91]

One of the ironies occurred toward the end of the war as described by Major General H. W. Slocum in *Century Magazine*. Slocum said, "During our stay in Raleigh, I witnessed a scene which to me was one of the most impressive of the war. It was the review by General Sherman of a division of colored troops. These troops passed through the principal streets of the city. They were well drilled, dressed in new and handsome uniforms, and with their bright bayonets gleaming in the sun they made a splendid appearance. The sides of the streets were lined with residents of the city and surrounding country, many of them, I presume, the former owners of some of these soldiers."[92]

As the United States Colored Troops moved south, the former slaves in the unit had a popular song that they would march to. Sung to the lyrics of the *Battle Hymn of the Republic*, the former slaves changed the lyrics to:

> *We are done with hoeing cotton,*
> *We are done with hoeing corn.*
> *We are colored Yankee soldiers,*
> *   As sure as you are born.*
> *When Massa hears us shouting,*
> *He will think 'tis Gabriel's horn,*
> *   As we go marching on.*[93]

Service to the Union war effort was not limited to African American men. The females also played an overlooked role in the war effort. They served in a variety of different capacities, from domestic services to nursing care. Approximately twenty thousand females worked in Northern military hospitals during the war and about 11 percent of these women were African American.[94]

At least one African American female served with combat soldiers. Maria Lewis served with the Eighth New York Cavalry for eighteen months during the war. She wore a regular uniform and carried a carbine and a sword.[95]

Harriet Tubman, an African American Underground Railroad leader whom we discussed in chapter three, also earned distinction in her service to the Union army. At the request of the Federal government she journeyed to Union-occupied portions of South Carolina and worked with newly freed slaves. She also worked as a nurse and some claim that she served as a Union scout or spy.[96] She received no pay for her military services, but was awarded a commendation. Tubman later tried to claim a military pension based on her service, but her pension application was rejected.[97]

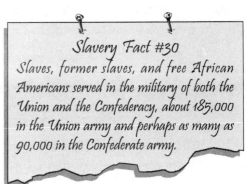

Slavery Fact #30

Slaves, former slaves, and free African Americans served in the military of both the Union and the Confederacy, about 185,000 in the Union army and perhaps as many as 90,000 in the Confederate army.

African Americans in the Confederate Army

The firing on Fort Sumter had just occurred; support throughout the South was strong. Rallies, parades, and enlistments were springing up throughout the new Confederate nation. There was pro-Confederate enthusiasm by African Americans from the start. After the firing on Fort Sumter, African Americans in Petersburg, Virginia, who had volunteered to work on fortifications in the Norfolk area, held a rally on the courthouse square. At the rally they were presented with one of the new Confederate flags by the former mayor, who promised them "a rich reward of praise, and merit, from a thankful people." In accepting the flag, one of the African American leaders said, "We are willing to aid Virginia's cause to the utmost of our ability . . . and we promise unhesitating obedience to all orders that may be given us."[98]

In New Orleans, the Southern spirit was also very strong. The Louisiana governor called on the state to raise eight thousand troops to defend the state from Northern invaders. Within hours of the governor's call ten prominent men in New Orleans called for a meeting at the Catholic Institute to discuss the need "to take arms and form themselves into companies for the defense of their homes."[99] Approximately two thousand men showed up for the meeting. These men were men, like Southerners throughout the Confederacy, who wanted to defend their homes and families; the only difference was these men were all African Americans.

By May, the free African Americans of New Orleans had raised five companies of volunteers, as the "Regiment of Free Men of Color." On January 8, 1862, the men, who had renamed themselves "The Native Guard," marched in a grand review of troops in New Orleans. By this time they had formed at least fourteen different companies of approximately one thousand men and marched down New Orleans streets, apparently under a Confederate battle flag. One of the New Orleans papers described the men as well drilled and in uniform.[100]

The Native Guard remained as a state militia unit, and the governor was apparently uncomfortable about sending the men into combat. In March of 1862, the governor asked for another ten thousand volunteers; the Native Guard offered their services, but the governor declined to accept them for active duty. By April of 1862 New Orleans fell to Union forces and for all practical purposes the Native Guard ceased to exist. After the Union occupation, some of the members of the Native Guard reformed, this time as Union forces, becoming the First Louisiana Native Guard, as described earlier in this chapter.

New Orleans was not unique in having free African Americans offer their services to the Confederate military. From Fort Smith, Arkansas, to Richmond, Virginia, Southern towns and cities were brimming with free African Americans that wanted to volunteer their services to the Confederate war effort. In Charleston, South

Carolina, one writer described it as "thousand Negroes who, so far from inclining to insurrection, were grinning from ear to ear at the prospect of shooting Yankees."[101] However, like in the North, their offer to help went unheeded.

The Confederate War Department steadfastly refused, except at the end of the war, to accept African Americans as combat soldiers. Like the United States Navy, the Confederate States Navy did not have the same prohibition. The Confederate navy accepted African Americans as long as the total number of African Americans on a ship did not exceed one-twentieth of the entire crew.[102]

African American men were used in a support capacity. Early in the war, the *Memphis Avalanche* reported a "procession of several hundred stout negro men," who were marching through the city "in military order, under command of Confederate officers." The men, however, marched not with rifled muskets but rather with "shovels, axes, blankets, etc." The newspaper seemed impressed with the African Americans, claiming, "A merrier set were never seen. They were brimful of patriotism, shouting for Jeff Davis and singing war songs." A few days later the *Avalanche* also reported that "Upwards of 1,000 negroes, armed with spades and pickaxes, have passed through the city within the past few days."[103]

Early on there was one official exception to the prohibition of African Americans formally joining the Confederate army. Those that were allowed in were musicians. From buglers, fifers, and drummers, African American musicians were common in the Confederate army. There were so many unofficial African American musicians that, in April of 1862, the Confederate Congress officially authorized their use. Unlike the Union army, the Confederate Congress agreed to pay the African Americans the same rate of pay as was paid to white musicians.[104]

The overall Confederate army prohibition seemed to have only a limited effect in stopping both free African Americans and slaves from entering into the war on the side of the Confederacy in a capacity other than a musician. It is quite obvious that Confederate officers largely ignored the ban on African Americans soldiers. Some slaves were not given an option, but were forced to work for the

Confederate war effort. Other slaves insisted that when their slave owner went to war they had the right to accompany him.

There are many examples of personal servants going off to war with either their slave owner or the son of their slave owner. A good example is Primus Kelly, who was a North Carolina born slave that ended up in Texas with his slave owner, John West. Kelly grew up with his slave owner's three sons and when war came the three West boys joined the Eighth Texas Cavalry, part of Terry's Texas Rangers. The regiment was to head east on a train from Houston, and the day they left, Kelly voluntarily showed up to join them. Kelly wore a Confederate uniform and carried a weapon and fought alongside the West boys. Twice one of the boys was wounded and Kelly made the journey back to Texas to take the injured West boy home; each time Kelly returned back to "his" unit. Kelly survived the war and ended up buying a small farm near the West land.[105]

Captain George Baylor, of the 12th Virginia Cavalry, had two personal servants, Tom and Overton, with him. At the 1863 Battle of Brandy Station, both of the slaves picked up arms and "joined in the company charges." During the charge they were able to capture an African American Union soldier. According to Baylor, the slaves were "highly delighted" with their prisoner and kept him for a number of months. They required their prisoner to care for Baylor's horses, collect firewood and water, as well as "do other chores about the camp."[106]

Perhaps the first Union officer killed in combat was killed by an African American Confederate. At the Battle of Big Bethel Church in Virginia in June of 1861, Union Major Theodore Winthrop was leading several regiments of Union soldiers against a Confederate position. Winthrop was killed, shot in the heart, while leading his men forward. Although the official Confederate battle report makes no mention of it,[107] some historians credit the deadly shot to an African American Confederate soldier, Sam, the slave of a Confederate captain.[108]

The first major battle of the war occurred in July of 1861 in northern Virginia, and there is no doubt of slave participation on the Southern side. The Battle of Manassas Junction or Bull Run was a Confederate victory and at least in a small part due to the efforts made by slaves. Confederate commander General Pierre G. T. Beauregard actively enlisted slave labor to help construct Confederate fortifications in and around Manassas Junction.[109] Also, in Wade Hampton's South Carolina unit, Hampton's Legion, they utilized African Americans as cooks.[110]

By 1862 it would appear that a large number of slaves and free African Americans were serving in the Confederate army. As the Confederate army moved through Frederick, Maryland, moving towards Sharpsburg, Maryland, and what would become the Battle of Sharpsburg or Antietam, Captain Issac Heysinger reported his observation of the Confederate forces marching through town. He estimated that there were "more than 64,000 men. Over 3,000 Negroes must be included in that number. These were clad in all kinds of uniforms, not only cast off or captured United States uniforms, but in coats with Southern buttons, State buttons, etc. They were shabby, but not shabbier or seedier looking than those worn by white men in the rebel ranks." Heysinger went on to describe how the African American Confederates were armed, supplied, and how they were well integrated within the Confederate units: "Most of the Negroes had arms, rifles, muskets, sabers, bowie knives, dirks, etc. They were supplied, in many instances, with knapsacks, haversacks, canteens, etc., and were manifestly an integral portion of the Southern Confederacy Army. They were seen riding on horses and mules, driving wagons, and promiscuously mixed up with all the rebel horde."[111]

The exact number of African Americans that served in the Confederate war effort will never be known for sure. Some historians cast doubt on African Americans serving the Confederate cause. Noted historian James McPherson, the author of *Battle Cry of Freedom* and other War Between the States books, commented on a claim of thirty thousand African Americans in the Confederate army, calling it "pure fantasy."[112] However, even to the casual student of the war, there were clearly a large number of slaves and free African Americans serving the Confederate military. As Leonard Haynes of Southern University commented, "When you eliminate the black Confederate soldier, you've eliminated the history of the South."[113]

One British eyewitness estimated in 1862 that there were thirty thousand African Americans as "servants" just in the Army of Northern Virginia.[114] Estimates range as high as ninety thousand African American men serving in the Confederate military, while other more conservative estimates put the number in the fifty to sixty thousand men range.[115] The accounts of African Americans in service to the Confederate army are numerous. An excellent source for various accounts of African American Confederate service is in the book *Forgotten Confederates: An Anthology About Black Southerners*, edited by, Charles K. Barrow, J. H. Segars, & R. B. Rosenburg. This book contains numerous accounts of African Americans supporting the Confederate military from period newspapers, military records, letters, and other firsthand accounts.

There is also very strong evidence that African Americans played more than just a support role on the Confederate side. From the *Official Records* of the war, which reflect Union battle reports describing Federal soldiers going up against armed African American Confederates, to comments by Frederick Douglass there is no question that African Americans saw combat serving the Confederate war effort. Douglass in 1861 described African Americans serving the Confederacy: "There are at the present moment, many colored men in the Confederate Army doing duty not only as cooks, servants, and laborers, but as real soldiers, having musket on their shoulders and bullets in their pockets, ready to shoot down loyal troops and do all that soldiers may do to destroy the Federal government and build up that of traitors and rebels."[116]

During Lee's Northern invasion in 1863, a Pennsylvania housewife questioned a North Carolina African American marching towards Gettysburg with his Confederate compatriots. She asked him if he was being treated well. He responded, "I live as I wish, and if I did not, I think I couldn't better myself by stopping here."[117]

One of the ultimate compliments paid to African American soldiers was from one of the South's preeminent and most feared cavalry officers, General Nathan Bedford Forrest. After the war Forrest commented on the African American soldiers that fought with him. Forrest said, " . . . these boys stayed with me . . . and better Confederates did not live."[118] That is extremely high praise from a

tough taskmaster who demanded much from the men who served
under him. Forrest, who rose from poverty to millionaire status prior
to the war, took forty-five slaves with him when he joined the Confederate army in 1861. After the war, Forrest would further describe
his slaves: "I said to forty-five colored fellows on my plantation that
I was going into the army; and that if they would go with me, if we
got whipped they would be free anyhow, and that if we succeeded
and slavery was perpetrated, if they would act faithful with me to
the end of the war, I would set them free. Eighteen months before
the war closed I was satisfied that we were going to be defeated,
and I gave those forty-five, or forty-four of them, their free papers
for fear I might be called (killed)."[119]

The Confederate Congress in early 1862 did allow for Confederate army units to use four slaves per company as cooks.[120]
The Confederate military later authorized the hiring of slaves from
their owners, at a rate of thirty dollars per month per slave, for
assisting the army in non-
combat roles. For whites, the
Confederate Congress passed
their first Conscription Act in
1862. The law, the first military draft in North America,
authorized that the president
could conscript, for a three-
year term, all white males between the ages of eighteen
and thirty-five who were not
legally exempt.[121]

> *Slavery Fact #31*
>
> *African Americans in the Union army served in segregated units and were paid less money than white soldiers. African Americans in the Confederate army served in integrated units and although not all were paid, when they were, they were paid the same as white soldiers.*

The following year the labor shortage in the South grew even
more critical and President Davis proposed using African Americans
as "wagoners, nurses, cooks, and other . . ."[122] Davis's suggestion resulted in an Impressment Bill being passed by the Confederate Congress in early 1864. That act allowed for up to twenty thousand
African Americans to be either drafted or impressed for Confederate military service. The legislation called first for all free African
Americans between the ages of eighteen and fifty to be subject to a

Jefferson Davis,

president of the Confederacy

National Archives

labor draft. If the twenty thousand could not be reached from free African Americans then the secretary of war was authorized to impress slaves from slave owners, provided that any single slave owner would not lose more than 20 percent of his or her slaves.[123] The impressment of slaves was not well received by some large slave owners. The *Richmond Examiner* tried to explain the refusal by some planters to part with their slaves. The paper explained that some planters' reluctance to allow their slaves to be used for Confederate service was "not so much to the employment of the Negro in itself, as to the shock to the rights of property which is involved."[124]

As the war dragged on, the South was simply running out of men. In Emory Thomas's *Confederate Nation*, he estimated that as of June 1864, the Confederate army in total had only two hundred thousand men present for duty, about one-third of what the Union army had and down nearly one hundred thousand men from June of 1863.[125] The war was simply taking its toll on the South. The manpower shortage was causing Confederate leaders to revisit the issue of using slaves as combat soldiers.

One of the first to propose such an idea was a Confederate major general in the Western Theater of the war, Patrick Cleburne. Cleburne was an Irish-born lawyer that had settled in Helena, Arkansas. In letters to his brother Cleburne clearly opined that the war was not one over slavery, but rather one over states' rights.[126] He quickly rose through the ranks of the Confederate army and was a division commander in the Army of Tennessee. His bold and tenacious military style led some to call him the "Stonewall Jackson of the West."

In January of 1864, Cleburne presented a bold plan. He said that he thought the South was losing the war primarily due to three reasons. First, he viewed the lack of manpower in the Confederacy compared to the North. He saw the North as having a near unlimited supply of men to draw upon versus "the inferiority of our army . . . in point of numbers," including the "training an army of 100,000 negroes as good as any troops."[127] Secondly, Cleburne saw the South disadvantaged as having only a single source of men for the Confederacy versus several different resources for the North. Cleburne said of the Union's manpower resources: "First, his own motley population; secondly, our slaves; and thirdly, Europeans whose hearts are fired into a crusade against us by fictitious pictures of the atrocities of slavery, and who meet no hindrance from their Governments in such enterprise, because these Governments are equally antagonistic to the institution."[128]

Finally, Cleburne saw the institution of slavery itself as the major cause of a potential defeat of the South. Cleburne said, "the fact that slavery, from being one of our chief sources of strength at the commencement of the war, has now become, in a military point of view, one of our chief sources of weakness."[129] He blamed slavery as the chief cause why key European nations, such as England and France, would not recognize the Confederacy and come to its aid. Cleburne pointed out that as Union troops invaded the South the disruption, factor it caused on slaves, some fleeing and causing general disruption, as well as the information source escaped slaves became to the Federal forces, describing it as "an omnipresent spy system, pointing out our valuable men to the enemy, revealing our positions, purposes, and resources, and yet acting so safely and secretly that there is no means to guard against it."[130]

In the same daring fashion that he showed on the battlefield, Cleburne proposed a plan to remedy the problems. He proposed the eventual freeing of all the slaves in the South that remain loyal to the Confederacy and to immediately begin training a large reserve of slaves for military service. Cleburne discussed his proposal, known as the "Cleburne Memorial," with his fellow Army of Tennessee officers. Predictably, the response was mixed. Cleburne's commanding officer, Joseph E. Johnston, decided not to forward the proposal to President Davis, however one of Cleburne's rivals took it upon himself to forward it to Davis, along with his letter expressing shock and outrage.

Davis saw the proposal as much too volatile for serious consideration. He attempted to bury the proposal in the War Department. Davis saw what the proposal advocated as far too explosive and that it had the potential to undermine one of the rights for which the South had left the Union.[131] The Confederacy's secretary of war wrote to General Johnston informing him that "the measures advocated in the memorial are considered to be little appropriate for consideration in military circles, and indeed in their scope pass beyond the bounds of Confederate action, and could under our constitutional system neither be recommended by the Executive to Congress nor be entertained by that body."[132] Not only intent on killing the idea, Johnston was ordered to suppress not only the plan, but even any further discussion of the proposal.

Cleburne followed orders and had copies of his proposal destroyed. Cleburne continued to excel on the battlefield, but his controversial plan would be like an albatross around him. He was passed over for army corps commander on several occasions, primarily due to the backlash over his slave proposal.[133] He was killed in combat at Franklin, Tennessee, on November 30, 1864.

In spite of Davis's balking at Cleburne's proposal in early 1864, by the end of the same year, Davis was "singing a remarkably similar tune." With its manpower nearly exhausted, Davis, in November, opened what would become the final session of the Confederate Congress with an astonishing proposal. Davis suggested to Congress that the precedent of using slaves had been established through impressments. Davis said that the time had come to acquire the slaves for public service. He proposed to compensate the slave owner, but in effect for the slave to become owned by the Confederate government.

Davis further told Congress that the slave should eventually be emancipated as a reward for faithful service. Davis asked Congress for authorization to purchase forty thousand slaves. He was not asking that the slaves become combat soldiers but held that in reserve. Davis said if the question of "the employment of the slave as (a) soldier" arose at a time when there were not sufficient numbers of whites to serve as soldiers, then "there seems no reason to doubt what should then be our decision."[134] Davis's proposal was attacked by many leading Southern newspapers, and ended up not being passed—armed slaves as Confederate soldiers remained too controversial.

When the new year of 1865 dawned, it dawned with the Confederacy slowly breathing its last breaths. Petersburg was nearly surrounded; Robert E. Lee's army was barely holding the city. If Petersburg fell then the Confederate capital of Richmond would fall—it would be the beginning of the end for the fledgling nation. Lee felt the time was right to arm the slaves. In a letter, dated January 11, 1865, to Andrew Hunter, Lee stated, "we must decide, whether slavery shall be extinguished by our enemies and the slaves used against us, or use them ourselves at the risk of the effects which may be produced upon our social institutions. My own opinion is that we should employ them without delay. I believe that with proper regulation they can be made efficient soldiers."[135]

Lee went on to give his thoughts about the potential of the slave soldier: "They possess the physical qualifications in an eminent degree. Long habits of obedience and subordination, coupled with the moral influence . . . furnish an excellent foundation for that discipline which is the best guaranty of military efficiency. Our chief aim should be to secure their fidelity."[136]

Was there to be a reward to the slave for fighting for the South? Lee felt it should be their freedom. In the letter he explained his position: "We should not expect slaves to fight for prospective freedom when they can secure it at once by going to the enemy, in whose service they will incur no greater risk than in ours. The reasons that induce me to recommend the employment of negro troops at all render the effect of the measures I have suggested upon slavery immaterial, and in my opinion the best means of securing the efficiency and fidelity of this auxiliary force would be to accompany the measure with a well-digested plan of gradual and general emancipation. As that will be the result of the continuance of the war, and will certainly occur if the enemy succeed, it seems to me most advisable to adopt it at once, and thereby obtain all the benefits that will accrue to our cause."[137]

Both Cleburne's and Lee's proposals remained difficult for some in the South to accept. With the Confederacy on the ropes, as Union forces began to close in on Richmond, some began to change their views. On February 9, 1865, a meeting occurred at the First African Baptist Church in Richmond, which would have seemed unthinkable at the start of the war. Over ten thousand people showed up; the majority could only gather outside the church and try to listen to the events inside. The church was filled predominately with whites and some African Americans. Attending the event was President Davis and other influential members of the Confederate government, including the Confederacy's Secretary of State Judah P. Benjamin. One major topic of discussion was using slaves as Confederate soldiers. Benjamin told the crowd, "Let us say to every Negro who wants to go into the ranks, go fight and you are free."[138] In spite of some cat calls, Benjamin's call was greeted with a preponderance of, "Let's try it," and "Now, now, now!"

There remained intense debate on the topic in the Confederate Congress. Finally on March 13, 1865, the Congress passed the "Act to Increase the Military Force of the Confederate States." It was not what Benjamin and others had asked for, but it did authorize the arming of slaves.[139] The bill created a quota of three hundred thousand African American males, between the ages of eighteen and forty-five, from both the ranks of slave and free African Americans, although only one-fourth of the slaves could come from a single state. The slaves had to be volunteers "rendered by their masters." The men would be treated on the same basis as white soldiers, with equal pay, clothing, rations, and allowances.[140] The promise of eventual emancipation, however, was not part of the act.

On March 13 the War Department issued General Order Number Fourteen and the recruitment of the African American combat units was begun. Within two days the *Richmond Dispatch* reported that the first African American company, under the new law, had been formed. The *Dispatch* wrote, after observing the new unit drilling, that they showed "as much aptness and proficiency . . . as is usually shown by any white troops we have ever seen."[141] The enthusiasm of the Richmond African Americans was not shared by all. One plantation mistress, Catherine Devereaux Edmondston of North Carolina, reported that some household servants overheard a discussion of the plan to draft slaves into the Confederate army. The next day the plantation was devoid of slaves.[142]

Lee was anxious for the infusion of new men. On April 2 he wrote President Davis, volunteering some of his officers "to recruit negro troops."[143] It was, however, too little too late, as time had simply run out on the Confederacy. On the same day Lee wrote his letter to Davis, the president was ordering the Confederate government to abandon Richmond. Lee would be forced to yield to overwhelming forces against him and surrender his Army of Northern Virginia a week later. By May 10, Davis was captured and the Confederacy would cease to exist as a nation.

At least twenty-eight slaves surrendered when Robert E. Lee surrendered his army. The men chose being paroled, along with their fellow white Confederate soldiers, over an offer of freedom.[144]

The African American Confederate soldier has been largely ignored in American history; fortunately his story is now being told. Initially, perhaps primarily for racist reasons, many ignored the African American Confederate, and today he seems to be still ignored as he does not represent a politically correct version of history. Regardless of the reason, the African American soldier, from both the ranks of slave and free, served the Confederate military and did so honorably and with valor, and his story should be a prominent part of American history.

In Arlington National Cemetery, outside of Washington, D.C., stands a monument to the Confederate cause. Located in Jackson Circle in the Cemetery, which contains the graves of over four hundred Confederate veterans, is a large monument honoring those that served the Confederacy. The monument, dedicated in 1914 by President Woodrow Wilson, contains a sculptured relief of faces of the Confederacy from the battle lines to the home front. Quite prominent on the monument is the likeness of an African American Confederate soldier.

The Slaves Back Home

If we recall from chapter five, there were not quite four million slaves in the South at the start of the war. What was life like for these men, women, and children? How many of them remained loyal to their slave owners?

Life was extremely difficult for all the people in the South during the war, whether slave or free, African American or white. The South was a nation at war, besieged by a much larger foe with far greater industry, commerce, and military might. The North, early on in the war, followed a plan designed by the ranking army officer at the war's onset, Winfield Scott, a Virginian, by the way. That plan, known as the Anaconda Plan, called for an extremely tight naval blockade of the entire South. The Anaconda Plan, when fully implemented, would mean that the South would have a difficult time in exporting goods to help finance and support her war effort, and have an equally difficult time in importing goods. The plan, which went into effect in 1861, took some time to implement, but by the latter half of the war it was causing severe shortages for the military and the Southern civilians. Life became most difficult in the South, again for the slave and for the free. Another major shortage for the South was manpower. The South needed all its able bodied men in the military service.

What of slave loyalty? As Union troops began to invade the South, what did the slaves do? The exact numbers will never be known, but it has been estimated that about a half million of the slaves left their slave owners as Union troops came.[145] If that estimate is correct it means that the overwhelming number of slaves remained with their slave owners. There were a variety of reasons for slave loyalty. Many of the slaves were simply afraid of the invading soldiers; after all, the South was just as much a home to the slaves as it was to the slave owners. There were certainly risks in leaving their homes where they grew up and the slave owner family that they had known all their lives. Many simply decided to stay where they were rather than risk joining invading strangers.

Many slaves looked at the advancing Federal soldiers more as invaders than as liberators. As invaders, the Union troops were often harsh in their treatment of the civilian population, African American or white, in the South. Wanton destruction of homes and crops, for "war reasons," and flat-out destruction, for retribution, and thievery were commonplace. One former slave, Henry D. Jenkins from South Carolina, referred to the Union soldiers as "a army dat seemed more concerned 'bout stealin' than they was 'bout de Holy War for de liberation of de poor African slave people."[146] Even slave cabins were not spared from thievery by Federal troops. One Union soldier, admonished by a slave woman for stealing her quilts when she thought he was supposed to be fighting for her freedom, told her, "You're a goddam liar. I'm fighting for fourteen dollars a month and the Union."[147] The slaves also saw gratuitous violence from the men in blue. There were many rapes of slave women by Federal soldiers. Union soldiers were rarely punished for these sexual assaults.[148]

Prior to Union invasion, Susan Dabney Smedes recalled plantation life during the war, "life went on as usual," and she described their slaves' actions in that they "went about their duties more conscientiously than before. They seemed to do better when there was trouble in the white family, and they knew there was trouble enough."[149] As the war caused countless hardships on the home front a South Carolinian slave owner on Christmas Day of 1864 stated that things were "wretched," but, "Our negroes are as orderly as usual. . . . They are anxious about the future & seem to sympathize with us in our distress."[150] Towards the end of the war, the owner of two South Carolina plantations wrote that Union troops had burned his house and destroyed his crops, but he also wrote, "I am happy to say my negroes have acted orderly and well all the time," and, "none going off excepting one or two Boys who accompanied the yanks for plunder but have returned home and appear quite willing to go to work." The other slaves had "acted nobly furnishing my family with provisions and return all they saved by begging the Yankees."[151]

A Pennsylvania-born editor of a Texas newspaper reported high praise throughout the war for slave loyalty. Writing in the *Bellville Countryman*, John P. Osterhout frequently gave tribute to slaves and cited examples of slave loyalty. Osterhout reported that slaves did what they could by financially supporting the Confederacy, some to a greater extent than whites. He reported that in Union-occupied

Louisville, Kentucky, authorities had arrested two African Americans for "aiding the Southern rebellion." Osterhout commented that "there is nothing singular to us in this, but such things must occasionally astonish the Yankees."[152]

Many stories were spread about the advancing Union forces; some were true and some were not. Remember, that in spite of Lincoln's Emancipation Proclamation, the typical Union soldier continued to have racist attitudes. Some slaves returned home after following the Union army; conditions in the refugee camps were at times atrocious. They were many accounts of atrocities committed on the slaves by the conquering Union soldiers. Often the history books tell of the Union soldiers invading the South joyously welcoming the teaming numbers of slaves they were freeing. Less often do we read about the numerous crimes committed against the slaves by their "liberators."

In past discussions we have described the racial bigotry exhibited by most Northern whites against African Americans. That bigotry typically manifested into verbal attacks or abuse but at times resulted in criminal behavior against slaves. One of the most mean-spirited expressions of racial hate during the war came from a Union soldier from Boston. Early in 1863, he wrote his brother from New Orleans, "As I was going along this afternoon a little black baby that could just walk got under my feet and it look so much like a big worm that I wanted to step on it and crush it, the nasty, greasy little vermin was the best that could be said of it."[153] Some of the Union soldiers made light of the slaves, and sometimes their fun, at the expense of the slaves, was crude with atrocious results. One soldier from Connecticut wrote, while in Virginia, that his comrades had taken two "niger wenches . . . turned them upon their heads, & put tobacco chips, sticks, lighted cigars & sand into their behinds."[154]

Court-martial records as well as other reports show that slave women were raped by Union soldiers, often to the cheers of the men that observed the crime. Early in the war a native of Germany, serving in the Union army, wrote of an incident he observed in South Carolina. "While on picket guard I witnessed misdeeds that made me ashamed of America." He wrote, "For example about five miles from the fort about 8–10 soldiers from the New York 47th Regiment chased some Negro women but they escaped, so they took a Negro girl about 7–9 years old, and raped her."[155]

The treatment that the slaves received from Union soldiers was not all bad. Some slaves endeared themselves to Union soldiers by providing intelligence information about Confederate troops or helping them with the lay of the land. Some of the slaves opened their cabins up to the Union troops, filling them with meals that were obviously far better than standard U.S. issue. Some of the Federal troops certainly had sympathy for the plight of people who were not free. One Union soldier in Louisiana wrote, "Visited during the day several plantations and saw enough of the horrors of slavery to make one an Abolitionist forever."[156]

But, as we have indicated, most of the slaves remained loyal to their owners. There was an interesting special bond that had developed between many slaves and their owners. Perhaps the comments of Booker T. Washington describe it the best. Washington wrote in his autobiography, *Up from Slavery*, about that unique relationship and bond. With the white males either dead or gone to war, many slaves felt it was up to them to help defend the plantation. Washington described life during the war: "In order to defend and protect the women and children who were left on the plantations when the white males went to war, the slaves would have laid down their lives. The slave who was selected to sleep in the 'big house' during the absence of the males was considered to have the place of honour. Any one attempting to harm 'young Mistress' or 'old Mistress' during the night would have had to cross the dead body of the slave to do so. I do not know how many have noticed it, but I think that it will be found to be true that there are few instances, either in slavery or freedom, in which a member of my race has been known to betray a specific trust."[157]

Freedom

In Texas it was known as "Juneteenth." It was on June 19, 1865, that the slaves in Texas learned that they were free. Union General Gordon Granger, along with approximately two thousand Union troops, arrived in Galveston, Texas. General Granger publicly announced that the slaves in the state were officially free. The term

"Juneteenth" is a combination of the words, June and nineteenth, and that day continues to be celebrated in Texas and in other Southern states.

Technically, not all slaves were freed as soon as the war was over. Prior to the end of the war, emancipation had been "piecemeal," following Union troops as they moved deeper and deeper into Confederate territory. By the end of the war, some of the border states, the exceptions being Delaware and Kentucky, had ended slavery on a state basis, but it took the thirteenth amendment to the United States Constitution to officially end slavery everywhere. The thirteenth amendment was relatively simple: "Neither Slavery, nor involuntary servitude, except as a punishment for crime whereof the party shall have been duly convicted, shall exist within the United States, or any place subject to their jurisdiction."

When the Confederacy ended in the spring of 1865, after four long years of war, much of the South was in ruin and life would never be the same again. The slaves were now freed, but most were totally unprepared for their newfound freedom. Thousands of former slaves migrated to the cities and towns or lived in shanty town camps outside Union army encampments. Some moved north to what they thought might be greater opportunities. Many of the former slaves became sick and others were literally starving to death. Something had to be done.

Just prior to the end of the war, in March of 1865, the United States government did something that was quite unprecedented; it went into the public subsistence business. The Bureau of Refugees, Freemen, and Abandoned Lands Bureau, better known as the "Freedmen's Bureau," was formed as a part of the War Department. The bureau was financed by a big tax on cotton.[158]

The bureau was given the assignment of providing food, clothing, and fuel to the "destitute and suffering refugees and their wives and children." It was originally only authorized for one year, but Congress extended the life of the bureau in 1866. Aid was available to both former slaves and whites. It was the first time that the government was involved in a massive public relief effort.

The Freedmen's Bureau also got into the land and education business. Abandoned land and land that had been confiscated by the Federal government or military was parceled out to former slaves by the bureau. The term "forty acres and a mule" was an early bureau plan to rent forty-acre plots to former slaves, from the confiscated lands. The former slaves would be given the opportunity to purchase the land at the end of three years, but the program was abandoned.

Although public schools were common in the Northern states, they were not in the South. One of the legacy's of the Freedmen's Bureau was an effort to educate illiterate former slaves through the founding of schools throughout the South. A number of free public schools in the South were founded as a result of the efforts of the bureau.

For many former slaves the solution was to stay right where they were. Their status simply changed from being a slave to being an employee. For those that stayed in the South change took time—years and even generations—before the promise of freedom equated equality. Becoming employees meant gaining new responsibilities and having to do things for oneself that was formerly done by others. Most former slave owners allowed the former slaves to stay on and become employees. One former slave, Laura Cornish, recalled the day when her former slave owner, Papa Day, called them all together. Cornish said, "One morin' Papa Day calls all us to de house and reads de freddom paper and say, 'De gov'ment don't need to tell you you is free, 'cause you been free all you days. If you wants to stay you can and if you wants to go, you can. But if you go, lots of white folks ain't gwine treat you like I does."[159]

Many stayed, but the lure of freedom and self-determination was too great; perhaps the old places reminded the former slaves too much of the old ways. Cornish remembered, "For de longest time, maybe two years, dey wasn't none of Papa Day's cullud folks what left, but den first one fam'ly den 'nother gits some land to make a crop on, and den daddy gits some land and us leaves, too. Maybe he gits de land from Papa Day, 'cause it not far from him plantation. Us sho' work hard on dat place, but I heard mama say lots of times she wishes we stay on Papa Day's place."[160]

Life would be hard for the ex-slaves, but they were free. Before slavery ended, perhaps one slave, after he escaped to freedom, said it the best to describe what freedom from slavery really meant. When questioned by a judge, this exchange ensued:

Slave: "Oh no. I had a good life there."

Judge: "Were you mistreated?"

Slave: "No. Old Masa and me was the greatest friends. Fished and hunted together."

Judge: "Did you have good food and housing?"

Slave: "Sure enough. Ham and 'taters. Molasses. My little cabin had roses over the door."

Judge: "I don't understand. Why did you run away?"

Slave: "Well your Honor, the situation is still open down there if you'd like to apply for it."[161]

Chapter Ten
The Legacy of Slavery

What is the America of today left with, nearly one hundred and forty years since slavery ended? Was it simply a horrible negative time in American history or was it a period of time where, in spite of the negatives, we see slavery from a different perspective? Hopefully, after reading this book the reader will have a better insight into American slavery and the life of the slave, as well as the slave owner.

For African Americans, in the twenty-first century, what is their legacy from the institution of slavery? Does American society in general owe the descendants of slaves for the bondage of their ancestors? Is the twenty-first century the time to "settle the account" and pay reparations to African Americans? And, what about white Americans, should they, as descendants of slave owners, although we now realize that most Southern whites were not slave owners, feel guilt and remorse for the actions of their ancestors?

These are difficult questions to ponder. What makes them so difficult to answer is that, as we have seen, slavery was not a uniform or perfectly consistent institution. That some slaves were mistreated is without question. That some slave owners were cruel and heartless individuals is not in doubt. That some slaves were treated as nearly equals in the slave owner's family is not in doubt. Does the fact that some slaves were mistreated and others were not, warrant reparations to the ancestors of the slaves?

I obviously have my own opinions; however, I leave it for the reader to make that decision for him or herself. Let us look at some of the issues one might consider in making a decision on the topic.

As we have seen in this book, the African American either as a slave or as a free person accomplished much and added greatly to make what America is today. Rather than as some historians have portrayed the slaves in America, lazy, insolent, and rebellious, what we find in fact is that most came to a new land to help clear, cultivate, and—although it was against his or her will—made the best of the situation and adapted to the "New World."

I think that the legacy of slavery in America is a proud history of African Americans' accomplishments. Should African Americans be celebrating the countless accomplishments of their race while held in bondage? The slaves accomplished so very much while being held in bondage under extraordinary conditions. It takes very special people to be able to overcome what African Americans have overcome, and the heritage of what the slaves were able to achieve is inspiring to all Americans.

And what of the descendants of slave owners? Should white America harbor guilt and pain because of what their ancestors did? First, white Americans need to put slavery into a proper perspective. As we said at the onset of this book, slavery is wrong and can never be justified. Yet, the world of the 1600s, 1700s, and the first half of the 1800s of America, had a very different perspective than what we have today. As we have seen, opposition to slavery took no real appreciable form until the 1830s; it was a generally accepted institution. White Americans should also be reminded that the vast majority of white Southerners simply did not even own slaves. Three out of four white Southerners today are not the descendants of slave owners.

The issue of reparation is fraught with many different dilemmas. What about the millions of Americans that are descendants of people who were not even in America during the period of slavery? Should their tax dollars be used? The same question can be asked of the descendants of those that served in the Northern army during the War Between the States. Should their tax dollars be used for reparation payments?

What about the free African Americans that owned slaves? Should their descendants be excluded from any reparation payment? Also, as we saw in chapter nine, what of the many African Americans that voluntarily served in the Confederate armed forces? Should the descendants of those men be excluded from reparation payments?

The greatest negative of slavery, once we get past the issue that by modern standards slavery was an abomination, is how the United States handled the South in the postwar years and the results it had on Southern race relations. Did the hardhanded Union occupation of the South during Reconstruction cause the close relationship between African Americans and whites to be severely damaged? Why has racial prejudice, North and South, been so slow in dying? Was the greater sin of the United States not slavery, but rather that of racial discrimination? Simply stated, slavery did not cause racism in America. The racist feelings and actions of Americans pre-existed slavery, and unfortunately, survived long after slavery died; in fact some would argue today that it still exists in the twenty-first century. If reparations are paid, should they be paid due to slavery or would they be more justified by the unequal treatment of African Americans for one hundred years after slavery ended? These are questions that American society will have to answer.

One common speculative question asked about slavery is, What would have happened to slavery had the War Between the States not occurred? What if the issues of 1860 and 1861 had been resolved, at least temporarily, through compromise? Would slavery have ended in the United States, and if so when? To gain insight into our speculative answer to the question, let us look at what happened in Brazil. Brazil received about 85 percent of all the slaves imported into the Western Hemisphere.[1] Brazil, like the American South, built its economy and its society on slavery. Brazil was one of the last places on Earth where slavery officially existed. Slavery in Brazil was not ended until 1888. As we have stated many times, world opinion had moved slavery from an accepted institution to one of moral disgust.

Would the same thing have happened in the South? Some historians, such as Phillips, have claimed that slavery by the onset of the War Between the States, was a dying institution, at least from an economic perspective. Later thought, *Time on the Cross*[2] and *Industrial Slavery in the Old South*,[3] would seem to suggest that the slavery system in the South was quite efficient and effective, from an economic perspective. What would have won out, economic considerations or moral indignation? At least in the short run, I think that economic factors would have allowed slavery to continue for at least a decade. But with increasing antislavery forces, the South losing its political clout and power in Washington, D.C., and with some type of a federally funded compensation program to slave owners, slavery would have ended peacefully in America. An emancipation plan that allowed for gradual emancipation and compensation would have eventually been accepted by Southerners—after all, they were realists.

The other theoretical question frequently asked is, What if the South had won the war, would we still have slavery today? The answer to that is no. Slavery in the South would have perhaps continued for another twenty years but it would have ended with, again, some governmental program to compensate slave owners. The South, as a member of the international community, would have been totally isolated from the rest of the world. The Confederate government would have succumbed to political pressures well before the turn of the nineteenth century.

Our original question was asked in chapter one. What was slavery like, the moonlight and magnolias of the old romantic South or the harsh Simon Legree South? Hopefully with this book the reader has learned it was neither. There were four million slave stories, and each varied. Life was hard and difficult for the slave, indeed life in the South was hard and difficult for almost everyone that resided there. The truth about slavery, once you cut through all the myths, is there, and like most things lies somewhere in the middle of the stereotyped extremes.

Appendix A
The Use of Resources

As was pointed out in the prologue of this book, the purpose of this book was not to present any dramatic new research on the life of the American slave. Instead, this book was crafted by using many different resources and presents a consolidated summary of the story of the institution of American slavery. The bibliography lists books and resources on American slavery. The notes section lists the specific sources for the material presented in this book.

As the reader will note from the recommended bibliography and from the referenced footnotes there are a variety of different resources to use in this study of American slavery. The following is a brief account of some of the key resources used in the book. Of specific interest are the resources used to fashion chapters six and seven, on the Life of the Slaves.

One of the earliest sources was by a chronicler from that time period who is an important source in learning about the slaves' life in the South. We have the opportunity to see the South through the eyes of Frederick Law Olmsted, a Northerner from New York. He was hired by the *New York Times*, at the time known as the *New York Daily Times*, to travel across the South and to report back to their readers his direct accounts about slavery.

Olmsted made three trips to the South, in 1852, 1853, and 1854, spending a total time of nearly fourteen months in the slave states. He visited almost all the slave states, including far-off Texas. He missed only the states of Arkansas and Florida. Olmsted sent back to the *Times* around seventy-five articles reporting to interested

Northern readers what he had learned about slavery and the Southern ways of life. The articles became the basis for four books about his Southern journeys; the best known of his books is *The Cotton Kingdom*, published in 1861.[1]

Olmsted was anything but objective in his reporting. He was staunchly antislavery in his views, although he differed from some abolitionists in that he favored the gradual emancipation of slaves. In spite of an antislavery bias, Olmsted was a firsthand observer, and we can learn from what he saw in the South.

Ulrich B. Phillips was a native Southerner whose work on the study of the American institution of slavery was the standard for nearly forty years. Phillips, a Yale professor of history, was the first researcher to produce both quantitative and qualitative information on slavery, based on an extensive review of Southern farm and plantation records. His findings were presented in a landmark book, *American Negro Slavery*, published in 1918, and in a subsequent book, *Life and Labor in the Old South*, published a decade or so later.

Phillips's work was recognized as exceptional by scholars in both the North and the South, and was the dominant work on the topic of slavery, at least until the 1950s. Although both books are very dated and many consider Phillips's early twentieth-century views today as racist, his writings include many firsthand accounts and contain much valuable research and information on slavery. One university history professor advised me to exclude anything written by Phillips in this book. He explained that Phillips's work is no longer well accepted in academia. What I found in reviewing both books is an exceptional wealth of information. Phillips's views may seem outdated today, but this does not discount his research and sources. As is described in the *American Negro Slavery* 1966 reprint's foreword by Eugene D. Genovese, "*American Negro Slavery* is not the last word on its subject; merely the indispensable first."[2]

Another excellent source about the life of slaves is from those that were actually held in slavery. What source will we use, since we have discounted many of the abolitionist-produced autobiographies and articles of ex-slaves (see chapter four)? An excellent source is the "Slave Narratives" compiled during the Depression era by the Federal Writers' Project (FWP), part of the Works Projects Administration. Some of the interviews were conducted by scholars from Fisk University and Southern University as early as in the 1920s.

The project interviewed former slaves as the interviewers transcribed their responses. Unfortunately, few sessions were taperecorded, so we are at the mercy of the interviewer for most of the responses. Over 2,200 interviews were conducted in seventeen states, by about three hundred interviewers. The result is a dramatic account of what slave life was like, from the voices of the former slaves themselves. The narratives were finally published in 1972. They consist of sixteen volumes in approximately 10,000 pages of about three and one-half million words.

The former slaves' stories range from recollections of terribly harsh treatment by their owners to truly kind and loving care from their slave owners. The majority of the recollections describe kind treatment, and the majority of the ex-slaves report positive recollections of their days as slaves. This book utilizes the FWP interviews rather than relying on the numerous autobiographies of ex-slaves written prior to the War Between the States. The FWP interviews did not have a political agenda to meet, as did the abolitionist sponsored ex-slave autobiographies. The FWP interviews are much broader, giving a better glimpse of slave life. The sheer volume of information from the FWP interviews dwarfs what can be found in the ex-slave autobiographies.

Some historians feel that some of the interviews were done with rose colored glasses or that those interviewed were intimidated by white interviewers. Noted historian C. Vann Woodward points out a number of concerns about the FWP interviews. He noted that the advanced age of those being interviewed perhaps caused a memory loss, resulting in reflections being more positive than they actually were. Woodward also questioned if former slaves were telling white interviewers what they wanted to hear.[3]

Woodward is correct that those interviewed were senior citizens, but such was the nature of the remaining former slaves—nearly two-thirds were over eighty. Because of their advanced age, had they forgotten how bad things really were? Typically, it is not the older memories that fade due to advanced age. If one does only a casual reading of the interviews, it is evident that their degree of recollection of slave life details is really rather amazing. What about the charge that they were telling white interviewers what they wanted to hear? Obviously some former slaves were not hesitant about telling white interviewers about harsh treatment. Of those that described compassionate and loving care, many gave accounts that obviously came from the heart. Whites were not the only ones that conducted the interviews. Of the interviewers, where race could be determined, about 27 percent were African American.[4]

One researcher actually compared responses from those being interviewed by African Americans versus those questioned by white interviewers. Using questions regarding the slaves' diets, it was found that the size of the farm or plantation the slaves were working on had more to do with the responses than the race of the interviewer. The difference of responses influenced by the interviewer's race was statistically insignificant.[5]

Another common complaint about the FWP interviews is that they were done during the harsh economic times of the 1930s 'depression. The thought is that since the nation was in the midst of severe economic hard times, the slaves were fondly recalling economic times that were better than their current situation. Some of the interviews were conducted in 1929, prior to the outbreak of the "Great Depression." A scholarly review of the interviews done post-depression as compared with pre-depression interviews showed the views of the two were very similar.[6] It would appear that current economic times had little or no effect on the recollections of the slaves.

As discussed in chapter four, with some exceptions, noted below, the author has not used the one hundred or so former slave autobiographies published prior to the War Between the States. We will not rehash that discussion other than to say we simply cannot ascertain what is fact and what is fiction in those bodies of work (see chapter four for a more detailed discussion of the topic).

Other firsthand accounts used in researching this book did include some ex-slave autobiographies. One of the first slave autobiographies was that of Gustavus Vassa, whose African name was Olaudah Equiano. His book, first published in 1789 in England, is unique in that it is one of the few accounts told by a native African old enough to remember his capture by slave traders. Also used was the firsthand account of Frederick Douglass, whose work is included as one of the slave autobiographies that the author of this book puts a bit more stock into. Douglass's book was one of the earlier autobiographies, and subsequent ex-slave autobiographies seem to be patterned on the Douglass book. Also included is the autobiography of Booker T. Washington, whose book *Up from Slavery* was written in 1901 and was not part of the abolitionists' propaganda.

In 1974 the book *Time on the Cross: The Economics of American Negro Slavery* by Robert William Fogel and Stanley L. Engerman was published. It was a landmark publication, written by two highly distinguished and prominent economic historians. The book carefully examined slave life using quantified data, massive computer-assisted research, and the best scientific principles of modern economics. The book produced some startling facts and conclusions, which differed from the more "modern" historical analysis of slavery. The authors themselves all but apologized for their findings, but being true to the scientific and research principles, which produced the book, presented the facts and hypotheses as they determined them.

The controversial book was attacked by unprecedented numbers of their learned colleagues in academia. What was wrong with the book? Why the attacks? Did the book distort the facts of slavery or was it merely attacked for presenting a "politically incorrect" view of slavery?

Time on the Cross perhaps was snagged, not in what it found in the nineteenth century, but rather in the race relations of the twentieth century and as such continues on today in the twenty-first century. One major difference between American slavery and slavery as it existed under the Romans, the Greeks, and in early European history is that all, with very few exceptions, of the slaves in the United States were black skinned. The racial discrimination, racial tensions, and unresolved racial issues that still linger today between black and white seem to prevent the truth from being told about American slavery without attack, least we offend one group or another.

What is presented in chapters six and seven are some of the observations of Olmsted, the reporting done by Phillips, information gleamed from the FWP's "Slave Narratives," and some of the conclusions of Fogel and Engerman, as well as numerous other sources. Putting it all together we get the best educated guess of a summary of what slave life was like in America, prior to the outbreak of the War Between the States. The goal of these chapters, as well as the entire book's, is again to weave what are the myths and what are the realities of slavery in the United States.

Numerous other books are utilized as resources. A now classic work on slavery was written by Kenneth Milton Stampp. Stampp's *Peculiar Institution* is an extensive account of American slavery, although it was written in the 1950s and is now a bit dated. Stampp was an early critic of Phillips and challenged some of his assumptions. Another good compendium on American slavery is the more recent work of Peter Kolchin: *American Slavery, 1619–1877*, published in 1993. One work, that is very well written, covers the life of all African Americans, slave or free. *Black Southerners 1619–1869* by John K. Boles was published in 1984 and is an authoritative and interesting book. Another book that has become a near classic is *Roll, Jordan, Roll* by Eugene D. Genovese. I disagree with a number of Professor Genovese's conclusions, such as his conclusion that the slaves in the South were in a constant passive resistance mode against their owners. In spite of disagreeing with some conclusions, this book is very ably written, well documented, and a thought-provoking read. The book includes numerous FWP slave interviews. *The Slave Community, Plantation Life in the Antebellum South* by John W. Blassingame provides a glimpse of Southern plantation life. This book frequently utilizes slave autobiographies, accounts that this author avoids due to their biased and often inaccurate reporting, but Blassingame's book is nevertheless an appealing read.

Another noteworthy book is *Many Thousands Gone*, published in 1998. This book, written by Ira Berlin, covers the first two hundred years of slavery in North America. A new book, published in 2001, is *Hard Road to Freedom* by James O. Horton and Lois E. Horton. This book chronicles the saga of African Americans from African slavery through the War Between the States and into the twentieth century. Although I have some disagreement with some of the Hortons' views, the book is very well written and interesting. Another book, similar to the Hortons', is *Before the Mayflower* by Lerone

Bennett, Jr. This book was originally written in 1962 and is now in its eighth edition. It tells the story of African Americans from capture in Africa to the early 1990s. Finally, one additional book worthy of mentioning is Robert William Fogel's 1989 *Without Consent or Contract*. Fogel, coauthor of *Time on the Cross*, updates some of the information provided in the earlier book and presents the political effort to end slavery, as well as making an effort to "ferret out the true story" of American slavery.

There are a number of good books relating to the Atlantic Slave trade. One major contribution to the understanding of the Atlantic slave trade business is the extensive 1997 book *The Slave Trade: The Story of the Atlantic Slave Trade: 1440-1870* by Hugh Thomas. One of the classic books, published in 1969, on the slave trade is *The Atlantic Slave Trade: A Census* by Philip D. Curtin. This book is a quantitative review of the slave trade to the Western Hemisphere. A newer work, which utilizes the new Trans-Atlantic Slave Trade Database, is David Eltis's *The Rise of African Slavery in the Americas*, published in 2000. Another interesting book that describes the slave trade to America is *The Middle Passage* by Herbert S. Klein. *Black Ivory: A History of British Slavery* by James Walvin describes the extent and importance of the British involvement in slave trade.

The Trans-Atlantic Slave Trade: A Database on CD-ROM is a new aid in the study of the slave trade from Africa to the Western Hemisphere. Published in 1999 by the Cambridge University Press, the database contains information on over twenty-seven thousand trans-Atlantic slave ship voyages made between 1595 and 1866. The searchable database contains information on each known voyage, such as the name of the vessel, number of slaves on board, number of crew members, ports and dates of departure and arrival. Unfortunately, the names of the slaves were not typically recorded, so this information is missing from the database, and thus the database will not directly help modern-day African Americans in their genealogical endeavors. Although not complete—one historian estimated it to be about 70 percent complete—the database is an important research tool to better understand the slave trade from Africa to the Western Hemisphere.

Numerous books, specializing in various aspects of slavery, were consulted in the writing of this book. Books such as *The Plantation Overseer, The Southern Plantation, The Ruling Race, A History of American Slaveholders, Masters without Slaves, Southern Planters in the Civil War and Reconstruction* give much insight into various aspects of American slavery. A relatively new book is *The Slaveholding Republic* by the late Don E. Fehrenbacher, a Pulitzer Prize-winning historian. This book, published in 2001, examines slavery from the perspective of the United States government from the Constitution to Abraham Lincoln. Another book published in 2001 is Michael Vorenberg's *Final Freedom*, which looks at the end of the War Between the States and the creation of the 13th Amendment to the Constitution. Collectively, these are important contributions to the total effort to gain insight into the lives of slaves. For detailed information about such specific topics, these books should be consulted.

For information on the free African Americans in America prior to the War Between the States, I recommend two books: *Slaves without Masters: The Free Negro in the Antebellum South* by Ira Berlin and *Black Slaveowners: Free Black Slave Masters in South Carolina, 1790–1860*, by Larry Koger, which takes a detailed and close look at the free African Americans in South Carolina.

For the War Between the States period, a number of different resources were used. The United States government published a 128-volume set of books on the War Between the States. *The War of the Rebellion: A Compilation of the Official Records of the Union and Confederate Armies*, better known as the "O.R.," was published between 1880–1901. This massive publication contains battle reports, correspondence of the war, from both sides. I recommend for a general reading on the war Shelby Foote's classic three-volume work, *The Civil War: A Narrative*. Foote is a marvelous writer who weaves a nonfiction account as though it were a bestselling novel. For the causes of the war, a new book published in 2001 by Charles B. Dew claims to prove that the war was fought over slavery. *Apostles of Disunion* attempts to demonstrate that efforts were made by Southern States already seceded from the Union to convince other Southern states to join them using the slavery issue as the key reason. The issue is far too complex to be adequately addressed by Dew's small 128-page book. For the reasons for fighting the war, I would recommend reading James M. McPherson's *What They Fought For, 1861–1865* and *The Confederate War* by Gary W. Gallagher, which is a very informative book.

The classic work on the African American contribution to the Union war effort is Dudley Taylor Cornish's *The Sable Arm: Negro Troops in the Union Army, 1861–1865*, published in 1966. A newer, less scholarly work is Joyce Hansen's *Between Two Fires: Black Soldiers in the Civil War*. Slave and free African American participation in the war from the Southern side is a relatively knew area of exploration. Forthcoming new research should be most interesting in this largely ignored and misunderstood area. For those interested in that area of study I recommend several books: *Forgotten Confederates, An Anthology about Black Southerners, Black Southerners in Gray,* and Ervin Jordan's, *Black Confederates and Afro-Yankees in Civil War Virginia.*

Appendix B
The Emancipation Proclamation

By the President of the United States of America:

A Proclamation.

Whereas, on the twenty-second day of September, in the year of our Lord one thousand eight hundred and sixty-two, a proclamation was issued by the President of the United States, containing, among other things, the following, to wit:

"That on the first day of January, in the year of our Lord one thousand eight hundred and sixty-three, all persons held as slaves within any State or designated part of a State, the people whereof shall then be in rebellion against the United States, shall be then, thenceforward, and forever free; and the Executive Government of the United States, including the military and naval authority thereof, will recognize and maintain the freedom of such persons, and will do no act or acts to repress such persons, or any of them, in any efforts they may make for their actual freedom.

"That the Executive will, on the first day of January aforesaid, by proclamation, designate the States and parts of States, if any, in which the people thereof, respectively, shall then be in rebellion against the United States; and the fact that any State, or the people thereof, shall on that day be, in good faith, represented in the Congress of the United States by members chosen thereto at elections wherein a majority of the qualified voters of such State shall have participated, shall, in the absence of strong countervailing testimony, be deemed conclusive evidence that such State, and the people thereof, are not then in rebellion against the United States."

Now, therefore I, Abraham Lincoln, President of the United States, by virtue of the power in me vested as Commander-in-Chief, of the Army and Navy of the United States in time of actual armed rebellion against the authority and government of the United States, and as a fit and necessary war measure for suppressing said rebellion, do, on this first day of January, in the year of our Lord one thousand eight hundred and sixty-three, and in accordance with my purpose so to do publicly proclaimed for the full period of one hundred days, from the day first above mentioned, order and designate as the States and parts of States wherein the people thereof respectively, are this day in rebellion again the United States, the following, to wit:

Arkansas, Texas, Louisiana, (except the Parishes of St. Bernard, Plaquemines, Jefferson, St. John, St. Charles, St. James Ascension, Assumption, Terrebonne, Lafourche, St. Mary, St. Martin, and Orleans, including the City of New Orleans) Mississippi, Alabama, Florida, Georgia, South Carolina, North Carolina, and Virginia, (except the forty-eight counties designated as West Virginia, and also the counties of Berkley, Accomac, Northampton, Elizabeth City, York, Princess Ann, and Norfolk, including the cities of Norfolk and Portsmouth[)], and which excepted parts, are for the present, left precisely as if this proclamation were not issued.

And by virtue of the power, and for the purpose aforesaid, I do order and declare that all persons held as slaves within said designated States, and parts of States, are, and henceforward shall be free; and that the Executive government of the United States, including the military and naval authorities thereof, will recognize and maintain the freedom of said persons.

And I hereby enjoin upon the people so declared to be free to abstain from all violence, unless in necessary self-defence; and I recommend to them that, in all cases when allowed, they labor faithfully for reasonable wages.

And I further declare and make known, that such persons of suitable condition, will be received into the armed service of the United States to garrison forts, positions, stations, and other places, and to man vessels of all sorts in said service.

And upon this act, sincerely believed to be an act of justice, warranted by the Constitution, upon military necessity, I invoke the considerate judgment of mankind, and the gracious favor of Almighty God.

In witness whereof, I have hereunto set my hand and caused the seal of the United States to be affixed.

Done at the City of Washington, this first day of January, in the year of our Lord one thousand eight hundred and sixty three, and of the Independence of the United States of America the eighty-seventh.

By the President: Abraham Lincoln

William H. Seward, Secretary of State.

Source: National Archives and Records Administration

Appendix C
The Constitution of the United States of America
Amendment 13
(Ratified December 6, 1865)

Section 1. Neither Slavery, nor involuntary servitude, except as a punishment for crime whereof the party shall have been duly convicted, shall exist within the United States, or any place subject to their jurisdiction.

Section 2. Congress shall have power to enforce this article by appropriate legislation.

Source: National Archives and Records Administration

Appendix D
The Constitution of the United States of America
Amendment 14
(Ratified July 9, 1868)

Section 1. All persons born or naturalized in the United States, and subject to the jurisdiction thereof, are citizens of the United States and of the State wherein they reside. No State shall make or enforce any law which shall abridge the privileges or immunities of citizens of the United States; nor shall any State deprive any person of life, liberty, or property, without due process of law; nor deny to any person within its jurisdiction the equal protection of the laws.

Section 2. Representatives shall be apportioned among the several States according to their respective numbers, counting the whole number of persons in each State, excluding Indians not taxed. But when the right to vote at any election for the choice of electors for President and Vice President of the United States, Representatives in Congress, the Executive and Judicial officers of a State, or the members of the Legislature thereof, is denied to any of the male inhabitants of such State, being twenty-one years of age, and citizens of the United States, or in any way abridged, except for participation in rebellion, or other crime, the basis of representation therein shall be reduced in the proportion which the number of such male citizens shall bear to the whole number of male citizens twenty-one years of age in such State.

Section 3. No person shall be a Senator or Representative in Congress, or elector of President and Vice President, or hold any office, civil or military, under the United States, or under any State, who, having previously taken an oath, as a member of Congress, or as an officer of the United States, or as a member of any State legislature, or as an executive or judicial officer of any State, to support the Constitution of the United States, shall have engaged in insurrection or rebellion against the same, or given aid or comfort to the enemies thereof. But Congress may by a vote of two-thirds of each House, remove such disability.

Section 4. The validity of the public debt of the United States, authorized by law, including debts incurred for payment of pensions and bounties for services in suppressing insurrection or rebellion, shall not be questioned. But neither the United States nor any State shall assume or pay any debt or obligation incurred in aid of insurrection or rebellion against the United States, or any claim for the loss or emancipation of any slave; but all such debts, obligations and claims shall be held illegal and void.

Section 5. The Congress shall have power to enforce, by appropriate legislation, the provision of this article.

Source: National Archives and Records Administration

Appendix E
The Constitution of the United States of America
Amendment 15
(Ratified February 3, 1870)

Section 1. The right of citizens of the United States to vote shall not be denied or abridged by the United States or by any State on account of race, color or previous condition of servitude.

Section 2. The Congress shall have power to enforce this article by appropriate legislation.

Source: National Archives and Records Administration

Appendix F
The L'Amistad Case

One slave ship uprising that has captured the imagination of many is what occurred on the ship *L'Amistad* in 1839. The events and subsequent court case captured the attention of the American public in the nineteenth century not unlike the O. J. Simpson murder trial did in the twentieth century. The American public was again reminded of the curious events of what occurred in the twentieth century by the popular 1997 movie *Amistad*.

I have not included the account of the *L'Amistad* events in the basic body of the book for several reasons. First, this book is about the institution of slavery from the perspective of the United States, and the *L'Amistad* case originally involved slaves transported to the Spanish colony of Cuba. Secondly, the events that transpired on the *L'Amistad* were atypical for several reasons. The slave uprising that unfolded on the *L'Amistad* did not take place on the trans-Atlantic crossing from Africa, but rather after the slaves had reached Cuba and had been sold. They were on their way, by ship, to another part of Cuba when the revolt took place. Also, the events occurred well after slave trading was outlawed by most nations.

I have included the events in this appendix due to the popularity of the subject matter, because the seizing of the *L'Amistad* was carried out by the United States Navy, and due to the fact that the subsequent court case wound its way through the U.S. judicial system.

The story of the *L'Amistad* case begins in Africa with the capture of a number of Africans, many from the Mende ethnic group in present-day Sierra Leone. One of those captured, at about age twenty-six, was a Mende African named Sengbe Pieh. Sengbe Pieh was captured by four other Africans who sold him to a member of the Vai ethnic group. The Vai were well known for their slave-trading activities. Sengbe Pieh was eventually sold to Portuguese slave traders. He and other slaves were loaded onto a Portuguese ship, *Teçora*, to begin the illegal voyage to the Western Hemisphere. In spite of the nations of the world banning slave trading, it still occurred as evidenced by the *Teçora* voyage that included Sengbe Pieh. Only the British, with their powerful navy, made any major effort to stop the trans-Atlantic slave trading.

The *Teçora*, with its human cargo, reached the waters off the coast of Cuba in 1839. Near Havana, the slaves were secretly unloaded and smuggled onto the Cuban mainland. Forty-nine of the slaves, including Sengbe Pieh, were purchased by a Cuban planter, Jose Ruiz. Ruiz and a companion, Pedro Montez, who also purchased several slaves from a different slave ship, decided to transport their slaves to southeastern Cuba by boat. All the slaves were given false government papers that indicated the slaves, fresh from Africa, were rather "Ladinos," slaves born in Cuba. To make the ruse all the more complete each slave was given a Spanish name, Sengbe Pieh became Jose Cinque.

The vessel *L'Amistad* was a Spanish schooner that would transport the fifty-three Africans, made up of forty-nine adult males, three young girls, and one young boy. In addition to Ruiz and Montez, the crew of the *L'Amistad* included the captain, Ramon Ferrer, his cabin boy, who was a sixteen-year-old slave, two Cuban crew members, and a mulatto cook. The trip, from Havana to Puerto Principe, would normally be only a few sailing days in duration. However, on the second day out, the winds shifted and Captain Ferrer realized the trip would take a bit longer. He ordered a cutting of slave food and the water rations to be reduced. Some of the slaves tried to drink more than their share, so Ruiz had the offenders strung up on deck and flogged by the crew members.

While on the main deck, Sengbe Pieh, now Jose Cinque, found a nail and carried it back to the slave deck. Using the nail to pick the lock on his chains he was able to free himself as well as the other slaves. In the cargo hold the slaves found ready-made arms, a shipment of steel sugar cane knives. The crew members were busy fighting a storm and did not realize that the slaves were free of their bonds and now armed.

Cinque waited until the predawn hours of the next day before launching their attack. The captain, cook, and likely the two Cuban crew members were killed. At least one, and perhaps as many as ten Africans were killed in the revolt. Spared were Ruiz and Montez. Since the Africans did not know how to navigate the boat, Ruiz and Montez were ordered by Cinque to stir the boat eastward, back towards Africa. Ruiz and Montes feigned compliance with the demand, deliberately slowing the vessel during the day and reversing course during the night.

Carried by the Gulf Stream the *L'Amistad* ended up moving more in a northerly direction, off the coast of the United States. After nearly two months at sea, with food and water nearly exhausted and some of the Africans already dead, Cinque ordered some of the slaves to go to shore to see if they could replenish their supplies. The shore party came upon two fishermen off Long Island, New York. While they were negotiating with the fishermen a United States Navy ship boarded *L'Amistad* and discovered what had happened nearly two months earlier. What the navy personnel found was Ruiz, Montez, the cabin boy, and thirty-nine surviving Africans. *L'Amistad* was forced to go to port at nearby New London, Connecticut.

The Africans were immediately imprisoned and a number of claims were filed for both the Africans and the ship. The captain of the U.S. Navy vessel, the two fishermen, the United States government, and of course Ruiz and Montez all filed various legal claims. The government's initial claim called for the Africans to be returned to Africa, since they were illegally taken from there. That claim was later revised, after President Martin Van Buren intervened, asking the court to return the slaves to Ruiz and Montez, due to treaty agreements between the United States and Spain. Also, the revised claim called for the adult Africans to be held for prosecution for murder at sea.

The plight of the Africans caught the fancy of the American public. Jailers charged admissions for local citizens to view the out-of-the-ordinary inmates. In September a play opened in New York

City that presented, to sell-out audiences, the intriguing saga of the Africans. Artists sketched their images, newspapers carried their story, and even wax figures were made of the Africans for public display. For over two years, abolitionists, including Lewis Tappan, raised money for the Africans, known in the United States as the "Amistads."

Before the case went to trial the court began to issue early rulings that worked to the advantage of the "Amistads." The Africans were ordered to be removed from jail. The court dismissed the claim of the fishermen and the navy officer and decreed that the issue for the court to decide was whether they were African-born or legal slaves in Cuba. If they were native to Africa they should be set free; if they were legal Cuban slaves then they should be turned over to Ruiz and Montez.

The case went to trial in January of 1840. The court ruled that the Africans were taken illegally and ordered their return, at government expense, to Africa, with the one exception of the cabin boy, who was found to be a legal Cuban slave. The court ordered him returned to Cuba. Apparently under the direction of President Van Buren, the government appealed the case. The case eventually reached the Supreme Court of the United States, where in March 1841, by an eight to one vote, the high court upheld most of the lower court's decision.

Part of the Supreme Court's decision ordered the Africans freed, but reversed the lower court's ruling that they be returned to Africa at government expense. After the abolitionists helped raise funds, on November 27, 1841, the thirty-five surviving Africans set sail from New York City for the long voyage home to Africa. They arrived in Sierra Leone in January of the following year. One of those that returned home was Cinque or Sengbe Pieh. Ironically, some reports state that he entered an odd business after his African return, that of a slave trader. Confirmation of this as fact has not been made.

Notes

Prologue

1. Harriet Chappell Owsley (ed.), *The South: Old and New Frontiers; Selected Essays of Frank Lawrence Owsley* (Athens: University of Georgia Press, 1969), p. 223.
2. Frank Lawrence Owsley, *Plain Folk of the Old South* (Baton Rouge: Louisiana State University Press, 1949), p. xv.

Chapter One

1. Thomas A. Bailey, "The Mythmakers of American History," *The Journal of American History* (June 1968), p. 5.

Chapter Two

1. David Chilton, *Productive Christians in an Age of Guilt Manipulators* (Tyler: Institute For Christian Economics, 1981), pp. 61–62.
2. Hugh Thomas, *The Slave Trade* (New York: Simon & Schuster, 1997), p. 37.
3. Ibid., p. 26.
4. Keith Bradley, *Slavery and Society at Rome* (Cambridge: Cambridge University Press, 1994), pp. 16–17.
5. Ibid., p. 19.
6. Robert W. Fogel and Stanley L. Engerman, *Time on the Cross* (Boston: Little, Brown and Company, 1974), p. 13.
7. Laura Foner and Eugene D. Genovese (eds.), *Slavery in the New World* (Englewood Cliffs: Prentice-Hall, Inc., 1969), p. 101.
8. Robert W. Fogel, *Without Consent or Contract: The Rise and Fall of American Slavery* (New York: W. W. Norton & Company, 1989), p. 17.
9. Kenneth M. Stampp, *The Peculiar Institution* (New York: Vintage Books, 1956), p. 16.
10. Thomas, p. 43.
11. John K. Boles, *Black Southerners 1619–1869* (Lexington: The University Press of Kentucky, 1984), p. 4.
12. Thomas, p. 27.
13. James Oliver Horton and Lois E. Horton, *Hard Road to Freedom: the Story of African Americans* (Rutgers: Rutgers University Press, 2001), p. 11.
14. Ibid., p. 41.
15. Boles, p. 1.
16. Thomas, p. 52.
17. Ulrich Bonnell Phillips, *American Negro Slavery* (Baton Rouge: Louisiana State University Press, 1966), p. 11.

18. Thomas, p. 56.
19. Ibid., p. 57.
20. Herbert S. Klein, *The Middle Passage: Comparative Studies in the Atlantic Slave Trade* (Princeton: Princeton University Press, 1978), pp. 4–5.
21. Ira Berlin, *Many Thousands Gone: The First Two Centuries of Slavery in North America* (Cambridge: The Belknap Press of Harvard University Press, 1998), p. 25.
22. Fogel, p. 17.
23. Philip D. Curtin, *The Atlantic Slave Trade: A Census* (Madison: The University of Wisconsin Press, 1969), p. 20.
24. Fogel, p. 17.
25. Velma Maia Thomas, *Lest We Forget* (New York: Crown Publishers, Inc., 1997), p. 2.
26. Stampp, p. 17.
27. Phillips, p. 1.
28. Ibid.
29. Ibid., p. 2.
30. V. Thomas, p. 2.
31. Fogel and Engerman, p. 30.
32. Ibid., p. 15.
33. H. Thomas, p. 83.
34. Ibid., p. 87.
35. Ibid., p. 89.
36. Phillips, p. 14 and H. Thomas, p. 89.
37. H. Thomas, p. 92.
38. Ibid., pp. 92–93.
39. Phillips, pp. 16–17.
40. H. Thomas, pp. 99–100.
41. V. Thomas, p. 2.
42. Horton and Horton, p. 8.
43. Lerone Bennett, Jr., *Before the Mayflower: A History of Black America, Sixth Edition* (New York: Penguin, 1988), p. 16.
44. Ibid., p. 16.
45. Horton and Horton, p. 9.
46. Bennett, p. 17.
47. Horton and Horton, p. 9.
48. Bennett, p. 18.
49. H. Thomas, p. 63.
50. Peter Kolchin, *American Slavery*, 1619–1877 (New York: Hill and Wang. 1993), p. 19.
51. H. Thomas, p. 58 and p. 74.
52. V. Thomas, p. 5.
53. H. Thomas, p. 60.
54. Ibid., pp. 372–73.
55. James Walvin, *Black Ivory: A History of British Slavery* (Washington, D.C.: Howard University Press, 1994), p. 28.
56. H. Thomas, p. 103.
57. Stampp, p. 17.
58. Kolchin, p. 11.
59. Fogel and Engerman, p. 15.

60. Curtin, p. 13.
61. David Eltis, Stephen D. Behrendt, David Richardson, and Herbert S. Klein, *The Trans-Atlantic Slave Trade: A Database on CD-ROM* (Cambridge: Cambridge University Press, 1999), p. 5.
62. Walvin, p. 317.
63. Fogel and Engerman, p. 15.
64. Boles, p. 31.
65. John R. Spears, *The American Slave-Trade* (Williamstown: Corner House Publishers, 1970), p. 69.
66. Ibid.
67. Kolchin, p. 18.
68. Stanley L. Engerman and Eugene D. Genovese (eds.), *Race and Slavery in the Western Hemisphere: Quantitative Studies* (Princeton: Princeton University Press, 1975), p. 12.
69. Klein, p. 236, and Boles, p. 30.
70. Boles, p. 30.
71. Fogel, p. 130.
72. Klein, pp. 86–87, 234.
73. H. Thomas, p. 424.
74. Klein, p. 87.
75. David Eltis, *The Rise of African Slavery in the Americas* (Cambridge: Cambridge University Press, 2000), p. 232.
76. H. Thomas, pp. 424–25.
77. Eltis, p. 228.
78. Spears, p. 4.
79. Francis B. Simkins and Charles P. Roland, *A History of the South* (New York: Alfred A. Knopf, 1972), p. 60.
80. Spears, p. 7.
81. U. B. Phillips, *Life and Labor in the Old South* (Boston: Brown, and Company, 1931), p. 25.
82. Gustavus Vassa, *The Interesting Narrative of the Life of Olaudah Equiano, or Gustavus Vassa, the African* (London: Printed For, And By The Author, 1794), p. 12.
83. Ibid., p. 52.
84. Ibid., p. 53.
85. Ibid., p. 61.
86. Ibid., pp. 70–71.
87. Curtin, p. 17.
88. Engerman and Genovese, p. 53.
89. Ibid.
90. Curtin, p. 25.
91. Ibid.
92. Klein, p. 7.
93. Phillips, *American Negro Slavery*, p. 21, and Walvin, p. 25.
94. Phillips, *American Negro Slavery*, p. 24.
95. Ottobah Cugoano, *Thoughts and Sentiments on the Evil and Wicked Traffic of the Slavery and Commerce of the Human Species* (London, 1787), p. 106.
96. Engerman and Genovese, p. 12.
97. Ibid., p. 13.
98. Klein, p. 12.

99. Engerman and Genovese, p. 20.
100. Ibid.
101. Ibid., p. 10.
102. Ibid., pp. 8, 10, 12.
103. Klein, p. 13.
104. Curtin, p. 216.
105. Spears, p. 8.
106. Ann Kellan, "Bones Reveal Little Known Tale of New York Slaves," CNN News Report, February 12, 1998, from: http://www.cnn.com/TECH/9802/12/t_t/burial.ground/.
107. Engerman and Genovese, p. 49.
108. Walvin, p. 317.
109. "Newport, R.I. and Triangle Trade: The Economic Implications Of The Rhode Island Slave Trade," www.providence.edu/afro/students/kane/triangle.txt
110. Engerman and Genovese, pp. 51–52.
111. Ibid., p. 78.
112. Curtin, pp. 282–83.
113. Ibid., p. 286.
114. Engerman and Genovese, p. 97.
115. Ibid., p. 123.
116. Walvin, p. 317.
117. Engerman and Genovese, p. 112.
118. Ibid., p. 36.
119. Eltis, pp. 185–86.
120. Engerman and Genovese, p. 112.
121. Ibid., p. 123.
122. Ibid., p. 116.
123. Walvin, p. 319.
124. Klein, p. 25.
125. H. Thomas, pp. 111–12.
126. Boles, p. 10.
127. Kolchin, p. 9.
128. Stampp, p. 16.
129. Kolchin, p. 7.
130. Philip D. Curtin, *The Rise and Fall of the Plantation Complex* (Cambridge: Cambridge University Press, 1990), p. 4.
131. Horton and Horton, p. 11.
132. Barbara L. Solow, "Sugar, Why Is Slavery Associated With Sugar?" *Encarta Reference Library 2002.*
133. Ibid.
134. Curtin, *The Rise and Fall of the Plantation Complex*, p. 43.
135. Fogel, p. 17.
136. Fogel and Engerman, p. 22.
137. Boles, p. 12.
138. Kolchin, p. 11.
139. Boles, p. 16.
140. Ibid., pp. 17–18.

141. Jeffrey R. Hummel, *Emancipating Slaves, Enslaving Free Men* (Chicago: Open Court, 1996), p. 9.

142. Phillips, *Life and Labor in the Old South*, p. 161.

143. Hummel, p. 9.

144. Stampp, p. 22.

145. Fogel, pp. 31–32.

Chapter Three

1. Don E. Fehrenbacher, *The Slaveholding Republic* (Oxford: Oxford University Press, 2001), p. 17.

2. Ibid., p. 18.

3. Ibid.

4. Boles, p. 55.

5. Kolchin, p. 71.

6. Boles, p. 57.

7. Kolchin, p. 78.

8. Hummel, p. 26.

9. Michael Vorenberg, *Final Freedom* (Cambridge: Cambridge University Press, 2001), p. 9.

10. Stampp, p. 25.

11. Clement Eaton, *The Growth of Southern Civilization* (New York: Harper & Brothers Publishers, 1961), pp. 26–27.

12. Fogel and Engerman, p. 44.

13. Kolchin, p. 96.

14. Fogel and Engerman, p. 44.

15. Hummel, p. 39.

16. Fogel and Engerman, p. 254.

17. Ibid., p. 44.

18. Ibid., p. 49.

19. Kolchin, pp. 22–23.

20. Stampp, p. 197.

21. Fogel and Engerman, p. 128.

Chapter Four

1. P. J. Staudenraus, *The African Colonization Movement, 1816–1865* (New York: Octagon Books, 1980), p. 1.

2. Leland Baldwin and Robert Kelley, *The Stream of American History* (New York: American Book Company, 1965), p. 265.

3. Eugene D. Genovese, *The Slaveholders' Dilemma: Freedom and Progress in Southern Conservative Thought, 1820–1860* (Columbia: University of South Carolina Press, 1995), p. 11.

4. Fogel, p. 265.

5. Ibid., p. 271.

6. Ibid., pp. 272–73.

7. Ibid., pp. 271–72.

8. Edward J. Renehan, Jr., *The Secret Six: The True Tale of the Men Who Conspired with John Brown* (New York: Crown Publishers, Inc., 1995), p. 137.

9. National Park Service History Series, "John Brown's Raid" (Washington, D.C.: U.S. Government Printing Office, 1978), p. 23.

10. Ibid., pp. 56–57.

11. David H. Donald, *Lincoln* (New York: Simon & Schuster, 1995), p. 239.

12. Ibid., p. 542.

13. Patrick Gerster and Nicholas Cords (Editors), *Myth and Southern History, Volume 2: The New South* (Urbana and Chicago: University of Illinois Press, 1989), p. 45.

14. Francis Pendleton Gaines, *The Southern Plantation: A Study in the Development and the Accuracy of a Tradition* (New York: Columbia University Press, 1924), p. 45.

15. Charles T. Davis and Henry Louis Gates, Jr., *The Slave's Narrative* (Oxford and New York: Oxford University Press, 1985), p. xxxii.

16. Ibid., pp. 152–53.

17. Charles L. Blockson, *The Underground Railroad* (New York: Prentice Hall Press, 1987), p. 138.

18. William Still, *The Underground Rail Road* (Philadelphia: Porter & Coates, 1872), pp. 81–85.

19. Constitution of the United States, Article 4, Section 2, Clause 3.

20. Stanley Campbell, *The Slave Catchers* (New York: W. W. Norton & Company, 1970), p. 7.

21. Forrest McDonald, *A Constitutional History of the United States* (New York: Franklin Watts, 1982), p. 112.

22. Larry E. Tise, *Proslavery: A History of the Defense of Slavery in America, 1701–1840* (Athens: The University of Georgia Press, 1987), p. 163.

23. Fogel, p. 274.

24. Ibid.

25. Ibid., p. 275.

26. Tise, p. 163.

27. Eugene D. Genovese, *The Political Economy of Slavery Studies in the Economy* and *Society of the Slave South* (Middletown: Wesleyan University Press, 1989), p. 159.

Chapter Five

1. Joseph Kennedy (ed.), *Population of the United States in 1860; Compiled from the Original Returns of the Eighth Census, Under the Direction of the Secretary of the Interior*, Washington, D.C., 1864 (Note: This and all other 1860 Census data are from this source, hereafter referred to as *1860 Census*).

2. James Oakes, *The Ruling Race: A History of American Slaveholders* (New York: Alfred A. Knopf, Inc., 1982), pp. 49–51.

3. Kennedy (ed.), *1860 Census*, p. xv.

4. Boles, p. 107.

Chapter Six

1. Norman R. Yetman (ed.), *Voices from Slavery* (New York: Holt, Rinehart And Winston 1970), p. 2.

2. Davis, and Gates, p. 49.

3. Kolchin, p. 113.

4. Ibid., p. 130.

5. Fogel and Engerman, p. 110.

6. Frederick Law Olmsted, *The Cotton Kingdom* (Edited by Arthur M. Schlesinger) (New York: Alfred A. Knopf, 1970), p. 190.

7. Ibid., p. 79.

8. Ibid., p. 111.

9. William D. Postell, *The Health of Slaves on Southern Plantations* (Gloucester: Peter Smith, 1970), p. 37.

10. Stampp, p. 165.

11. Eaton, p. 59.

12. George P. Rawick (ed.), *The American Slave: A Composite Autobiography* (Westport: Greenwood Publishing Group, Inc., 1972), vol. 16, p. 286.

13. T. L. Baker and Julie P. Baker (eds.), *The WPA Oklahoma Slave Narratives* (Norman: University Of Oklahoma Press, 1996), pp. 107–17.

14. Ibid., p. 87.

15. Fogel and Engerman, pp. 114–15.

16. Fogel, p. 133.

17. Ibid.

18. Ibid., p. 136.

19. Ibid., pp. 140–41.

20. William H. Russell, *My Diary North and South* (Boston, 1863), p. 126.

21. Baker and Baker, p. 69.

22. Phillips, *Life* and *Labor*, p. 197.

23. Baker and Baker, p. 69.

24. Postell, p. 41.

25. Kolchin, p. 114.

26. Baker and Baker, p. 338.

27. W. C. Corsan, *Two Months in the Confederate States* (Baton Rouge: Louisiana State University Press, 1996), p. 43.

28. Ibid.

29. Postell, p. 41.

30. Fogel and Engerman, pp. 116–17.

31. Frederick Douglass, *My Bondage and My Freedom* (New York: Auburn Miller, Orton and Mulligan, 1855), p. 135.

32. Baker and Baker, p. 270.

33. G. Bailey, N. Maynor, and P. Cukor-Avila (eds.), *The Emergence of Black English* (Philadelphia: John Benjamins Publishing Co., 1991), pp. 29–37.

34. Postell, p. 42.

35. James Oakes, p. 37.

36. Kolchin, p. 114.

37. Fogel and Engerman, p. 116.

38. Olmsted, p. 181.

39. Stampp, p. 293.

40. Olmsted, p. 161.

41. Rawick, vol. 5, pp. 236–46.

42. Rawick, vol. 16, p. 223.

43. Fogel and Engerman, p. 116.

44. Ibid., p. 42.

45. Eugene D. Genovese, *Roll, Jordan, Roll: The World the Slaves Made* (New York: Pantheon Books, 1974), p. 8.

46. Kolchin, p. 109.

47. Stanley M. Elkins, *Slavery: A Problem in American Institutional and Intellectual Life* (Chicago: University of Chicago Press, 1959), pp. 128–29.

48. Fogel and Engerman, pp. 209–10.
49. Eaton, p. 57.
50. Stampp, pp. 54–55.
51. Bertha S. Dodge, *Cotton: The Plant That Would Be King* (Austin: University of Texas Press, 1984), pp. 117–18.
52. Ibid., p. 118.
53. Kolchin, p. 103.
54. Eaton, p. 57.
55. Rawick, *Supplemental Series Two*, Vol. 1, p. 287.
56. Ibid., pp. 104–5.
57. Clement Eaton, *The Waning of the Old South Civilization* (Athens, University of Georgia Press, 1968), p. 25.
58. Kolchin, p. 105.
59. Fogel and Engerman, p. 200.
60. Phillips, *Life and Labor in the Old South*, pp. 306–7.
61. Stampp, p. 38.
62. Olmsted, p. 438.
63. John Spencer Bassett, *The Plantation Overseer, As Shown in His Letters* (Northampton: Smith College, 1925), p. 12.
64. Fogel, p. 47.
65. Bassett, p. 4.
66. Olmsted, p. 43.
67. Bassett, p. 8.
68. Ibid., p. 178.
69. Ibid., p. 185.
70. Ibid., p. 186.
71. Frederick Law Olmsted, *A Journey in the Seaboard Slave States* (New York: Dix and Edwards, 1856), pp. 601–2.
72. C. Vann Woodward (ed.) *Mary Chesnut's Civil War* (New Haven: Yale University Press, 1981), p. 29.
73. Stampp, p. 353.
74. Fogel and Engerman, pp. 132–33.
75. Ibid., p. 133.
76. Olmsted, *Seaboard*, p. 508.
77. John W. Blassingame, *The Slave Community: Plantation Life in the Antebellum South* (New York: Oxford University Press, 1972), p. 84.
78. Ira Berlin, *Many Thousands Gone*, p. 58.
79. Kolchin, p. 27.
80. Berlin, *Many Thousands Gone*, pp. 191–92.
81. Kennedy, *1860 Census*, various pages.
82. Robert S. Starobin, *Industrial Slavery in the Old South* (New York: Oxford University Press, 1970), p. 11.
83. Ibid., pp. 13–18.
84. Ibid., pp. 157–58.
85. Richard C. Wade, *Slavery in the Cities: the South 1820–1860* (London and Oxford: Oxford University Press, 1964), p. 23.
86. Hummel, p. 42.

87. Wade, p. 45.

88. Fogel and Engerman, p. 56.

89. Phillips, *Life* and *Labor*, p. 181.

90. Ibid., p. 182.

91. Ibid., p. 186.

92. Eaton, *Growth of Southern Civilization*, p. 64.

93. Starobin, p. 11, 50.

94. Ibid., p. 50.

95. Wade, pp. 75–77.

96. Rawick, *Supplemental Series One*, Vol. 1, p. 14.

97. Ibid., p. 290.

98. Rawick, vol. 16, p. 286.

99. Genovese, *Roll, Jordan, Roll*, pp. 350–51.

100. Olmsted, *Cotton Kingdom*, pp. 255–56.

101. Ibid., p. 349.

102. Corsan, pp. 57–58.

103. Genovese, *Roll, Jordan, Roll*, p. 191.

104. Kennedy, *1860 Census*, p. xv.

105. Ibid., p. xv.

106. Kolchin, p. 77.

Chapter Seven

1. Rawick, *North Carolina Narratives*, pp. 286–87.

2. Ibid., pp. 287–88.

3. Thomas E. Will, "Weddings on Contested Grounds: Slave Marriage in the Antebellum South," *Historian*, Fall 1999, Vol. 62, Issue 1, p. 99.

4. Ibid.

5. Ibid.

6. Rawick, pp. 288.

7. Olmsted, *The Cotton Kingdom*, pp. 357–58.

8. Stampp, p. 342.

9. Phillips, *Life and Labor in the Old South*, p. 270.

10. Will, p. 99.

11. Fogel and Engerman, p. 127–28.

12. Ibid., pp. 136–37.

13. Rawick, pp. 79–80.

14. Kolchin, pp. 125–26.

15. Fogle and Engerman, p. 49.

16. Eaton, *Growth of Southern Civilization*, p. 51.

17. Douglass, pp. 40–42.

18. Rawick, pp. 14–15.

19. Stampp, pp. 57–58.

20. Kolchin, p. 60.

21. Ibid., p. 94.

22. Ibid., p. 112.

23. Blassingame, p. 167.

24. Genovese, *Roll, Jordan, Roll*, pp. 357–58.

25. Ibid., p. 359.

26. Eaton, *The Waning of the Old South Civilization*, p. 12.

27. Stampp, p. 231.

28. Phillips, *Life and Labor in the Old South*, p. 211.

29. Booker T. Washington, *Up from Slavery* (New York: Doubleday & Company, Inc., 1901), pp. 12–13.

30. Ibid., pp. 13–14.

31. Phillips, *Life and Labor in the Old South*, p. 215.

32. Rawick, *North Carolina Narratives*, p. 290.

33. Olmsted, *A Journey in the Seaboard Slave States*, pp. 17–18.

34. Kolchin, p. 192.

35. Genovese, *Roll, Jordan, Roll*, p. 126.

36. Ibid., p. 124.

37. Stampp, p. 307.

38. Fogel and Engerman, p. 121.

39. Bill Bynum, "Discarded Diagnoses," *The Lancet*, November 4, 2000, Vol. 356, Issue 9241, p. 1615.

40. William D. Postell, p. 81.

41. Kolchin, p. 114.

42. Rawick, vol. 16, p. 298.

43. Fogel and Engerman, p. 120.

44. Stampp, pp. 311–12.

45. Ibid., p. 311.

46. Fogel and Engerman, p. 122.

47. Stampp, pp. 313–14.

48. William D. Postell, p. 114.

49. Boles, pp. 99–100.

50. Fogel and Engerman, pp. 123–24.

51. Ibid., p. 125.

52. Bell I. Wiley, "Slavery," *American History Illustrated*, April, 1970, p. 11.

53. Stampp, p. 214.

54. Ibid., p. 208.

55. Wiley, p. 11.

56. Baker and Baker, p. 96.

57. Rawick, vol. 16, p. 260.

58. Washington, pp. 6–7.

59. Phillips, *Life and Labor in the Old South*, p. 198.

60. Olmsted, *The Cotton Kingdom*, pp. 348–49.

61. McPherson, James M., *Abraham Lincoln and the Second American Revolution* (Oxford: Oxford University Press, 1991), p. 16.

62. Ibid., p. 17.

63. James Oakes, *The Ruling Race: A History of the American Slaveholders* (New York: Alfred A. Knopf, 1982), p. 107.

64. Charles C. Jones, *The Religious Instruction of the Negroes in the United States* (New York: Negro Universities Press, 1969), p. 274.

65. Moses M. Henkle, *Primary Platform of Methodism; or, Exposition of the General Rules* (Louisville: Southern Methodist Book Concern, 1853), p. 191.

66. Olmsted, *Cotton Kingdom*, p. 467.

67. Wiley, p. 15.

68. Rawick, vol. 16, p. 291.

69. Phillips, *Life and Labor in the Old South*, p. 201.

70. Rawick, p. 9.

71. Woodward, pp. 213–14.

72. Kolchin, p. 116.

73. Woodward, p. 213.

74. Fogel and Engerman, p. 40.

75. Stampp, p. 338.

76. Douglass, p. 118.

77. Genovese, *Roll, Jordan, Roll*, p. 316.

78. Stampp, p. 125.

79. Ibid., p. 210.

80. Phillips, *Life* and *Labor*, p. 166.

81. Ibid., p. 165.

82. Wiley, p. 16.

83. Genovese, *Roll, Jordan, Roll*, p. 34.

84. Ibid.

85. Ibid., p. 37.

86. Phillips, *Life and Labor*, p. 180.

87. Hummel, p. 39.

88. Eaton, *The Waning of the Old South Civilization*, p. 49.

89. Phillips, *American Negro Slavery*, pp. 230–31.

90. Ibid., p. 231.

Chapter Eight

1. Larry Koger, *Black Slaveowners: Free Black Slave Masters in South Carolina, 1790–1860* (Jefferson: McFarland and Co., 1985), pp. 9–11.

2. Ira Berlin, *Slaves without Masters* (New York: The New Press, 1974), pp. 11–12.

3. Phillips, *Life and Labor in the Old South*, p. 170.

4. Berlin, p. 6.

5. Eric Foner, *Politics and Ideology in the Age of the Civil War* (Oxford: Oxford University Press, 1980), p. 78.

6. Fogel and Engerman, pp. 243–44.

7. Foner, p. 77, and Fogel and Engerman, pp. 243–44.

8. Fogel and Engerman, p. 244.

9. Berlin, p. 235.

10. Kennedy, *1860 Census*, various pages.

11. Kolchin, p. 82.

12. Eaton, *Growth of Southern Civilization*, pp. 86–87.

13. Phillips, *Life and Labor in the Old South*, p. 171.

14. Oakes, p. 47, and Berlin, p. 4.

15. Stampp, pp. 194–95.

16. Eaton, *Growth of Southern Civilization*, p. 94.

17. Koger, p. 1.

18. Ibid., pp. 10–11.

19. Ibid., p. 23.

20. James R. Kennedy and Walter D. Kennedy, *The South Was Right* (Baton Rouge: Land And Land, 1991), p. 55.

21. Carter G. Woodson, "Free Negro Owners of Slaves in the United States in 1830," Journal of Negro History, vol. 9 (January 1924), p. 42.

22. Koger, p. 82.

23. Kennedy and Kennedy, p. 56.

24. Eaton, *Growth of Southern Civilization*, p. 93.

25. Alonford James Robertson, *Free Blacks in the United States*, Encarta Reference Library, 2002.

26. Koger, p. 144.

27. Ibid., p. 167.

28. Marian Aguiar, *Brown Fellowship Society*, Encarta Reference Library, 2002.

29. Berlin, pp. 274–75, and Oakes, p. 49.

30. Oakes, p. 49.

Chapter Nine

1. J. Jeffery Auer (ed.), *Antislavery and Disunion, 1858–1861: Studies in the Rhetoric of Compromise and Conflict* (Gloucester: Peter Smith, 1968), p. 29.

2. George Baker (ed.), *The Works of William H. Seward* (Boston, 1884), pp. 289–302.

3. Charles Dew, *Apostles of Disunion: Southern Secession Commissioners and the Causes of the Civil War* (Charlottesville: University of Virginia Press, 2001), p. 4.

4. Edgar Lee Masters, *Lincoln: the Man* (Columbia: The Foundation For American Education, 1997), p. 371.

5. Robert W. Johannsen, *Lincoln, the South, and Slavery: The Political Dimension* (Baton Rouge and London: Louisiana State University Press, 1991), p. 124.

6. James M. McPherson, *Why They Fought For, 1861–1865* (Baton Rouge: Louisiana State University Press, 1994), p. 18.

7. Jeffrey Rogers Hummel, "Why Did Lincoln Choose War," *North & South*, Sept. 2001, Vol. 4, No. 7, p. 41.

8. Thomas J. DiLorenzo, *The Real Lincoln* (New York: Forum, 2002), p. 31.

9. Avery Craven, *The Repressible Conflict, 1830–1861* (Baton Rouge: Louisiana State University Press, 1939), p. 64.

10. Leland Baldwin and Robert Kelley, p. 328.

11. Abraham Lincoln, Inaugural Address, March 4, 1861.

12. Ibid.

13. Ibid.

14. DiLorenzo, p. 3.

15. Ibid., pp. 15–16.

16. Ibid., p. 14.

17. Ibid., p. 18.

18. Donald, p. 284.

19. Glenn F. Williams, "Under the Despot's Heel," *America's Civil War Magazine*, May 2000, p. 27.

20. Donald, p. 307.

21. Ibid., p. 314.

22. Ibid., pp. 314–17.

23. Ibid., p. 343.

24. *An Act for the Release of certain Persons held to Service or Labor in the District of Columbia*, National Archives.

25. Paul M. Angle (ed.), *Herndon's Life of Lincoln* (New York: Premier Books, 1961), p. 245.

26. Donald, pp. 367–68.

27. Ibid., p. 368.

28. John Gauss, "Give The Blacks Texas," *Civil War Times Illustrated*, May–June 1990.

29. Baldwin and Kelley, p. 353.

30. Ibid., pp. 351–53.

31. Donald, p. 375.

32. Koger, p. 190.

33. James L. Roark, *Masters without Slaves: Southern Planters in the Civil War and Reconstruction* (New York: W. W. Norton & Company, 1977), p. 75.

34. Koger, p. 407.

35. *The Emancipation Proclamation*, National Archives.

36. James G. Randall, *Lincoln the President: Springfield to Gettysburg, Vol. Two* (New York: Dodd, Mead & Company, 1945), p. 189.

37. Baldwin and Kelley, p. 353.

38. Koger, p. 190.

39. William C. Harris, "After the Emancipation Proclamation: Lincoln's Role In The Ending Of Slavery," *North & South Magazine*, Dec. 2001, Vol. 5, No. 1, p. 45.

40. Ibid.

41. *The Emancipation Proclamation*, National Archives.

42. Frederick Douglass, "The Glorious Morning of Liberty," *The Douglass Monthly*, Jan. 1863.

43. Ibid.

44. Jefferson Davis, Address to the Confederate Congress, January 12, 1863.

45. Shelby Foote, *The Civil War: A Narrative, Vol. 2* (New York: Vintage Press, 1986), pp. 151–52; and James M. McPherson, *Battle Cry of Freedom* (New York: Oxford University Press, 1988), p. 602.

46. Foote, p. 636.

47. J. D. Haines, "Eyewitness to War," *America's Civil War Magazine*, May 2000, pp. 70–71.

48. Eric Foner, *Reconstruction: America's Unfinished Revolution 1863–1877* (New York: Harper & Row Publishers, 1988), p. 33.

49. Ibid.

50. Ibid.

51. Budge Weidman, *Prologue*, Vol. 29, No. 2, "Preserving the Legacy of the United States Colored Troops," p. 91.

52. Versalle F. Washington, *Eagles on Their Buttons: A Black Infantry Regiment in the Civil War* (Columbia: University of Missouri Press, 1999), p. x.

53. Ervin L. Jordan, *Black Confederates and Afro-Yankees in Civil War Virginia* (Charlottesville: University Press of Virginia, 1995), p. 264.

54. McPherson, p. 563.

55. Dudley Taylor Cornish, *The Sable Arm: Negro Troops in the Union Army, 1861–1865* (New York: W. W. Norton, 1966), pp. 17–18.

56. McPherson, p. 563.

57. Joyce Hansen, *Between Two Fires: Black Soldiers in the Civil War* (New York: Franklin Watts, 1993), pp. 46–48.

58. Weidman, p. 91.

59. Washington, p. 7.

60. Weidman, p. 91.

61. Ibid.

62. Washington, p. 7.

63. Cornish, p. 46.

64. Ibid., pp. 46–47.

65. Emancipation Proclamation, see appendix D.

66. Hansen, pp. 52–53.

67. McRae, Jr., Bennie J., "United States Colored Troops, A Brief History," *Lest We Forget,* Apr. 1995, p. 2.

68. Cornish, p. 130.

69. Weidman, p. 92.

70. Harris, p. 47.

71. Donald, p. 431.

72. Washington, pp. 14–15.

73. Randall C. Jimerson, *The Private Civil War: Popular Thought during the Sectional Conflict* (Baton Rogue: Louisiana State University Press, 1988), p. 93.

74. Ibid.

75. Bell Irvin Wiley, *The Life of Billy Yank: The Common Soldier of the Union* (Baton Rouge: Louisiana State University Press, 1981), p. 109.

76. Ibid.

77. Jimerson, p. 108.

78. Hansen, p. 96.

79. Jordan, p. 271.

80. Cornish, p. 195.

81. Hansen, p. 55.

82. Charles Rice, "The Bull Whip Mutiny," *Civil War Times Illustrated,* Feb. 2002, pp. 38–43, 62.

83. Martin Robison Delany, *The Condition, Elevation, Emigration, and Destiny of the Colored People of the United States, Politically Considered* (Philadelphia: 1852), p. 209.

84. Jordan, p. 269.

85. Eric Foner, *Reconstruction: America's Unfinished Revolution 1863–1877* (New York: Harper & Row Publishers, 1988), p. 8.

86. Encarta Reference Library 2002, *Civil War, American.*

87. Wiley, *The Life of Billy Yank: The Common Soldier of the Union,* p. 314.

88. Jordan, p. 272.

89. McPherson, p. 686.

90. Cornish, p. 156.

91. Christian A. Fleetwood, "The Negro As A Soldier," Speech given November 11, 1895 at the Negro Congress, Atlanta, Ga (Library of Congress).

92. Garry James, "Infantryman, U.S. Colored Troops, 1864," *Arms Gazette,* March 1977, p. 53.

93. Genovese, *Roll, Jordan, Roll,* p. 157.

94. Jane E. Schultz, "African American Women in Civil War Hospital Work," *The Journal of Civil War Medicine,* Jan./Feb. 1997, Vol. 1, No. 1, p. 3.

95. Jordan, p. 269.

96. Hansen, p. 23.

97. Ibid.

98. Obatala, J. K., "The Unlikely Story of Blacks Who Were Loyal To Dixie," *Smithsonian Magazine*, 9, 1979, p. 94.

99. Richard Rollins (ed.) *Black Southerners in Gray* (Murfreesboro: Southern Heritage Press, 1994), p. 39.

100. Ibid., pp. 40–41.

101. Charles Wesley, *The Collapse of the Confederacy* (New York: Associated Publishers, 1937), p. 244.

102. Charles K. Barrow, J. H. Segars, and R. B. Rosenburg (eds.), *Forgotten Confederates: An Anthology About Black Southerners* (Atlanta: Southern Heritage Press, 1995), p. 4.

103. Cornish, p. 16.

104. Rollins, p. 10.

105. Rollins, p. 17.

106. Obatala, p. 99.

107. *War of the Rebellion: A Compilation of the Official Records of the Union and Confederate Armies* (hereafter referred to as *O.R.*), Washington, D.C. 1880–1901, ser. I, vol. XI, pp. 93–97.

108. Barrow, Segars, and Rosenburg, p. 19.

109. Ibid., p. 61.

110. William C. Davis, *Battle at Bull Run* (Garden City: Doubleday & Company, Inc., 1977), p. 28.

111. Barrow, Segars, and Rosenburg, p. 22.

112. Tony Horwitz, "Shades of Gray: Did Blacks Fight Freely For the Confederacy," *Wall Street Journal*, May 8, 1997, p. 1A.

113. Barrow, Segars, and Rosenburg, p. 3.

114. Rollins, p. 76.

115. Barrow, Segars, and Rosenburg, p. 3.

116. Ibid., p. 10.

117. Foote, p. 443.

118. William S. Fitzgerald. "We Will Stand By You," *Civil War Times Illustrated*, Nov.–Dec. 1993, pp. 71–72.

119. Robert Selph Henry, *Nathan Bedford Forrest: First with the Most* (New York: Mallard Press, 1991), p. 14.

120. Wilfred Buck Yearns, *The Confederate Congress* (Athens: University of Georgia Press, 1960), p. 111.

121. Emory M. Thomas, *The Confederate Nation: 1861–1865* (New York: Harper Torchbooks 1979), p. 152.

122. Yearns, p. 111.

123. Ibid., p. 112.

124. Roark, p. 79.

125. Thomas, p. 261.

126. Barbara C. Ruby, "General Patrick Cleburne's Proposal to Arm Southern Slaves," *Arkansas Historical Quarterly*, Autumn, 1971, pp. 194–95.

127. *O.R.* ser. I, vol. LII, pt. II, p. 587.

128. Ibid.

129. Ibid.

130. Ibid., p. 588.

131. William C. Davis, *Jefferson Davis: The Man and His Hour* (New York: Harper Collins, 1991), p. 541.

132. *O.R.*, ser. I, vol. LII, pt. II, p. 606.

133. Wiley Sword, *Southern Invincibility* (New York: St. Martin's Press, 1999), p. 247.

134. Davis, *Jefferson Davis*, p. 597.

135. *O.R.*, ser. IV, vol. III, p. 1013.

136. Ibid.

137. Ibid.

138. Eli N. Evans, *Judah P. Benjamin, The Jewish Confederate* (New York: The Free Press, 1988), p. 285.

139. Thomas, p. 296.

140. Jordan, p. 242.

141. Thomas, p. 297.

142. Genovese, *Roll, Jordan, Roll*, pp. 129–30.

143. Clifford Dowdey and Louis Manarin (eds.), *Wartime Papers of R. E. Lee* (New York: Bramhall House, 1961), p. 927.

144. Barrow, Segars, and Rosenburg, p. 68.

145. Ibid., p. 14.

146. Genovese, *Roll, Jordan, Roll*, p. 153.

147. Ibid., p. 153.

148. Ibid.

149. Roark, p. 81.

150. Ibid.

151. Ibid.

152. Randy J. Sparks, *Southwestern Historical Quarterly*, "John P. Osterhout, Yankee, Rebel, Republican," Oct. 1986, p. 121.

153. Wiley, *The Life of Billy Yank: The Common Soldier of the Union*, p. 109.

154. Ibid., p. 114.

155. Ibid., p. 115.

156. Ibid.

157. Washington, p. 13.

158. Baldwin and Kelley, p. 366.

159. Rawick, vol. 16, pt. 1, p. 255.

160. Ibid., p. 256.

161. Hummel, p. 41.

Chapter Ten

1. Kolchin, p. 22.

2. Fogel and Engerman, pp. 158–257.

3. Starobin, pp. 154–58.

Appendix A

1. Frederick Law Olmsted, *The Cotton Kingdom*, pp. ix–xxxiv.

2. Phillips, *American Negro Slavery*, p. xxi.

3. Davis, and Gates, pp. 48–59.

4. Yetman, p. 358.

5. Fogel, pp. 177–78.

6. Ibid., p. 177.

Bibliography

Aguiar, Marian. *Brown Fellowship Society*, Encarta Reference Library, 2002.

An Act for the Release of certain Persons held to Service or Labor in the District of Columbia, National Archives.

Angle, Paul M. (Editor). *Herndon's Life of Lincoln*. New York: Premier Books, 1961.

Auer, J. Jeffery (Editor). *Antislavery and Disunion, 1858–1861: Studies in the Rhetoric of Compromise and Conflict*. Gloucester: Peter Smith, 1968.

Bailey, G., N. Maynor, and P. Cukor-Avila (Editors). *The Emergence of Black English*. Philadelphia: John Benjamins Publishing Co., 1991.

Bailey, Thomas A. "The Mythmakers of American History," *The Journal of American History* (June 1968).

Baker, George (Editor). *The Works of William H. Seward*. Boston, 1884.

Baker, T. L., and Julie P. Baker (Editors). *The WPA Oklahoma Slave Narratives*. Norman: University of Oklahoma Press, 1996.

Baldwin, Leland, and Robert Kelley. *The Stream of American History*. New York: American Book Company, 1965.

Barrow, Charles K., J. H. Segars, and R. B. Rosenburg (Editors). *Forgotten Confederates: An Anthology about Black Southerners*. Atlanta: Southern Heritage Press, 1995.

Basler, Roy (Editor). *The Collected Works of Abraham Lincoln*. New Brunswick: Rutgers University Press, 1953.

Bassett, John Spencer. *The Plantation Overseer, As Shown in His Letters*. Northampton: Smith College, 1925.

Bennett, Lerone, Jr. *Before the Mayflower: A History of Black America, Sixth Edition.* New York: Penguin, 1988.

Berlin, Ira. *Many Thousands Gone: The First Two Centuries of Slavery in North America.* Cambridge: The Belknap Press of Harvard University Press, 1998.

————. *Slaves without Masters.* New York: The New Press, 1974.

Blassingame, John W. *The Slave Community: Plantation Life in the Antebellum South.* New York: Oxford University Press, 1972.

Blockson, Charles L. *The Underground Railroad.* New York: Prentice Hall Press, 1987.

Boles, John K. *Black Southerners 1619-1869.* Lexington: The University Press of Kentucky, 1984.

Bradley, Keith. *Slavery and Society at Rome.* Cambridge: Cambridge University Press, 1994.

Bynum, Bill. "Discarded Diagnoses," *Lancet*, Nov. 4, 2000, Vol. 356, Issue 9241, p. 1615.

Campbell, Stanley. *The Slave Catchers.* New York: W. W. Norton & Company, 1970.

Chilton, David. *Productive Christians in an Age of Guilt Manipulators.* Tyler: Institute For Christian Economics, 1981.

Cornish, Dudley Taylor. *The Sable Arm: Negro Troops in the Union Army, 1861–1865.* New York: W. W. Norton, 1966.

Corsan, W. C. *Two Months in the Confederate States* (Edited by Benjamin H. Trask). Baton Rouge: Louisiana State University Press, 1996.

Craven, Avery. *The Repressible Conflict, 1830–1861.* Baton Rouge: Louisiana State University Press, 1939.

Cugoano, Ottobah. *Thoughts and Sentiments on the Evil and Wicked Traffic of the Slavery and Commerce of the Human Species.* London: 1787.

Curtin, Philip D. *The Atlantic Slave Trade: A Census.* Madison: The University Of Wisconsin Press, 1969.

————. *The Rise and Fall of the Plantation Complex.* Cambridge: Cambridge University Press, 1990.

Davis, Charles T., and Henry Louis Gates, Jr. *The Slave's Narrative.* Oxford and New York: Oxford University Press, 1985.

Davis, William C. *Battle at Bull Run.* Garden City: Doubleday and Company, Inc., 1977.

————. *Jefferson Davis: The Man and His Hour.* New York: Harper Collins, 1991.

Delany, Martin Robison. *The Condition, Elevation, Emigration, and Destiny of the Colored People of the United States, Politically Considered.* Philadelphia: 1852.

Dew, Charles. *Apostles of Disunion: Southern Secession Commissioners and the Causes of the Civil War.* Charlottesville: University Press of Virginia, 2001.

DiLorenzo, Thomas J. *The Real Lincoln.* New York: Forum, 2002.

Dodge, Bertha S. *Cotton: The Plant That Would Be King.* Austin: University of Texas Press, 1984.

Donald, David H. *Lincoln.* New York: Simon & Schuster, 1995.

Douglass, Frederick. *My Bondage and My Freedom.* New York: Auburn Miller, Orton and Mulligan, 1855.

————. "The Glorious Morning of Liberty," *The Douglass Monthly,* January, 1863.

Dowdey, Clifford, and Louis Manarin (Editors). *Wartime Papers of R. E. Lee.* New York: Bramhall House, 1961.

Eaton, Clement. *The Growth of Southern Civilization.* New York: Harper & Brothers Publishers, 1961.

————. *The Waning of the Old South Civilization.* Athens: University of Georgia Press, 1968.

Elkins, Stanley M. *Slavery: A Problem in American Institutional and Intellectual Life.* Chicago: University of Chicago Press, 1959.

Eltis, David. *The Rise of African Slavery in the Americas.* Cambridge: Cambridge University Press, 2000.

Eltis, David, Stephen D. Behrendt, David Richardson, and Herbert S. Klein. *The Trans-Atlantic Slave Trade: A Database on CD-ROM.* Cambridge: Cambridge University Press, 1999.

Engerman, Stanley L., and Eugene D. Genovese (Editors). *Race and Slavery in the Western Hemisphere: Quantitative Studies*. Princeton: Princeton University Press, 1975.

Evans, Eli N. *Judah P. Benjamin, The Jewish Confederate*. New York: The Free Press, 1988.

Fehrenbacher, Don E. *The Slaveholding Republic: An Account of the United States Government's Relations to Slavery* (Compiled and Edited by Ward M. McAfee). Oxford: Oxford University Press, 2001.

Fitzgerald, William S. "We Will Stand By You," *Civil War Times Illustrated*, Nov.-Dec. 1993, pp. 71-72.

Fleetwood, Christian A. "The Negro As A Soldier," Speech given November 11, 1895, at the Negro Congress, Atlanta, Ga., Library of Congress.

Fogel, Robert W. *Without Consent or Contract: The Rise and Fall of American Slavery*. New York: W. W. Norton & Company, 1989.

Fogel, Robert W., and Stanley L. Engerman. *Time on the Cross*. Boston: Little, Brown and Company, 1974.

Foner, Eric. *Politics and Ideology in the Age of the Civil War*. Oxford: Oxford University Press, 1980.

————. *Reconstruction: America's Unfinished Revolution 1863–1877*. New York: Harper & Row Publishers, 1988.

Foner, Laura, and Eugene D. Genovese (Editors). *Slavery in the New World*. Englewood Cliffs: Prentice-Hall, Inc., 1969.

Foote, Shelby. *The Civil War: A Narrative, Vol. 2, Fredericksburg to Meridian*. New York: Vintage Press, 1986.

Franklin, John Hope, and Alfred A. Moss. *From Slavery to Freedom: A History of African Americans, Eighth Edition*. New York: Alfred A. Knopf, 2000.

Gaines, Francis Pendleton. *The Southern Plantation: A Study in the Development and the Accuracy of a Tradition*. New York: Columbia University Press, 1924.

Gauss, John. "'Give The Blacks Texas," *Civil War Times Illustrated*, May–June 1990.

Genovese, Eugene D. *Roll, Jordan, Roll: The World the Slaves Made*. New York: Pantheon Books, 1974.

———. *The Political Economy of Slavery Studies in the Economy & Society of the Slave South*. Middletown: Wesleyan University Press, 1989.

———. *The Slaveholders' Dilemma: Freedom and Progress in Southern Conservative Thought, 1820–1860*. Columbia: University of South Carolina Press, 1995.

Gerster, Patrick, and Nicholas Cords (Editors). *Myth and Southern History, Volume 2: The New South*. Urbana and Chicago: University of Illinois Press, 1989.

Haines, J. D. "Eyewitness to War," *America's Civil War Magazine*, May 2000.

Hansen, Joyce. *Between Two Fires: Black Soldiers in the Civil War*. New York: Franklin Watts, 1993.

Harris, William C. "After the Emancipation Proclamation: Lincoln's Role in the Ending of Slavery," *North & South Magazine*, Dec. 2001, Vol. 5, No. 1.

Henkle, Moses M. *Primary Platform of Methodism; Or, Exposition of the General Rules*. Louisville: Southern Methodist Book Concern, 1853.

Henry, Robert Selph. *Nathan Bedford Forrest: First with the Most*. New York: Mallard Press, 1991.

Horton, James Oliver, and Lois E. Horton. *Hard Road to Freedom: The Story of African Americans*. Rutgers: Rutgers University Press, 2001.

Horwitz, Tony. "Shades of Gray: Did Blacks Fight Freely for the Confederacy," *Wall Street Journal*, May 8, 1997, p. 1A.

Hummel, Jeffrey R. *Emancipating Slaves, Enslaving Free Men*. Chicago: Open Court, 1996.

———. "Why Did Lincoln Choose War," *North & South*, Sept. 2001, Vol. 4, No. 7.

James, Garry. "Infantryman, U.S. Colored Troops, 1864," *Arms Gazette*, March 1977.

Jimerson, Randall C. *The Private Civil War: Popular Thought during the Sectional Conflict.* Baton Rouge: Louisiana State University Press, 1988.

Johannsen, Robert W. *Lincoln, the South, and Slavery: The Political Dimension.* Baton Rouge and London: Louisiana State University Press, 1991.

Jones, Charles C. *The Religious Instruction of the Negroes in the United States.* New York: Negro Universities Press, 1969.

Jordan, Ervin L. *Black Confederates and Afro-Yankees in Civil War Virginia.* Charlottesville: University Press of Virginia, 1995.

Kellan, Ann. "Bones Reveal Little Known Tale of New York Slaves," CNN News Report, February 12, 1998, from: http://www.cnn.com/TECH/9802/12/t_t/burial.ground

Kennedy, James R., and Walter D. Kennedy. *The South Was Right.* Baton Rouge: Land And Land, 1991.

Kennedy, Joseph (Editor). *Population of the United States in 1860; Compiled from the Original Returns of the Eighth Census,* Under the Direction of the Secretary of the Interior, Washington, D.C., 1864.

Klein, Herbert S. *The Middle Passage: Comparative Studies in the Atlantic Slave Trade.* Princeton: Princeton University Press, 1978.

Koger, Larry. *Black Slaveowners: Free Black Slave Masters in South Carolina 1790–1860.* Jefferson: McFarland and Co., 1985.

Kolchin, Peter. *American Slavery, 1619–1877.* New York: Hill and Wang, 1993.

McDonald, Forrest. *A Constitutional History of the United States.* New York: Franklin Watts, 1982.

McPherson, James M. *Abraham Lincoln and the Second American Revolution.* Oxford: Oxford University Press, 1991.

———. *Battle Cry of Freedom.* New York: Oxford University Press, 1988.

———. *What They Fought For, 1861–1865.* Baton Rouge: Louisiana State University Press, 1994.

McRae, Jr., Bennie J. "United States Colored Troops, A Brief History," *Lest We Forget,* April 1995.

Masters, Edgar Lee. *Lincoln: The Man*. Columbia: The Foundation For American Education, 1997.

National Park Service History Series "John Brown's Raid." Washington, D.C.: U.S. Government Printing Office, 1978.

Oakes, James. *The Ruling Race: A History of American Slaveholders*. New York: Alfred A. Knopf, Inc., 1982.

Obatala, J. K. "The Unlikely Story of Blacks Who Were Loyal to Dixie," *Smithsonian Magazine*, 9, 1979.

Olmsted, Frederick Law. *A Journey in the Seaboard Slave States*. New York: Dix and Edwards, 1856.

———. *The Cotton Kingdom* (Edited by Arthur M. Schlesinger). New York: Alfred A. Knopf, 1970.

Owsley, Frank Lawrence. *Plain Folk of the Old South*. Baton Rouge: Louisiana State University Press, 1949.

Owsley, Harriet Chappell (Editor). *The South: Old and New Frontiers; Selected Essays of Frank Lawrence Owsley*. Athens: University of Georgia Press, 1969.

Phillips, Ulrich Bonnell. *American Negro Slavery*. Baton Rouge: Louisiana State University Press, 1966.

———. *Life and Labor in the Old South*. Boston: Brown, and Company, 1931.

Postell, William D. *The Health of Slaves on Southern Plantations*. Gloucester: Peter Smith, 1970.

Randall, James G. *Lincoln the President: Springfield to Gettysburg, Volume Two*. New York: Dodd, Mead & Company, 1945.

Rawick, George P. (Editor). *The American Slave: A Composite Autobiography*. Westport: Greenwood Publishing Group, Inc., 1972.

Renehan, Jr., Edward J. *The Secret Six: The True Tale of the Men Who Conspired with John Brown*. New York: Crown Publishers, Inc., 1995.

Rice, Charles. "The Bull Whip Mutiny," *Civil War Times Illustrated*, February 2002.

Roark, James L. *Masters without Slaves: Southern Planters in the Civil War and Reconstruction*. New York: W. W. Norton & Company, 1977.

Robertson, Alonford James. *Free Blacks in the United States*. Encarta Reference Library, 2002.

Rollins, Richard (Editor). *Black Southerners in Gray*. Murfreesboro: Southern Heritage Press, 1994.

Ruby, Barbara C. "General Patrick Cleburne's Proposal to Arm Southern Slaves," *Arkansas Historical Quarterly*, Autumn, 1971.

Russell, William H. *My Diary North and South*. Boston, 1863.

Schultz, Jane E. "African-American Women in Civil War Hospital Work," *The Journal of Civil War Medicine*, Jan./Feb. 1997, Vol. 1, No. 1.

Simkins, Francis B., and Charles P. Roland. *A History of the South*. New York: Alfred A. Knopf, 1972.

Solow, Barbara L. "Sugar, Why Is Slavery Associated With Sugar?" Encarta Reference Library, 2002.

Spears, John R. *The American Slave-Trade*. Williamstown: Corner House Publishers, 1970.

Stampp, Kenneth M. *The Peculiar Institution*. New York: Vintage Books, 1956.

Starobin, Robert S. *Industrial Slavery in the Old South*. New York: Oxford University Press, 1970.

Staudenraus, P. J. *The African Colonization Movement, 1816–1865*. New York: Octagon Books, 1980.

Still, William. *The Underground Rail Road*. Philadelphia: Porter & Coates, 1872.

Sword, Wiley. *Southern Invincibility*. New York: St. Martin's Press, 1999.

Thomas, Emory M. *The Confederate Nation: 1861–1865*. New York: Harper Torchbooks, 1979.

Thomas, Hugh. *The Slave Trade*. New York: Simon & Schuster, 1997.

Thomas, Velma Maia. *Lest We Forget*. New York: Crown Publishers, Inc., 1997.

Tise, Larry E. *Proslavery: A History of the Defense of Slavery in America, 1701–1840*. Athens: The University of Georgia Press, 1987.

Vassa, Gustavus. *The Interesting Narrative of the Life of Olaudah Equiano, or Gustavus Vassa, The African*. London: Printed For, And By The Author, 1794.

Vorenberg, Michael. *Final Freedom: The Civil War, the Abolition of Slavery, and the Thirteenth Amendment*. Cambridge: Cambridge University Press, 2001.

Wade, Richard C. *Slavery in the Cities: The South 1820–1860*. London and Oxford: Oxford University Press, 1964.

Walvin, James. *Black Ivory: A History of British Slavery*. Washington, D.C.: Howard University Press, 1994.

War of the Rebellion: A Compilation of the Official Records of the Union and Confederate Armies, Washington, D.C. 1880–1901.

Washington, Booker T. *Up from Slavery*. New York: Doubleday & Company, Inc., 1901.

Washington, Versalle F. *Eagles on their Buttons: A Black Infantry Regiment in the Civil War*. Columbia: University of Missouri Press, 1999.

Weidman, Budge. *Prologue*, Vol. 29, No. 2, "Preserving the Legacy of the United States Colored Troops."

Wesley, Charles. *The Collapse of the Confederacy*. New York: Associated Publishers, 1937.

Wiley, Bell Irvin. *The Life of Billy Yank: The Common Soldier of the Union*. Baton Rouge: Louisiana State University Press, 1981.

———."Slavery," *American History Illustrated*, April, 1970.

Will, Thomas E. "Weddings on Contested Grounds: Slave Marriage in the Antebellum South," *Historian*, Fall 1999, Vol. 62, Issue 1, p. 99.

Williams, Glenn F. "Under the Despot's Heel," *America's Civil War Magazine*, May 2000.

Woodson, Carter G. "Free Negro Owners of Slaves in the United States in 1830," Journal of Negro History, Jan. 1924, Vol. 9.

Woodward, C. Vann (Editor). *Mary Chesnut's Civil War*. New Haven: Yale University Press, 1981.

Yearns, Wilfred Buck. *The Confederate Congress*. Athens: University of Georgia Press, 1960.

Yetman, Norman R. (Editor). *Voices from Slavery*. New York: Holt, Rinehart And Winston, 1970.

Index